INTERMITTENT FASTING FOR *WOMEN OVER 50*

The complete guide to reactivate metabolism, lose weight and counteract signs of aging with 210 easy to prepare recipes and a 21-day meal plan

By

Rachel Rodriguez

TABLE OF CONTENTS

WHAT IS INTERMITTENT FASTING?

Intermittent fasting (IF) is essentially restricting the diet to a specific time period. There are some IF variants to pick from. Choose the kind that best suits your lifestyle, and then consult with your doctor.

Daily Directions. This is the most common IF condition. The everyday routine normally follows a 16/8 or 18/6 pattern. This involves eating regular, healthy meals for 6 to 8 hours a day and fasting for the other 16 to 18 hours. This has been found to be the most long-lasting process.

You can begin by experimenting with various timings. A 12/12 diet consists of 12 hours of feeding followed by 12 hours of fasting. When you're ready, you'll move on to a more rigid schedule.

5:2 Directions. This plan requires you to eat healthy, balanced meals five days a week and limit your calories to 500-600 calories two days a week. It's unclear if it's best to eat all of your calories at once or spread them out over the course of the day, so do what feels right to you.

Alternate day Directions. If you choose this type, you can normally eat every other day. You should only eat 25% of the daily calorie needs on fasting days. On fasting days, for example, if you usually eat 1,800 calories a day, you will only consume 450 calories.

24-hour Directions. This procedure necessitates a complete 24-hour fast before feeding again. Many that use this method swift from morning to breakfast or lunch to lunch only once or twice a week.

Proceed with caution if you use this type. This solution can induce intense irritability, nausea, and headaches, and it may not be the best choice for you.

WHY INTERMITTENT FASTING FOR WOMEN OVER 50 WORKS?

It can be odd that just changing your eating habits will help you lose weight. Nonetheless, fasting has a beneficial effect on our bodies. Your fat reserves are used as calories when your body goes into fasting mode, enabling you to use body fat for energy.

Naturally, just because you aren't fasting doesn't mean you can eat whatever you want. For better outcomes, stick to whole grains, unrefined carbs, and lean proteins. Remember to consume calorie-free beverages, including black coffee, tea, and water during fasting! You will also find that you are more relaxed at meals and enjoy your food more.

- You've already fasted for long periods of time in your life.
- If you've ever eaten dinner but then slept late the next day and didn't feed again until noon, you've fasted for 16+ hours.
- This is because everybody eats instinctively. They simply may not feel hungry in the morning.

BEFORE YOU GET STARTED

Consult your doctor before you start. If you have a serious condition or are taking medication, this is especially important. When you get sick, you must stop.

Maintain an uncomplicated approach. Fasting is described as drinking only plain water (flat or carbonated), black coffee, or unsweetened tea during this experiment.

Keep it easy. Prepare your regular meals during your eating time. In my experience, intermittent fasting works well when combined with a low-carb, high-fat diet made up of real, whole foods. However, for the time being, completing a project quickly is more critical than releasing the perfect combination to maximize profits.

The time (i.e. 7 p.m.) is mentioned for brevity's sake. You are in no obligation to do so. You have complete freedom to adjust the times to meet your requirements.

Are you talking about the days of the week? Fasting on weekdays, in my mind, is more convenient because it is more structured and has fewer variables. It's possible that this isn't the case for you. You're looking forward to the days when you think to yourself, "Where did the time go?" and "I didn't remember to eat!"

It's perfectly acceptable to make mistakes. Please, first and foremost, forgive yourself. You can pick up where you left off or start from the beginning. Make the most straightforward choice to get back on track. The next...

Many people agree that the 16/8 system is the most convenient and simplest way to do intermittent fasting; you may want to start there.

You could progress to more advanced fasts such as 24-hour fasts 1–2 times a week (Eat-Stop-Eat) or eating 500–600 calories 1–2 days a week if you find fasting comfortable and feel safe (5:2 diet).

Another choice is to fast if possible — just skip meals when you aren't hungry or don't have time to prepare them.

There's no need to follow a strict intermittent fasting plan to reap the benefits.

Experiment with different approaches before you find one that you like and that suits your schedule.

You can start with the 16/8 approach and work your way up to longer fasts. It's important to experiment to find a method that works for you.

Should You Try It?

Intermittent fasting is not needed for everyone.

It's just one of the healthy lifestyle improvements you can make. Consuming real food, exercise, and having an adequate sleep are the most important things to focus on.

If you dislike the idea of fasting, you should ignore this book and continue to do what works for you.

There is no such thing as a one-size-fits-all diet when it comes to nutrition. The best diet for you is one that you can stick to for an extended period of time.

Intermittent fasting is beneficial to some individuals but not to others. Checking out which political party you belong to is the easiest way to find out.

If you feel good when fasting and believe it to be a sustainable form of eating, fasting can be a very useful strategy for losing weight and enhancing your fitness.

WHAT ARE THE BENEFITS OF INTERMITTENT FASTING?

Weight loss isn't the only advantage of intermittent fasting. Fasting is an old tradition that is still observed in some civilizations today.

Health benefits are a welcome side effect of IF, and many of them are particularly beneficial to women's health.

- **Musculoskeletal health.** This group includes conditions like osteoporosis, arthritis, and lower back pain. Thyroid hormone production has been shown to be increased by fasting. This would help to increase bone integrity and avoid bone fractures.

- **Metabolic health.** In their fifties, both women hit menopause. Menopause can cause hormonal changes in the body, which can result in an increase in belly fat, cholesterol, and glucose levels. Fasting will help you lose weight, lower your blood pressure, and decrease your cholesterol, all of which will increase your insulin response. Fasting will also aid in the maintenance of a balanced metabolism as you age.

- **Mental health.** Mental stability has been shown to benefit from fasting. It can help with anxiety, stress, and the physical ups and downs that come with menopause. Fasting has since been found to improve self-esteem and reduce stress levels.

Other proven benefits of IF include:

- Improved memory
- Tissue health
- Physical performance
- Heart health

WHAT ARE THE TYPES OF INTERMITTENT FASTING AND HOW TO PREPARE PROPERLY TO SET YOUR WAY TO ONE SUCCESSFUL TRANSFORMATION?

It's awesome that there are so many different ways to do IF. If this is something you like doing, you'll be able to choose one that suits your needs best, improving your chances of success.

Here are four:

1. THE TWICE-A-WEEK METHOD – 5:2

This approach to intermittent fasting focuses on restricting calories to 500 calories for two days a week. The other five days of the week, you eat a healthy, nutritious meal.

On non-fasting days, a 200-calorie meal is served, and on fasting days, a 300-calorie meal is served. When fasting, it's crucial to focus on high-fibre and high-protein foods to keep you full while keeping your calorie intake down.

You can fast on any two days (for example, Tuesdays and Thursdays) as long as a non-fasting day falls between them. Consume the same number of calories that you would on a regular day.

2. ALTERNATE DAY FASTING

Any other day, this modification involves "adjusted" fasting. On fasting days, for example, keep your calorie intake to 500 calories, or around 25% of your caloric intake. Switch to your regular, healthy diet on non-fasting days. (There are some strict variations to this technique, such as consuming 0 calories instead of 500 on alternate days.)

People who observed the IF pattern for six months had significantly higher LDL (or bad) cholesterol levels after another six months off the diet, according to one study.

3. TIME-RESTRICTED EATING

This option allows you to set fasting and feeding windows. For example, imagine fasting for 16 hours a day and only being able to eat for eight.

Since most people fast while sleeping, this approach is efficient. It's practical because it helps you to extend your overnight fast by skipping breakfast and not eating again until lunchtime. What are some of the most widely used techniques?

16/8 method: Only eating between 11 a.m. and 7 p.m. or noon and 8 p.m.

14/10 method: Only eating between 10 a.m. and 8 p.m.

This IF procedure can be done as many times as you like, or even once or twice a week, depending on your tastes.

It may take a few days to find the right feeding and fasting windows for this strategy, particularly if you're really busy or if you wake up hungry for breakfast.

"For many people who want to try intermittent fasting for the first time, this form of fasting is a safer bet."

4. THE 24-HOUR FAST (OR EAT: STOP: EAT METHOD)

For this type, you must fast for a full 24 hours. It's only done once or twice a week, too. The vast majority of people fast from breakfast to lunch or lunch to lunch. Nausea, headaches, irritability, appetite loss, and reduced energy are also possible side effects of this version of IF.

You will revert to a normal, healthy diet on non-fasting days if you use this method.

MISTAKES TO AVOID WHEN YOU UNDERTAKE INTERMITTENT FASTING

So the study is pretty impressive, but there are some crucial points to remember while intermittent fasting, as well as some frequent errors that may prevent it from being as successful as it should be.

Here are five typical intermittent fasting errors, as well as how to prevent them entirely.

1 GOING INTO IT TOO SOON

When you're merely extending your natural evening short, the 16:8 intermittent fasting mechanism seems easy, but it can be jarring if you jump right in. You don't want to fast for the whole 16 hours if this is the first time dealing with prolonged fasting. Instead, start by skipping breakfast for an hour or two to see how your body responds. You should steadily increase the amount of time you spend on what sounds good to you.

2 NOT HYDRATING ENOUGH

You'll want to stay hydrated by drinking plenty of water during your fasting period! If you drink a good portion of your daily water intake at mealtimes, it's possible to forget because you don't want to get dehydrated. Often have a reusable water bottle on you and refill it as required.

What about coffee, though?

If you can't imagine waking up without a cup of coffee in the morning, you might be wondering if you can still get it during intermittent fasting.

During their fasting period, some people only drink water, while others drink black coffee (this means no added sugar or milk). Caffeine can help alleviate feelings of hunger for a short period of time, which some people find helpful, despite the lack of hard evidence to back this up.

If that cup of coffee is part of your everyday routine and helps you get through your fasting period, enjoy it in moderation (one cup) and plain.

NEGLECTING NUTRITIOUS FOODS ONCE FAST ENDS

This is a big one because what you eat when you've finished fasting matters a lot! As far as possible, we want to focus on wholesome and nutrient-dense foods.

Beginning with your first post-intermittent fasting meal, feed your body the foods it craves — your body will thank you!

Here are some delectable meal suggestions to help you break your fast:

- Scrambled eggs on gluten-free toast with dark leafy vegetables, tomato, and half an avocado
- Salmon filet served with quinoa and asparagus.
- Chicken breast with quinoa, broccoli, and balsamic vinegar on the side.

4 EATING TOO MUCH

There's even the common mistake of eating too much after the fasting period has ended. If you get hungry after intermittent fasting, it's a smart idea to have a nutritious meal cooked and ready to go; this way, you'll be less likely to reach for anything unhealthy.

NOT ADDING HEALTHY LIFESTYLE HABITS TO IT

Intermittent fasting is not a diet, and it should not be mistaken for one. It should not be used in lieu of other healthy lifestyle activities.

We should preferably be caring for all aspects of our health, which necessitates a normal self-care routine, exercise, and sufficient sleep.

BEST EXERCISES TO DO DURING INTERMITTENT FASTING FOR GETTING THE MOST OUT OF THIS TYPE OF DIET

If you're attempting intermittent fasting (IF) or fasting for a specific reason and still want to exercise, there are a few pros and cons to consider when working out when fasted.

According to some research, fasting exercise affects muscle biochemistry and metabolism, which are linked to insulin sensitivity and blood sugar level consistency.

Research also supports eating and exercising quickly until digestion or absorption. For people with type 2 diabetes or metabolic syndrome, this is particularly important.

According to Chelsea Amengual, MS, RD, manager of Fitness Programming & Nutrition at Virtual Health Partners, one advantage to fasting is that the glycogen (stored carbohydrates) would more likely be lost, causing you to burn more fat. Count on this reliable source to fuel your workout.

Would the prospect of burning more fat appeal to you? Remember the following before jumping on the fasted cardio bandwagon.

Suppose you work out while fasting, the body will continue to break down muscle in order to use protein for food, according to Amengual. "Plus, you're more likely to touch a wall," she says, "which means you won't have as much stamina and won't be able to work out as hard or do as well."

Intermittent fasting and long-term exercise, according to Priya Khorana, EdD, a diet trainer at Columbia University, are not ideal. "As your body runs out of calories and energy, your metabolism slows down."

GETTING IN AN EFFECTIVE GYM SESSION WHILE FASTING

There are some things you can do to make your workout more successful if you want to do IF by continuing to exercise.

1. THINK THROUGH TIMING

Registered dietician Christopher Shuff says there are three things to remember when it comes to making your fasting workout more successful: whether you can exercise before, after, or after the fueling window.

A well-known type of IF is the 16:8 protocol. The concept is to eat something for 8 hours and then fast for 16 hours.

"Training out before the window is better for someone who does well during exercise on an empty stomach," he explains, "while working out during the window is best for someone who does not want to exercise on an empty stomach but still wants to take advantage of post-workout nutrition." Throughout, Shuff says, it is the ideal moment for both success and relegation.

2. CHOOSE THE TYPE OF WORKOUT BASED ON YOUR MACROS

According to Lynda Lippin, a licensed personal trainer and master Pilates instructor, it's important to keep track of the macronutrients you ingest when exercising and what you eat afterwards.

Power workouts, for example, require more carbs on the day of the workout, while cardio/HIIT [high-intensity interval training] can be done on a lower carb day, explains.

3. EAT THE RIGHT MEALS AFTER YOUR WORKOUT TO BUILD OR MAINTAIN MUSCLE

The best way to balance IF and fitness, according to Dr Niket Sonpal, is to plan your workouts during your feeding periods while your nutrition levels are at their peak.

"And if you do a lot of heavy lifting, the body requires protein to assist with recovery afterwards," he adds.

Within 30 minutes after the strength training workout, Amengual advises consuming carbohydrates and about 20 grams of protein.

HOW CAN YOU SAFELY EXERCISE WHILE FASTING?

Any weight loss or wellness program's success is measured by its potential to be maintained over time. When doing IF, you must be cautious if your primary goal is to lose body weight while maintaining your fitness. Here are a few pointers from the pros to get you started.

Within an hour after your medium- to a high-intensity workout, eat a snack.

This is where the value of meal planning becomes apparent. It's crucial, according to Khorana, to schedule a meal to coincide with a medium- to high-intensity workout. As a result, your body will be able to rely on glycogen stores to fuel your workout.

STAY HYDRATED

Fasting does not imply dehydration. In reality, you should drink more water while fasting.

KEEP YOUR ELECTROLYTES UP

recommends coconut water as a low-calorie hydration source. "It replenishes electrolytes, has a low-calorie count, and tastes pretty good," he says. Gatorade and sports drinks are rich in sugar, so limit the intake.

KEEP THE INTENSITY AND DURATION FAIRLY LOW

If you start to feel dizzy or light-headed after working too long, take a break. It's important to pay attention to the body.

CONSIDER THE TYPE OF FAST

Lippin suggests performing low-intensity exercises like yoga while you're doing a 24-hour intermittent intense:

- Walking
- Restorative Yoga
- Gentle Pilates

The majority of the 16-hour fasting window is spent in the evening, sleeping, and early in the morning if you're doing the 16:8 hard, so sticking to a certain type of exercise isn't as important.

MEAL PLAN WITH 21 DAYS

It can be daunting at first, but sleep accounts for at least eight hours of the sixteen hours. There is also a significant amount of downtime between dinner and bedtime, which adds up. Just be gentle with yourself, and your body can soon adjust to your new eating habits. What better way to get started right away than to plan out what you'll eat during your eight-hour meal window?

DAY 1

MEAL # 1: CHIA PUDDING

Preparation Time: 50 minutes

Cooking Time: 5 minutes

Total Time: 10 Minutes

Chia Overnight Oats are a delicious combination of chia seeds, oats, and almond milk. So easy and convenient for a good breakfast on the go! YUMMY!

INGREDIENTS:

- 1/2 Cup Quaker Oats Rolled Oats
- 1/4 Cup Chia Seeds
- 1 Cup Milk or Water
- Pinch of Salt and Cinnamon
- Maple Syrup or Other Sweetener to Taste
- 1 Cup Frozen Berries of Choice (Or Yesterday's Smoothie Leftovers)
- Yoghurt for Topping
- Berries for Topping

DIRECTIONS:

1. In a jar with a lid, combine the peas, almonds, milk, salt, and cinnamon. Refrigerate for at least one hour.
2. Blend the berries until smooth. (I usually incorporate this into my smoothie routine, but I either use leftover smoothie or make a big batch of smoothie because I have some left over for the oats.) You are not obligated to do so, but it is a nice way to add some colour and fruit.)
3. Toss oats with frozen berry puree and top with yoghurt, more berries, nuts, cinnamon, or whatever else you want.

NUTRITION FACT: Calories Per Serving 516: Total Fat 16.5g: Cholesterol 0mg: Sodium 602mg: Total Carbohydrate 78.1g: Dietary Fiber 26.1g: Sugars 20.8g: Protein 14.8g

Snack: Fruit of choice

MEAL #2: CHINESE CHICKEN SALAD

Preparation Time: 4 minutes

Cooking Time: 5minutes, 59 seconds

Total Time: 10 Minutes

INGREDIENTS

For the dressing:
- One teaspoon minced garlic
- 1/4 cup reduced-sodium soy sauce
- Two tablespoons rice vinegar
- 1 1/2 tablespoons honey
- Pinch of ground ginger
- For the salad:
- 1 cup cooked chicken breast, chopped or shredded
- 1 cup shelled edamame beans, cooked according to package directions and cooled
- Two medium bell peppers, diced
- 1 cup shredded carrots
- 4 cups tricolour coleslaw mix

- 1/2 cup chopped cilantro
- Three green onions, chopped, optional
- 1/4 cup toasted almonds, optional
- One tablespoon sesame seeds, optional

DIRECTIONS
1. To make the dressing, combine the garlic, soy sauce, rice vinegar, sugar, and ginger in a small cup.
2. In a big mixing bowl, combine the chicken, edamame, bell peppers, carrots, and coleslaw blend. Toss all together.
3. Toss the salad with the dressing and toss until it is evenly covered. Mix in the cilantro once more.
4. If wanted, top with green onions, toasted almonds, and sesame seeds.
5. Serve right away, or let it cool for the best flavour.

Nutrition Fact: Calories Per Serving 400: Total Fat 13.5g: Cholesterol 0mg: Sodium 602mg: Total Carbohydrate 70.1g: Dietary Fiber 26.1g: Sugars 20.8g: Protein 14.8g

MEAL #3: SPICY CHICKEN CHILLI

Preparation Time: 4 minutes

Cooking Time: 5minutes, 59 seconds

Total Time: 10 Minutes

INGREDIENTS

- One tablespoon canola oil
- 1 cup chopped red onion
- 1 cup chopped green pepper
- Two cloves garlic, finely chopped
- Two jalapeños, thinly sliced
- 1-1/2 pounds ground chicken
- 1/4 cup chili powder
- 2 cups canned crushed tomatoes
- 1 tablespoon chicken stock
- 1 tablespoon brown sugar
- 1 tablespoon apple cider vinegar
- 1 tablespoon hot sauce
- 1 tablespoon salt
- 2 cans dark red kidney beans, drained
- To garnish: (optional)
- Cilantro

DIRECTIONS

1. Heat the canola oil in a big Dutch oven over high heat. Combine the onion, tomato, jalapeos, and garlic in a large mixing bowl. Cook, stirring sometimes, until the onion is soft (about five minutes.)
2. Cook, stirring to break up any lumps, until the chicken has lost its pink hue (about five minutes). Cook for one minute after adding the chili powder.
3. Combine the onions, broth, sugar, mustard, hot sauce, and salt in a mixing bowl. Reduce to a low heat, cover, and cook, stirring often, until the chili has thickened (about 45 minutes.)
4. Cook, stirring sometimes, until the beans are cooked through, about 15 minutes. For the last 15 minutes of cooking, remove the cover.
5. Garnish with your own garnish and enjoy!

Nutrition Fact: Calories Per Serving 324: Total Fat 16.5g: Cholesterol 0mg: Sodium 602mg: Total Carbohydrate 50.1g: Dietary Fiber 26.1g: Sugars 18.8g: Protein 12.8g

DAY 2

MEAL # 1 : MINT CHIP PROTEIN SHAKE

Preparation Time: 2 minutes

Cooking Time: 2 minutes, 59 seconds

Total Time: 10 Minutes

INGREDIENTS

- 3/4 cup nonfat Greek yogurt
- 1/4 cup fresh mint, tightly packed
- 1 cup almond milk
- 1/4 cup dark chocolate chips
- 1 cup baby spinach
- 1 tablespoon maple syrup
- 2 cups ice

DIRECTIONS

1. Combine all of the ingredients in a blender until creamy, then serve.

Nutrition Fact: Calories Per Serving 337: Total Fat 18.5g: Cholesterol 0mg: Sodium 72mg: Total Carbohydrate 68.1g: Dietary Fiber 30.1g: Sugars 15.8g: Protein 14.8g

Snack: Nuts

MEAL #2: VEGAN CHICKPEA CURRY

Preparation Time: 4 minutes

Cooking Time: 5minutes, 59 seconds

Total Time: 10 Minutes

6 servings

To get the best spice out of this recipe, you'll need a slow cooker. If you don't have a slow cooker, steam the curry in a stockpot for one hour.

INGREDIENTS
Curry:
- 1 teaspoon olive oil
- 1/2 yellow onion, chopped
- 1 clove garlic, minced
- 1 tablespoons minced ginger
- 15-ounce can chickpeas (about 1 1/2 cups)
- 2 cups canned or boxed chopped tomatoes
- 2 cups small cauliflower florets
- 1 sweet potato, peeled and diced
- 1 can light coconut milk
- 1 cup vegetable broth
- 1 tablespoon garam masala
- 1/2 tablespoon curry powder
- 1 teaspoon salt
- 2 cups lightly packed baby spinach, chopped

Coconut rice:
- 1 1/2 cups uncooked brown basmati rice
- 1 can light coconut milk
- 1/2 cup water
- 1/4 teaspoon salt

DIRECTIONS

1. In a skillet, heat the oil and sauté the onions, garlic, and fresh ginger for seven minutes.
2. Apply the remaining ingredients, minus the spinach, to the onion mixture in the slow cooker.
3. Heat for six hours on low (or on high for four hours).
4. Stir in the spinach just before serving and cook for another five minutes.
5. To make the rice, follow these steps:
6. In a saucepan, combine the rice, coconut milk, water, and salt. Bring to a boil on high heat, then cover, reduce to low heat, and cook for 40 minutes. Enable the curry to cool for 10 minutes after turning off the fire. Serve with rice if desired.

Nutrition Fact: Calories Per Serving 398: Total Fat 16.5g: Cholesterol 0mg: Sodium 602mg: Total Carbohydrate 78.1g: Dietary Fiber 26.1g: Sugars 20.8g: Protein 14.8g

Snack: Fruit of choice

MEAL #3: MEXICAN TEMPEH QUINOA SALAD

Preparation Time: 10 minutes
Cooking Time: 34 minutes, 59 seconds
Total Time: 10 Minutes
Yield 4 to 6 servings

INGREDIENTS

- 1 cup quinoa
- 2 cups water
- 1 tablespoon olive oil
- 1/2 onion, chopped
- 1 red pepper, diced
- 1 (8-oz.) package tempeh, diced into bite-size pieces
- 1 cup salsa
- Juice from one lime
- 1 teaspoon cumin
- 1/4 teaspoon cayenne pepper
- 1/4 teaspoon salt
- 1/4 teaspoon pepper
- 1 black beans can
- 1 cup fresh corn (or frozen)
- 1/2 cup cherry tomatoes, halved
- 2 tablespoons fresh cilantro
- Salt and pepper, to taste
- 1 avocado, diced

DIRECTIONS

1. In a sealed pot over high heat, combine the quinoa and water. Reduce to a low heat and cook for 20 minutes, or until the water has been absorbed and the quinoa is soft.
2. Prepare the tempeh while the quinoa is frying. In a medium-sized skillet, heat the oil and add the chopped onion. 5 minutes in the oven
3. Combine the diced red pepper, tempeh, salsa, lime juice, cumin, cayenne pepper, and salt and pepper in a large mixing bowl.
4. Cook the tempeh mixture for about 15 minutes, stirring periodically.
5. Once the quinoa and tempeh are all cooked, combine them in a glass dish. Mix in the rice, corn, onions, cilantro, and a pinch of salt and pepper. Serve with a few chopped avocado slices on top.
6. Enjoy on its own or as a tasty burrito filling.

NUTRITION

Calories per serving 353

DAY 3

Snack: Yogurt

MEAL #1: VEGAN VANILLA PROTEIN SHAKE

Preparation Time: 2 minutes
Cooking Time: 2 minutes, 59 seconds
Total Time: 10 Minutes
Yield 1 smoothie

INGREDIENTS

- 1/2 cup soft tofu
- 1 cup vanilla soy milk
- 1 frozen banana
- 1/2 tablespoon peanut butter

DIRECTIONS

1. In a blender, combine all of the ingredients and process for one minute, or until smooth. Have fun!

Nutrition Fact: Calories Per Serving 328: Total Fat 16.5g: Cholesterol 0mg: Sodium 602mg: Total Carbohydrate 78.1g: Dietary Fiber 26.1g: Sugars 20.8g: Protein 14.8g

MEAL #2: TUNA SALAD PITA SANDWICHES

Preparation Time: 10 minutes
Cooking Time: 34 minutes, 59 seconds
Total Time: 10 Minutes
Yield 4 to 6 servings

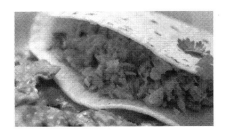

INGREDIENTS

- 2 whole-wheat pitas
- 1 can tuna canned in water without salt
- Lemon juice from 2 wedges
- 2 tsps olive oil
- 1/2 small onion diced (purple or red onion adds color)
- 1/2 cup diced red bell pepper
- 1 tbsp chopped parsley
- Salt and pepper

DIRECTIONS

1. Open the tuna can, empty it, and put it in a mixing bowl.
2. Combine the lemon juice and olive oil in a mixing bowl.
3. Combine the bell pepper, onion, and parsley in a large mixing bowl.
4. Season with salt and pepper to taste.
5. Put it in a pita and enjoy it!

Nutrition Fact: Calories Per Serving 230: Total Fat 16.5g: Cholesterol 0mg: Sodium 602mg: Total Carbohydrate 78.1g: Dietary Fiber 4.5g: Sugars 20.8g: Protein 14.8g

MEAL #3: ASIAN FRIED "RICE"

Preparation Time: 10 minutes
Cooking Time: 34 minutes, 59 seconds
Total Time: 10 Minutes
Yield 4 servings

INGREDIENTS

- 3 slices bacon, crosscut into 1/4-inch pieces
- 1 medium cauliflower head, cut into uniform pieces
- 2 large eggs
- Kosher salt
- Freshly ground black pepper
- 2 tablespoons ghee (or fat of choice)
- 1 small yellow onion, minced
- 4 ounces cremini mushrooms, thinly sliced
- 1-inch piece of fresh ginger, grated (about 1 tablespoon)
- 2 tablespoons coconut aminos
- 1 teaspoon coconut vinegar
- 1 teaspoon Paleo-friendly fish sauce (I used Red Boat Fish Sauce)

- 2 scallions, thinly sliced
- 2 tablespoons chopped cilantro

DIRECTIONS

1. In a big skillet over medium heat, cook the bacon, stirring periodically. With a slotted spoon, pass the crispy bacon to a paper-towel-lined plate once it has crisped up, about 15 minutes.
2. When the bacon is crisping, pulse the cauliflower in a food processor until it's the size of rice grains. Don't overdo it, however. We don't like cauliflower in liquid form.
3. Whisk the eggs in a shallow bowl of salt and pepper to taste. Make a thin egg omelet by pouring the eggs into the hot bacon drippings. Remove the omelet from the skillet and cut it into ribbons before setting it aside.
4. In the same skillet over medium-high heat, melt the ghee and add the onions, along with a pinch of kosher salt and pepper. Add the sliced mushrooms after the onions have softened and become transparent, around 5 minutes. Apply the grated ginger after the mushrooms have browned and swirl for 30 seconds to integrate.
5. Mix in the cauliflower "rice," season with a pinch of salt then pepper, and combine the ingredients. Cover the skillet with a lid, reduce the heat to medium, and cook for around 5 minutes with the lid on. When the "rice" is soft but not mushy, it's over.
6. With the coconut aminos, coconut vinegar, and fish sauce, season to taste. Mix in the scallions, cilantro, sliced omelet, and a pinch of salt and pepper before eating.

Nutrition Fact: Calories Per Serving 230: Total Fat 16.5g: Cholesterol 0mg: Sodium 602mg: Total Carbohydrate 78.1g: Dietary Fiber 4.5gr: Sugars 20.8g: Protein 12.5g

DAY 4

MEAL # 1: EGG MUFFINS

Preparation Time: 10 minutes
Cooking Time: 34 minutes, 59 seconds
Total Time: 10 Minutes
Servings: 3

INGREDIENTS

- 12 eggs
- half teaspoon of sea salt

- nonstick cooking spray
- 1 cup fresh spinach
- 1 cup sliced mushrooms
- 1/4 cup sliced green onion
- 2 cups shredded cheese

DIRECTIONS

1. Preheat the oven to 350 degrees Fahrenheit. In a liquid mixing cup, crack eggs. Combine the eggs and salt in a mixing bowl.
2. Using ghee, grease a 12-cup muffin pan. Fill each muffin cup halfway with spinach, mushrooms, green onion, and cheese, then carefully spill eggs over the tops until almost full (leave 1/4-inch space).
3. Bake for 20-25 minutes, or until a wooden pick inserted in the middle comes out clean. When the egg muffins come out of the oven, they will seem to be soufflé, but they will sink after a few minutes. Allow them to cool in the muffin tin for a few minutes before carefully removing each muffin with a rubber spatula.
4. Allow to cool completely before transferring to a resealable plastic container. refrigerant

Nutrition Fact: Calories Per Serving 520: Total Fat 38.7g: Cholesterol 803mg: Sodium 952mg: Total Carbohydrate 3.41g: Dietary Fiber 26.1g: Sugars 20.8g: Protein 39.9g

MEAL #2: BROCCOLI SLAW SALAD

Preparation Time: 2 minutes
Cooking Time: 2 minutes, 59 seconds
Total Time: 10 Minutes
Yield 1 salad

INGREDIENTS

- 1/2 cup plain yogurt
- 1 teaspoon lemon juice
- 1 tablespoon apple cider vinegar
- 2 tablespoons blue cheese crumbles
- 2 cups broccoli slaw (I used Trader Joe's)
- 2 ounces chicken breast, grilled or baked
- 1 teaspoon sliced green onions

DIRECTIONS

1. In a shallow tub, combine the milk, lemon juice, apple cider vinegar, and blue cheese crumbles. Mix thoroughly.
2. Add the broccoli slaw to a separate dish, then pour in the dressing and stir well until the slaw is finely covered.
3. Place the chicken breast on top of the slaw and garnish with green onions. Take pleasure in it.!

Nutrition Fact: Calories Per Serving 313: Total Fat 16.5g: Cholesterol 0mg: Sodium 602mg: Total Carbohydrate 78.1g: Dietary Fiber 6.1g: Sugars 20.8g: Protein 34.2g

MEAL #3: LEMON GARLIC CHICKEN DRUMSTICKS

Preparation Time: 10 minutes
Cooking Time: 34 minutes, 59 seconds
Total Time: 10 Minutes
Yield 3-4 servings

INGREDIENTS

- Kosher salt
- Pepper, freshly cracked
- 10-16 skin-on chicken drumsticks
- 1 tablespoon olive oil
- 4 tablespoons butter
- 3 garlic cloves, finely chopped
- Zest of 1 lemon, plus 1 tablespoon lemon juice
- 2 tablespoons parsley, chopped

DIRECTIONS

1. Season the drumsticks generously with salt and pepper, and set aside for 30 minutes at room temperature, if time permits. Until frying, pat the drumsticks dry with paper towels.
2. Preheat a 12-inch heavy-bottomed skillet over medium-high heat (preferably not nonstick). Use two smaller skillets if you don't have a large enough skillet. Combine the oil and half of the butter in a mixing bowl. Brown the drumsticks on both sides in batches in the foaming butter; pass the browned drumsticks to a plate.
3. Reduce the heat to medium-low, return all of the drumsticks to the skillet(s), cover, and cook for 20-25 minutes, rearranging the drumsticks every 5-10 minutes to ensure even cooking. Remove the lid from the pan and stir in the remaining butter, garlic, lemon zest, and lemon juice. Toss the drumsticks gently to cover them. Remove the skillet from the heat and set aside for a few minutes to allow the flavors to meld (this also allows the chicken to rest). Serve immediately with a parsley garnish.

Nutrition Fact: Calories Per Serving 441: Total Fat 28.8g: Cholesterol 0mg: Sodium 602mg: Total Carbohydrate 78.1g: Dietary Fiber 26.1g: Sugars 20.8g: Protein 42.6g

DAY 5

MEAL #1: 50-CALORIE CHOCOLATE COCONUT PROTEIN BALLS

Preparation Time: 4 minutes
Cooking Time: 14 minutes, 59 seconds
Total Time: 10 Minutes
Yield 24 balls

INGREDIENTS
- 1 cup raw almonds
- 1 cup golden raisins
- 1 1/2 scoops chocolate plant-based protein powder (1 scoop is about 35 grams; I used Vega)
- 1/8 teaspoon sea salt
- 2 tablespoons unsweetened shredded coconut

DIRECTIONS
1. In a food processor or high-powered blender, combine almonds. For a few minutes, process the nuts until a smooth almond butter develops.
2. Mix in the raisins until they are almost smooth.
3. Blend in the protein powder and salt until it is well mixed.
4. Roll the dough into 24 balls, then roll each one in shredded coconut and put on a plate or pan.
5. Enjoy right now, or chill for at least 20 minutes if you want a firmer quality. Keep those balls that haven't been consumed in an airtight jar.

Nutrition Fact: Calories Per Serving 53: Total Fat 16.5g: Cholesterol 0mg: Sodium 602mg: Total Carbohydrate 78.1g: Dietary Fiber 26.1g: Sugars 20.8g: Protein 14.8g

Snack: Boiled eggs

MEAL #2: TACO SALAD

Preparation Time: 4 minutes
Cooking Time: 5minutes, 59 seconds
Total Time: 10 Minutes
Servings: 2

INGREDIENTS

- 1 tablespoon olive oil
- 1/2 jalapeño, seeded and thinly sliced
- 1 clove of garlic, minced
- 1/2 pound of ground beef
- 3/4 teaspoon plus 1/2 teaspoon cumin
- 1/2 teaspoon chili powder
- 3/4 teaspoon plus 1/2 teaspoon salt
- 1/2 teaspoon plus 1/4 teaspoon black pepper
- 1 head of red leaf lettuce
- 1/2 cup canned black beans, rinsed
- 3/4 cup cotija cheese, crumbled
- 3 radishes, thinly sliced
- 2 green onions, thinly sliced
- 1 cup tortilla chips, crumbled
- 1 cup cherry tomatoes, halved
- 5 tablespoons extra-virgin olive oil
- 1 large lime, juiced
- 3 tablespoons minced cilantro

DIRECTIONS

1. In a big sauté pan, heat the olive oil. Cook for about a minute after adding the jalapeos and garlic.

2. 3/4 teaspoon cumin, chili powder, 3/4 teaspoon cinnamon, and 1/2 teaspoon pepper are added to the ground beef. Cook for 10 minutes, stirring to break up the ground beef. Remove from the equation.

3. Lettuce should be washed and dried. Dismantle. Divide the mixture in two big pots. Arrange the rice, cheese, radishes, green onions, peas, and tortilla chips in an even layer on the plate. In two separate pans, divide the ground beef mixture.

4. Combine 1/2 teaspoon cumin, 1/2 teaspoon cinnamon, 1/4 teaspoon black pepper, and minced cilantro in a separate shallow cup. Combine the lime juice and olive oil in a mixing bowl. Combine all ingredients in a mixing bowl.

5. Toss the salads together after pouring the dressing generously over them.

Nutrition Fact: Calories Per Serving 556: Total Fat 24%: Cholesterol 113mg: Sodium 150mg: Total Carbohydrate 48.1g: Dietary Fiber 26.1g: Sugars 20.8g: Protein 50.8g

MEAL #3: THAI CITRUS CHICKEN SALAD

Preparation Time: 4 minutes
Cooking Time: 5minutes, 59 seconds
Total Time: 10 Minutes
Yield 3 servings

INGREDIENTS

For the salad:

- One chicken breast, about 7 to 8 ounces, cubed
- One clove garlic, minced
- 1 1/2 cup Napa cabbage, shredded
- 1 cup red cabbage, shredded
- 1 cup papaya, cut into matchsticks
- 1 cup carrots, shredded
- 1/2 cup daikon, shredded
- 1/4 cup green onion, minced
- 1/4 cup cilantro, chopped
- 1 tablespoon olive oil
- Salt
- Pepper
- 1/2 lime, cut into wedges
- For the dressing:
- 1 tablespoon fresh lime juice
- 1 tablespoon soy sauce
- 1 tablespoon fish sauce
- 1 teaspoon rice vinegar
- 1 teaspoon sugar
- 1/2 teaspoon olive oil
- 2 cloves garlic, minced
- 1/2 to 1 jalepeno, or to taste

DIRECTIONS

1. Season cubed chicken breast with salt and pepper, as well as garlic minced. Allow for a few minutes of rest.
2. Heat olive oil in a skillet or pan over medium-high heat.
3. When the oil is thick, add the chicken breasts and brown on both sides, turning periodically. When it's done, about seven minutes later, remove it. Put aside to cool after squeezing the juice from a lime wedge on the chicken.
4. Combine the remaining salad ingredients in a big mixing cup (red and Napa cabbage, carrots, papaya, daikon, green onion, and cilantro). Remove from the equation.
5. Combine all salad dressing ingredients in a small bowl and stir to combine.
6. Blend the dressing before it is emulsified in a blender.
7. Toss the salad with the chicken and dressing and toss to combine. Serve with a wedge of lime.

Nutrition Fact: Calories Per Serving 223: Total Fat 16.5g: Cholesterol 0mg:

Sodium 602mg: Total Carbohydrate 78.1g: Dietary Fiber 3.5g: Sugars 20.8g: Protein 24.1g

DAY 6

MEAL #1: KARLIE KLOSS'S PROTEIN SMOOTHIE

Preparation Time: 0 minutes
Cooking Time: 1minutes, 59 seconds
Total Time: 10 Minutes
Yield 1 smoothie

INGREDIENTS

- 1 cup of almond milk preferably unsweetened
- A scoop of chocolate protein powder
- 1 banana
- A cup of blackberries

DIRECTIONS

1. In a blender, combine all ingredients and blend until smooth.
2. Enjoy!

Nutrition Fact: Calories Per Serving 398: Total Fat 16.5g: Cholesterol 0mg: Sodium 602mg: Total Carbohydrate 78.1g: Dietary Fiber 26.1g: Sugars 20.8g: Protein 14.8g

MEAL #2: AVOCADO CHICKEN SALAD

Preparation Time: 4 minutes
Cooking Time: 5minutes, 59 seconds
Total Time: 10 Minutes

Yield Makes 1 sandwich; Total Time 4 minutes, 59 seconds

INGREDIENTS

For the chicken salad:

- 1/4 avocado
- 2 tablespoons plain yogurt
- 1 teaspoon lemon juice
- 3/4 cup shredded chicken, precooked
- For the sandwich:
- 1 whole wheat English muffin

- Handful of lettuce or sunflower sprouts
- 2 slices tomato

DIRECTIONS

1. Mash the avocado with the yogurt and lemon juice in a shallow bowl until well mixed.
2. Add the chicken to the bowl and toss it about with a spoon until it's evenly covered.
3. Serve the chicken salad over lettuce or break between two English muffins with a tomato slice and sunflower sprouts.

Nutrition Fact: Calories Per Serving 420**:** Total Fat 16.5g**:** Cholesterol 0mg**:** Sodium 602mg**:** Total Carbohydrate 78.1g**:** Dietary Fiber 26.1g**:** Sugars 20.8g**:** Protein 15.8g

MEAL #3: MEDITERRANEAN QUINOA SALAD

Preparation Time: 4 minutes
Cooking Time: 5minutes, 59 seconds
Total Time: 10 Minutes

Yield 2 servingsTotal Time 4 minutes, 59 seconds

INGREDIENTS

For the dressing:

- 3 tablespoons lemon juice
- 2 tablespoons red wine vinegar
- 1/2 tablespoon olive oil
- Pinch of oregano
- For the salad:
- 1 cup quinoa, cooked
- 2 cups spinach
- 1 red pepper, diced
- 10 grape tomatoes, halved
- 10 kalamata olives, sliced
- 1/4 cup feta cheese

DIRECTIONS

1. In a small mug, whisk together all of the dressing ingredients. Remove from the equation.
2. Combine the quinoa, spinach, and about half of the prepared seasoning in a large mixing dish.

Using a wooden spoon, thoroughly combine the ingredients.

3. In a mixing dish, combine the red pepper, onions, olives, and the remaining dressing. Mix thoroughly.

4. Refrigerate or eat right away after folding in the feta!

Nutrition Fact: Calories Per Serving 397**:** Total Fat 16.5g**:** Cholesterol 0mg**:** Sodium 602mg**:** Total Carbohydrate 70.1g**:** Dietary Fiber 30.1g**:** Sugars 20.8g**:** Protein 14.8g

DAY 7

MEAL #1: PALEO BREAKFAST BAR

Preparation Time: 4 minutes
Cooking Time: 5minutes, 59 seconds
Total Time: 10 Minutes
These delectable breakfast bars are packed with nutrients and plant-based protein! Perfect for anytime you need to "grab and go" for your meal!

Ingredients
- 1 cup desiccated coconut
- 1/2 cup shelled hemp seeds
- 1/2 cup sesame seeds
- 1/2 cup pumpkin seeds
- 1 1/2 cups mixed nuts, chopped into small chunks (I added cashews, walnuts, almonds &

pistachios to a high-powered blender and pulsed for a few seconds)
- 1/2 cup raisins
- 1 tsp ground cinnamon
- 1/2 cup cashew butter, or nut butter of your choice
- 4 tbsp maple syrup or date paste
- 1 tsp vanilla extract

Directions
1. Preheat the oven to 180 degrees Celsius (350 degrees Fahrenheit) and line a brownie pan with parchment paper.
2. Combine the coconut, beans, almonds, raisins, and cinnamon in a big mixing cup.
3. Melt the cashew butter and maple syrup in a big saucepan over medium heat. Remove from the heat and stir in the vanilla extract until it is well mixed and smooth.
4. Mix the contents of the bowl with the contents of the saucepan until it is well mixed. If necessary, a drop of water may be added to make it hold together.
5. To make a smooth, even sheet, transfer to the brownie tin and press down as tightly as possible.
6. Preheat oven to 350°F and bake for 15 minutes, or until golden brown.
7. Allow for full cooling before cutting into 12 strips. Keep for up

to a week in an airtight tin. Have fun!

Nutrition Fact: Calories Per Serving 340**:** Total Fat 16.5g**:** Cholesterol 0mg**:** Sodium 602mg**:** Total Carbohydrate 20.8g**:** Dietary Fiber 3.3g**:** Sugars 20.8g**:** Protein 10.8g

Snack: Carrots and hummus

MEAL #2: SMASHED AVOCADO CHICKPEA SALAD

Preparation Time: 4 minutes
Cooking Time: 5minutes, 59 seconds
Total Time: 10 Minutes

Yield 4 servingsTotal Time 14 minutes, 59 seconds

Ingredients

- 1 ripe avocado
- 1/4 cup tahini or Goddess Salad Dressing
- Juice from 1/2 a lemon (or 1 lemon if you prefer)
- 15-ounce can of chickpeas, rinsed and drained
- 1/2 cucumber, diced
- 2 stalks celery, chopped
- 1 large carrot, chopped
- 2 tablespoons fresh dill
- 3 tablespoons salted sunflower seeds
- Sea salt and pepper, to taste
- 2 English muffins
- 8 cherry tomatoes, halved

Directions

1. In a mixing dish, combine the avocado, tahini, lemon juice, and chickpeas. Smash these ingredients with a fork or a potato masher until coarsely mashed.
2. Mix together the cucumber, celery, carrot, dill, and sunflower seeds. Salt and pepper to taste.
3. Serve 1/4 of the chickpea mixture on half of a toasted English muffin with four cherry tomato slices on top, and enjoy!

Nutrition Fact: Calories Per Serving 485**:** Total Fat 16.5g**:** Cholesterol 0mg**:** Sodium 602mg**:** Total Carbohydrate 78.1g**:** Dietary Fiber 26.1g**:** Sugars 20.8g**:** Protein 14.8g

MEAL #3: PEANUT CHICKEN AND VEGGIES

Preparation Time: 15 minutes
Cooking Time: 10 minutes

Total Time: 25 Minutes

SERVINGS: 4 servings, about 7 cups

INGREDIENTS

For the Peanut Sauce:
- 1/3 cup creamy peanut butter
- 1 tablespoon sesame oil
- 1 tablespoon freshly squeezed lime juice
- 2 cloves garlic minced
- 1 tablespoon minced fresh ginger
- 1 tablespoon low-sodium soy sauce
- 2 teaspoons honey
- 5-6 tablespoons water
- Half teaspoon of red pepper flakes
- For the Chicken and Stir Fry Veggies:
- Two cups cooked shredded chicken, about 8 ounces; if the chicken has not yet been cooked.
- 1 tbsp olive oil (extra virgin)
- Three cups chopped broccoli florets (approximately 1 small head or 8 ounces)

- Two big red bell peppers, thinly sliced
- Two medium carrots, peeled and cut into 1/8-inch coins
- One small bunch sliced green onions, white and green bits separated
- 1 cup shelled edamame (frozen or thawed)
- Two minced garlic cloves
- 1 tbsp fresh ginger, minced
- One tbsp soy sauce (low sodium)
- Blue rice quinoa, soba noodles, or brown rice noodles, cooked

DIRECTIONS

1. Whisk together the sauce ingredients in a shallow saucepan over medium heat: peanut butter, sesame oil, lime juice, garlic, ginger, soy sauce, sugar, 5 tablespoons sugar, and red pepper flakes. Heat, stirring constantly, until the sauce is smooth and slightly thickens. If the sauce is so thick, thin it out with a little more water. Toss in the chicken to coat it in the sauce and heat it through. To keep the chicken warm, turn off the heat and cover the saucepan.

2. Meanwhile, in a big nonstick skillet or wok, melt the olive oil over medium high heat. Broccoli, bell pepper, carrots, and the white

and light green portions of the green onions can all be added at this stage. Cook the vegetables for 6 to 8 minutes, or until crisp tender. Toss in the edamame, garlic, ginger, soy sauce, and green onions' green bits. Cook for an extra minute, stirring to coat.

3. Spoon the rice into separate cooking bowls to eat. Add the vegetables, peanut chicken, and any other desired toppings to the top. Enjoy while it's still hot.

Notes

1. Refrigerate leftovers for up to 4 days or freeze them for up to 3 months.
2. Do you like peanut sauce or anticipate consuming any of the recipe's leftovers? I'd recommend making 1.5 times the sauce, or even double it if you're married to my peanut-sauce-loving husband. Toss only enough sauce with the chicken to cover it evenly, then set aside the remainder for eating or repurposing leftovers.
3. Replace the chicken with Crispy Tofu or chickpeas to make it vegetarian or vegan.
4. To keep it gluten-free, replace the soy sauce with gluten-free tamari.

Serve with a gluten-free grain like rice or quinoa.

Nutrition Fact: Calories Per Serving 507: Total Fat 21.5g: Cholesterol 0mg: Sodium 603mg: Total Carbohydrate 48.1g: Dietary Fiber 7.1g: Sugars 11.8g: Protein 31.8g

DAY 8

MEAL # 1: EGG SCRAMBLE WITH SWEET POTATOES (SEE RECIPE IN THE RECIPES SECTION)

Preparation Time: 4 minutes
Cooking Time: 5minutes, 59 seconds
Total Time: 10 Minutes

MEAL #2: GREEK CHICKPEA WAFFLES

Preparation Time: 4 minutes
Cooking Time: 5minutes, 59 seconds
Total Time: 10 Minutes

INGREDIENTS:
- A third of a cup chickpea flour
- 1/2 teaspoon baking soda
- 1/2 teaspoon salt
- 3/4 cup plain, 2% greek yogurt

- Six big eggs
- To serve, combine tomatoes, cucumbers, scallions, olive oil, parsley, milk, and lemon juice (optional)
- Seasoned with salt and pepper

DIRECTIONS:

1. Preheat the oven to 200 degrees Fahrenheit. Preheat the oven to 350°F and put a wire rack over a rimmed baking dish. Preheat a waffle iron according to the manufacturer's instructions.
2. Combine the rice, baking soda, and salt in a big mixing cup. Whisk together the yogurt and eggs in a shallow cup. Combine the wet and dry products in a mixing bowl.
3. Spray the waffle iron lightly with nonstick cooking spray. Drop 14 to 12 cup batter into each part of the iron in batches and cook for 4 to 5 minutes, until golden brown. Heat the waffles by placing them in the oven. Continue for the remaining hitter.
4. Waffles may be topped with the savory tomato mixture or a dollop of soft almond butter and berries.

Nutrition Fact: Calories Per Serving 412: Total Fat 18.5g: Cholesterol 0mg: Sodium 602mg: Total Carbohydrate 24.1g: Dietary Fiber 26.1g: Sugars 20.8g: Protein 35.8g

MEAL #3: PB&J OVERNIGHT OATS

Preparation Time: 4 minutes
Cooking Time: 5minutes, 59 seconds
Total Time: 10 Minutes

INGREDIENTS:
- 1/4 cup rolled oats (quick-cooking)
- 1/2 cup of 2% milk
- 3 tablespoons smooth peanut butter
- 1/4 cup raspberries, crushed
- 3 tablespoons entire raspberries

DIRECTIONS:

1. Combine the oats, cream, peanut butter, and crushed raspberries in a medium mixing dish. Stir until the mixture is almost smooth.
2. Refrigerate overnight, covered. Cover and top with whole raspberries in the morning.

Nutrition Fact: Calories Per Serving 455: Total Fat 28.5g: Cholesterol 0mg: Sodium 602mg: Total Carbohydrate 36.1g: Dietary Fiber 26.1g: Sugars 20.8g: Protein 20.8g

DAY 9

MEAL #1: TURMERIC TOFU SCRAMBLE

INGREDIENTS:
- 1 pound portobello mushroom
- Three or four cherry tomatoes
- 1 tbsp olive oil and additional for cleaning
- Seasoned with salt and pepper
- 1/2 block (14-oz) tofu that is firm
- 1/4 teaspoon turmeric powder
- A pinch of garlic powder
- 1/2 thinly sliced avocado

Directions:
1. Preheat the oven to 400 degrees Fahrenheit. Brush the mushrooms and tomatoes with oil and put them on a baking sheet. Salt and pepper to taste. Roast for about 10 minutes, or until the vegetables are tender.
2. Meanwhile, combine the tofu, turmeric, garlic powder, and a pinch of salt in a medium mixing cup. Using a fork, mash the potatoes. 1 tablespoon olive oil, heated in a big skillet over medium heat Cook, stirring regularly, until the tofu mixture is solid and egg-like, around 3 minutes.
3. Serve the tofu with the mushroom, onions, and avocado on a plate.

Nutrition Fact: Calories Per Serving 431: Total Fat 33.5g: Cholesterol 0mg: Sodium 602mg: Total Carbohydrate 17.1g: Dietary Fiber 26.1g: Sugars 20.8g: Protein 21.8g

MEAL #2: AVOCADO RICOTTA POWER TOAST

Preparation Time: 4 minutes
Cooking Time: 5minutes, 59 seconds
Total Time: 10 Minutes

Total time: 5 minutes | Servings: 1

INGREDIENTS:
- 1 slice whole-grain bread
- ¼ ripe avocado, smashed
- 2 tbsp ricotta
- Pinch crushed red pepper flakes
- Pinch flaky sea salt

Directions:
1. The bread should be toasted. Avocado, ricotta, crushed red pepper flakes, and sea salt are served on top. Serve with fried or

hard-boiled eggs and yogurt or berries on the side.

Nutrition Fact: Calories Per Serving 288: Total Fat 17.5g: Cholesterol 0mg: Sodium 602mg: Total Carbohydrate 29.1g: Dietary Fiber 26.1g: Sugars 20.8g: Protein 10.8g

MEAL #3: TURKISH EGG BREAKFAST

Total time: 13 minutes | Servings: 2

INGREDIENTS:
- 2 tbsp olive oil
- ¾ cup diced red bell pepper
- ¾ cup diced eggplant
- Pinch each of salt and pepper
- 5 large eggs, lightly beaten
- ¼ tsp paprika
- Chopped cilantro, to taste
- 2 dollops plain yogurt
- 1 whole-wheat pita

DIRECTIONS:

2. Heat the olive oil in a big nonstick skillet over medium high heat. Combine the bell pepper, eggplant, and salt and pepper in a mixing bowl. Sauté for about 7 minutes, or before softened.
3. Add the eggs, paprika, and season to taste with salt and pepper. Cook until the eggs are lightly scrambled, stirring often.
4. Serve with a dollop of yogurt and pita bread, garnished with minced cilantro.

Nutrition Fact: Calories Per Serving 469: Total Fat 29.5g: Cholesterol 0mg: Sodium 602mg: Total Carbohydrate 25.1g: Dietary Fiber 26.1g: Sugars 20.8g: Protein 14.8g

DAY 10

MEAL #1: ALMOND APPLE SPICE MUFFINS
Preparation Time: 4 minutes
Cooking Time: 5minutes, 59 seconds
Total Time: 10 Minutes

Total time: 15 minutes | Servings: 5

INGREDIENTS:

- ½ stick butter
- 2 cups almond meal
- 4 scoops vanilla protein powder
- 4 large eggs
- 1 cup unsweetened applesauce
- 1 tbsp cinnamon
- 1 tsp allspice
- 1 tsp cloves
- 2 tsp baking powder

DIRECTIONS:

1. Preheat the oven to 350 degrees Fahrenheit. Melt the butter in a small microwave-safe bowl on low power for around 30 seconds.
2. Combine all of the remaining ingredients with the melting butter in a big mixing cup. Using cupcake liners or coat 2 muffin tins with nonstick cooking spray.
3. Fill the muffin tins about 34 complete with the batter, being careful not to overfill. This recipe should yield 10 muffins.
4. Preheat the oven to 350°F and bake one tray for 12 minutes. If you overbake the muffins, they will become too dry. Remove the first tray from the oven when it's done baking and repeat for the second muffin tin.

Nutrition Fact: Calories Per Serving 484: Total Fat 31.5g: Cholesterol 0mg: Sodium 602mg: Total Carbohydrate 78.1g: Dietary Fiber 26.1g: Sugars 20.8g: Protein 40.8g

MEAL #2: TURKEY TACOS

Preparation Time: 4 minutes
Cooking Time: 5minutes, 59 seconds
Total Time: 10 Minutes

Total time: 25 minutes | Servings: 4

INGREDIENTS:

- 2 tsp oil
- 1 small red onion, chopped
- 1 clove garlic, finely chopped
- 1 lb. Extra-lean ground turkey
- 1 tbsp sodium-free taco seasoning

- 8 whole-grain corn tortillas, warmed
- ¼ cup sour cream
- ½ cup shredded mexican cheese
- 1 avocado, sliced
- Salsa, for serving
- 1 cup chopped lettuce

DIRECTIONS:

1. Heat the oil in a big skillet over medium-high heat. Cook, stirring occasionally, until the onion is tender, about 5 to 6 minutes. Cook for 1 minute after adding the garlic.
2. Cook, breaking up the turkey with a spoon until it is almost orange, about 5 minutes. 1 cup water, taco seasoning, and taco seasoning Cook for 7 minutes, or until the liquid has been decreased by slightly more than half.
3. To serve, stuff the tortillas with turkey, sour cream, cheese, tomato, salsa, and lettuce.

Nutrition Fact: Calories Per Serving 472: Total Fat 27.5g: Cholesterol 0mg: Sodium 602mg: Total Carbohydrate 30.1g: Dietary Fiber 26.1g: Sugars 20.8g: Protein 28.8g

MEAL #3: HEALTHY SPAGHETTI BOLOGNESE

Preparation Time: 4 minutes
Cooking Time: 5minutes, 59 seconds

Total Time: 10 Minutes

INGREDIENTS:

- 1 spaghetti squash, big
- 3 tablespoons olive oil
- 1/2 teaspoon garlic powder
- Kosher salt and black pepper
- 1 finely chopped small onion
- 11/4 pound field turkey
- 4 garlic cloves, finely chopped
- 8 oz. cut small cremini mushrooms
- 3 cups diced new tomatoes (or 2 15-oz cans)
- 1 (8-oz) can no-sugar-added low-sodium tomato sauce
- basil, freshly chopped

DIRECTIONS:

1. Preheat the oven to 400 degrees Fahrenheit. Remove the seeds from the spaghetti squash and cut it in half lengthwise. Each half should be rubbed with 1/2 tbsp oil and seasoned with garlic powder, 14 tsp salt, and 14 tsp pepper. Roast until tender, 35 to 40 minutes, skin-side up on a rimmed

baking dish. Allow 10 minutes for cooling.

2. Meanwhile, heat the remaining 2 tablespoons oil in a big skillet over medium heat. Cook, stirring regularly, for 6 minutes, until the onion is tender, seasoning with 14 tsp salt and pepper. Cook, breaking up the turkey into small pieces with a spoon, until browned, around 6 to 7 minutes. Cook for 1 minute after adding the garlic.

3. Place the turkey on one side of the pan and the mushrooms on the other. Cook for 5 minutes, stirring regularly, until the mushrooms are tender. Combine with the turkey. Simmer for 10 minutes after adding the tomatoes and tomato sauce.

4. Scoop out the squash and place it on plates as the sauce simmers. Serve with a dollop of turkey Bolognese and a sprinkling of basil, if desired.

Nutrition Fact: Calories Per Serving 450: Total Fat 23.5g: Cholesterol 0mg: Sodium 602mg: Total Carbohydrate 78.1g: Dietary Fiber 26.1g: Sugars 20.8g: Protein 32.8g

Day 11

DAY 11

MEAL # 1: CHICKEN WITH FRIED CAULIFLOWER RICE

Preparation Time: 4 minutes
Cooking Time: 5minutes, 59 seconds
Total Time: 10 Minutes

Total time: 35 minutes | Servings: 4

INGREDIENTS:

- Grapeseed oil two tbsp
- 1 ¼ lb. Pounded to even thickness chicken breast (boneless & skinless)
- Four eggs, beaten
- Two finely chopped red bell peppers
- 2 small carrots, finely chopped 1 onion, finely chopped 2 garlic cloves, finely chopped 4 scallions, finely chopped + more for serving
- 1/2 cup thawed frozen peas
- Four cups "rice" cauliflower
- 2 tablespoons low-sodium soy sauce

- 2 tablespoons rice vinegar
- Kosher salt and black pepper

DIRECTIONS:
1. 1 tablespoon oil, heated in a big, deep skillet over medium-high heat Cook the chicken for 3 to 4 minutes per hand, or until golden brown. Until chopping, move to a cutting board and set aside for 6 minutes. In the same pan, add the remaining 1 tbsp oil. Add the eggs and scramble for 1 to 2 minutes, or until just set; switch to a dish.
2. Add the bell pepper, carrot, and onion to the skillet and cook, stirring often, until only tender, about 4 to 5 minutes. Cook for 1 minute after adding the garlic. Toss with peas and scallions.
3. Toss together the cauliflower, soy sauce, rice vinegar, salt, and pepper. Allow the cauliflower to sit for 2 to 3 minutes, without stirring, before it begins to brown. Combine the sliced chicken and eggs in a mixing bowl.

Nutrition Fact: Calories Per Serving 427: Total Fat 16.5g: Cholesterol 0mg: Sodium 602mg: Total Carbohydrate 25.1g: Dietary Fiber 26.1g: Sugars 20.8g: Protein 45.8g

MEAL #2: SHEET PAN STEAK
Preparation Time: 4 minutes
Cooking Time: 5minutes, 59 seconds
Total Time: 10 Minutes

INGREDIENTS:
- 1 pound cut and halved small cremini mushrooms
- 1 1/4 pound broccolini cluster, trimmed and sliced into 2-inch lengths
- Four garlic cloves, finely chopped
- 3 tablespoons olive oil
- 14 teaspoon red pepper flakes (or a bit more for extra kick)
- Kosher salt and black pepper
- 2 1-inch-thick New York strip steaks (approximately 112 pound total), trimmed of excess fat
- 1 15-oz can rinsed low-sodium cannellini beans

DIRECTIONS:
1. Preheat the oven to 450 degrees Fahrenheit. Toss the mushrooms, broccolini, garlic, grease, red

pepper flakes, and 14 tsp salt and pepper on a wide rimmed baking dish. Preheat the oven to 350°F and roast the baking sheet for 15 minutes.

2. To make way for the steaks, push the mixture to the pan's sides. Place the steaks in the middle of the pan and season with 14 tsp salt and pepper. Roast the steaks until they're roasted to your liking, around 5 to 7 minutes per side for medium-rare. Allow 5 minutes for the steaks to sit on a cutting board before slicing.

3. Toss the beans with the rest of the ingredients on the baking dish. Roast for 3 minutes, or until thoroughly cooked. With the beef, serve beans and vegetables.

Nutrition Fact: Calories Per Serving 464**:** Total Fat 22.5g**:** Cholesterol 0mg**:** Sodium 602mg**:** Total Carbohydrate 26.1g**:** Dietary Fiber 26.1g**:** Sugars 20.8g**:** Protein 42.8g

Meal #3: Pork Tenderloin with Butternut Squash and Brussels Sprouts
Preparation Time: 4 minutes
Cooking Time: 5minutes, 59 seconds
Total Time: 10 Minutes

Total time: 50 minutes | Servings: 4

INGREDIENTS:

- 1 ¾ lb. pork tenderloin, trimmed
- Salt
- Pepper
- 3 tbsp canola oil
- 2 sprigs fresh thyme
- 2 garlic cloves, peeled
- 4 cups Brussels sprouts, trimmed and halved
- 4 cups diced butternut squash

DIRECTIONS:

1. Preheat the oven to 400 degrees Fahrenheit. Season the tenderloin with salt and pepper all over. 1 tbsp oil, heated in a big cast-iron pan over medium warm. When the oil begins to glow, apply the tenderloin and sear for 8 to 12 minutes, or until golden brown on all sides. Place on a plate to cool.

2. Add the thyme and garlic to the pan with the remaining 2 tbsp oil and simmer for 1 minute, or until

fragrant. Combine the Brussels sprouts, butternut squash, and a generous pinch of salt and pepper in a large mixing bowl. Cook, stirring regularly, for 4 to 6 minutes, or until the vegetables are slightly browned.

3. Place the tenderloin on top of the vegetables and bake it. Roast for 15 to 20 minutes, or until the vegetables are tender and a meat thermometer inserted into the thickest portion of the tenderloin reads 140°F.

4. Carefully remove the pan from the oven while wearing oven mitts. Allow for 5 minutes of resting time before slicing and serving the tenderloin with the vegetables. To serve as a hand, toss greens with a balsamic vinaigrette.

Nutrition Fact: Calories Per Serving 401: Total Fat 15.5g: Cholesterol 0mg: Sodium 602mg: Total Carbohydrate 25.1g: Dietary Fiber 26.1g: Sugars 20.8g: Protein 44.8g

DAY 12

MEAL #1: WILD CAJUN SPICED SALMON

Preparation Time: 4 minutes
Cooking Time: 5minutes, 59 seconds
Total Time: 10 Minutes

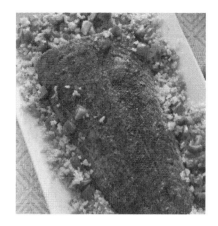

INGREDIENTS:

- 1 1/2 pound fillet of wild Alaskan salmon
- Taco sauce and no sodium
- 1/2 head cauliflower (approximately 1 pound), cut into florets
- One head broccoli (approximately 1 pound), cut into florets
- 3 tablespoons olive oil
- 1 teaspoon garlic powder
- Four medium diced tomatoes

DIRECTIONS:

1. Preheat the oven to 375 degrees Fahrenheit. In a baking dish, place the salmon. Mix the taco seasoning with 12 cup water in a shallow tub. Pour the mixture over the salmon and bake for 12 to 15 minutes, or until it is opaque within.

2. Meanwhile, pulse the cauliflower and broccoli in a food processor (in batches if necessary) until finely chopped and "riced."

3. Heat the oil in a big skillet over medium heat. Cook, flipping sometimes, until the cauliflower and broccoli are only soft, about 5 to 6 minutes.

4. Serve the salmon with tomatoes on top of the "rice."

Nutrition Fact: Calories Per Serving 408: Total Fat 23.5g: Cholesterol 0mg: Sodium 602mg: Total Carbohydrate 78.1g: Dietary Fiber 26.1g: Sugars 20.8g: Protein 42.8g

MEAL #2: PORK CHOPS WITH BLOODY MARY TOMATO SALAD

Preparation Time: 4 minutes
Cooking Time: 5minutes, 59 seconds
Total Time: 10 Minutes

INGREDIENTS:
- 2 tbsp olive oil
- 2 tbsp red wine vinegar
- 2 tsp Worcestershire sauce
- 2 tsp prepared horseradish, squeezed dry
- ½ tsp Tabasco
- ½ tsp celery seeds
- Kosher salt
- 1 pint cherry tomatoes, halved
- 2 celery stalks, very thinly sliced
- ½ small red onion, thinly sliced
- 4 small bone-in pork chops (1 in. thick, about 2¼ lb total)
- Pepper
- ¼ cup finely chopped flat-leaf parsley
- 1 small head green-leaf lettuce, leaves torn

DIRECTIONS:
1. Preheat the grill to medium-high heat. Whisk together the oil, vinegar, Worcestershire sauce, horseradish, Tabasco, celery seeds, and 14 teaspoon salt in a big mixing cup. Combine the peppers, celery, and onion in a mixing bowl.

2. 5 to 7 minutes per hand, season the pork chops with 12 tsp per salt and pepper and grill until golden brown and only cooked through.

3. Toss the tomatoes with the parsley and serve over the pork and greens. Serve with mashed cauliflower or potatoes as a side dish.

Nutrition Fact: Calories Per Serving 400: Total Fat 23.5g: Cholesterol 0mg: Sodium 602mg: Total Carbohydrate 8.1g: Dietary Fiber 26.1g: Sugars 20.8g: Protein 39.8g

MEAL #3: LOW-CARB CHICKEN STIR FRY

3 tbsp low sodium soy sauce, 1 tbsp honey, 2 tsp lemon juice, 2 tbsp sesame oil, 1 tbsp cornstarch, 2 tsp sesame seeds, 1 tbsp extra virgin olive oil, 566 g boneless and skinless chicken breasts, 1

onion medium, 1-inch finely chopped ginger root, 2 cups broccoli florets, 1/4 tsp black pepper

This serves 4 people

Nutrition Fact: Calories Per Serving 256**:** Total Fat 16.5g**:** Cholesterol 41mg**:** Sodium 602mg**:** Total Carbohydrate 28.1g**:** Dietary Fiber 26.1g**:** Sugars 20.8g**:** Protein 5.8g

DAY 13

Turkey Sausage with Pepper and Onions (See recipe in the recipes section)
Courgette and mint frittata (See recipe in the recipes section)
Chicken Meatballs and Green Beans in Tomato Broth (See recipe in the recipes section)

DAY 14

MEAL #1: HUMMUS BREAKFAST BOWL | POWERBOWL

Preparation Time: 4 minutes
Cooking Time: 5minutes, 59 seconds
Total Time: 10 Minutes

INGREDIENTS

- Two tbsp. diced bell pepper, every color
- One cup kale, stems cut and leaves chopped
- One tablespoon olive oil 1/4 cup diced roma tomatoes
- 1/4 cup cooked brown rice or quinoa
- One teaspoon hummus
- two egg whites
- one tsp sunflower seeds

DIRECTIONS

1. In a big skillet over medium melt, heat the olive oil. When the pan is warmed, add the kale.
2. After 3-4 minutes, add the tomatoes and peppers to the kale. Add another 4-5 minutes to the cooking time.
3. Lightly whisk the egg before gradually adding the kale and peppers. Scramble the eggs until they're no longer runny.
4. Fill a serving bowl halfway with rice or quinoa, then finish with vegetables and an egg. Sprinkle the sunflower seeds on top of the hummus. Have fun!

Nutrition Fact: Calories Per Serving 354: Total Fat 18.5g: Cholesterol 0mg: Sodium 602mg: Total Carbohydrate 34.1g: Dietary Fiber 26.1g: Sugars 20.8g: Protein 14.8g

MEAL #2: BAKED LEMON SALMON AND ASPARAGUS FOIL PACK

Preparation Time: 4 minutes
Cooking Time: 5minutes, 59 seconds
Total Time: 10 Minutes

INGREDIENTS

- 16 to 24 ounces salmon filets 4 pieces
- 1 pound asparagus fresh, about 1 inch of bottom ends trimmed off
- 1 teaspoon kosher salt
- 1/2 teaspoon ground black pepper
- 2 tablespoons olive oil
- 1/4 cup lemon juice fresh
- 1 tablespoon thyme fresh, chopped
- 2 tablespoons parsley fresh, chopped
- 2 tablespoons lemon zest

DIRECTIONS

1. Preheat oven to 400 degrees Fahrenheit.
2. Spray 4 big sheets of foil with nonstick spray and position on a flat surface. Place the asparagus in a single sheet, side by side, in each of the packages. Add part of the salt and pepper to taste.
3. On top of each asparagus bed, place a salmon filet. Drizzle with the remaining salt and pepper, as well as the olive oil, lemon juice, and thyme. Fold each side of the foil sheets up carefully to form a packet around the salmon and put in a single layer on a baking sheet. 15 minutes in the oven.
4. Remove the packets from the oven and carefully open each one, being mindful of the steam that will be emitted! On top, strew lemon zest and parsley. Serve and have fun!
5. Notes For more spice, try this recipe on the grill instead of in the oven!

Nutrition Fact: Calories Per Serving 386: Total Fat 26.5g: Cholesterol 78mg: Sodium 5582mg: Total Carbohydrate 7.1g: Dietary Fiber 26.1g: Sugars 3.8g: Protein 32.8g

MEAL #3: CHICKEN AND BROCCOLI STIR-FRY

Preparation Time: 4 minutes
Cooking Time: 5minutes, 59 seconds
Total Time: 10 Minutes

INGREDIENTS

- 3 tablespoons lite soy sauce optional tamari
- 1 tablespoon honey
- 2 teaspoons lemon juice
- 2 tablespoons sesame oil
- 1 tablespoon cornstarch or flour
- 2 teaspoons sesame seeds
- 1 tablespoon extra virgin olive oil
- 1 1/4 pounds boneless and skinless chicken breasts cubed
- 1 onion medium, coarsely chopped
- 1 1-inch ginger root peeled and finely chopped
- 2 cups broccoli florets
- 1/4 teaspoon black pepper

DIRECTIONS

1. Combine the soy sauce, honey, lemon juice, sesame oil, and cornstarch in a mixing bowl. Set aside the combination.
2. Toast sesame seeds in a big skillet or wok over medium-low heat for 2 minutes, or until fragrant. Put aside the toasted seeds in a cup.
3. In the same pan, heat the olive oil over medium heat and cook the chicken until it is finely golden. Combine the onions, ginger, broccoli, and pepper in a large mixing bowl. 4 minutes of sautéing Reduce the fire to medium-low and toss in the soy sauce mixture. Cook for no longer than 5 minutes, or until sauce reaches target thickness. Serve with toasted sesame seeds as a garnish. Have fun!
4. For brown rice or quinoa, serve the Chicken and Broccoli Stir-Fry.

Nutrition Fact: Calories Per Serving 3256: Total Fat 18.5g: Cholesterol 0mg: Sodium 602mg: Total Carbohydrate 15.1g: Dietary Fiber 26.1g: Sugars 6.8g: Protein 35.8g

DAY 15

MEAL # 1: 4-INGREDIENT PROTEIN PANCAKES

Preparation Time: 4 minutes
Cooking Time: 5minutes, 59 seconds
Total Time: 10 Minutes

INGREDIENTS

- 1/2 cup mashed banana
- three egg whites
- a quarter teaspoon baking powder
- Optional: 1 tablespoon vanilla protein powder, 1 tablespoon chocolate protein powder

DIRECTIONS

1. In a mixing cup, whisk together all of the ingredients until smooth.
2. Heat a skillet over medium heat, lightly sprayed with nonstick spray. 1/4 cup batter should be poured into the tub. Cook for 3 to 4 minutes, or until the middle of the pancakes begins to bubble. Cook for another 2 to 3 minutes after carefully flipping. Remove the pancake from the pan until it is done cooking and repeat the procedure until all of the batter has been consumed. In between pancakes, spray the skillet with nonstick spray as desired.

3. Fresh fruit, sugar, or your favorite almond butter can be added to the top! Have fun!

Nutrition Fact: Calories Per Serving 57: Total Fat 1.5g: Cholesterol 0mg: Sodium 602mg: Total Carbohydrate 6.1g: Dietary Fiber 26.1g: Sugars 20.8g: Protein 7.8g

Turkey Sausage with Pepper and Onions (See recipe in the recipes section)
Chicken Meatballs and Green Beans in Tomato Broth (See recipe in the recipes section)

DAY 16

Cauliflower and ribeye steak fajitas (See recipe in the recipes section)
NO-BEAN KETO chill (See recipe in the recipes section)
Smoky beef stew (See recipe in the recipes section)

DAY 17

Honey Lime Rainbow Fruit Salad (See recipe in the recipes section)
Keto Low Carb Vegetable Soup Recipe (See recipe in the recipes section)
Chicken Meatballs and Green Beans in Tomato Broth (See recipe in the recipes section)

DAY 18

BREAKFAST: CREAMY GREEN SMOOTHIE WITH A HINT OF MINT

Preparation Time: 4 minutes
Cooking Time: 5minutes, 59 seconds
Total Time: 10 Minutes

This dessert-like smoothie is made with clean and whole foods, making this the best green drink out there!
Prep Time: 5 minutes
Total Time: 5 minutes

INGREDIENTS

- 3 romaine heart leaves
- 14 honeydew melon cubed, 1" cubes recommended
- 1/2 avocado ripe, seeded and peeling removed
- 1 banana ripe, frozen, slice before freezing
- 2 teaspoons honey optional
- 1 1/2 cups buttermilk low fat
- 2 mint leaves fresh, more for garnish
- 8 to 10 ice wedges

DIRECTIONS

1. In a mixer, combine all of the ingredients and mix until smooth and fluffy. 2 teaspoons whipped topping, if desired For a delicious bonus, try our 100 percent Clean Whipped Topping recipe! If needed, top with cinnamon.

NUTRITION

Serving: 1cup | Calories: 207kcal | Carbohydrates: 29g | Protein: 6g | Fat: 9g | Saturated Fat: 3g | Cholesterol: 13mg | Sodium: 145mg | Potassium: 691mg | Fiber: 5g | Sugar: 21g | Vitamin A: 2739IU | Vitamin C: 8mg | Calcium: 151mg | Iron: 1mg |

Red lentil & sweet potato pâté (See recipe in the recipes section)
Baked Salmon in Foil (See recipe in the recipes section)

DAY 19

Smoky beef stew (See recipe in the recipes section)
Turkey & spring onion wraps(See recipe in the recipes section)
Turkey Sausage with Pepper and Onions(See recipe in the recipes section)

DAY 20

Potato drop scones with grilled bacon and tomato(See recipe in the recipes section)
Chicken noodle miso soup(See recipe in the recipes section)
Boiled egg with rye bread soldiers

Preparation timeless than 30 mins
Cooking time less than 10 mins
Serves 2

INGREDIENTS

- 2 medium eggs
- 2 slices dark rye bread (pumpernickel)
- 5g unsalted butter, for spreading
- Sea salt and ground black pepper

DIRECTIONS

2. Bring a medium saucepan half-filled with water to a boil. Return the pot to a boil after gently adding the eggs to the water with a slotted spoon.
3. For a soft-boiled egg, cook the eggs in boiling water for 4-5 minutes.
4. Toast the bread, spread it with a thin layer of butter, and cut it into thin soldiers while the eggs are frying.
5. Place the eggs in egg cups on small plates and serve. Remove the tops and season with salt and pepper to taste. To dip, serve with the troops.

Nutrition Fact: Calories Per Serving 160: Total Fat 16.5g: Cholesterol 40mg: Sodium 602mg: Total Carbohydrate 78.1g: Dietary Fiber 26.1g: Sugars 20.8g: Protein 14.8g

DAY 21

Salmon and bulgur wheat pilaf(See recipe in the recipes section)
Toasted crumpets and warm spiced berries with yoghurt and honey(See recipe in the recipes section)
Blackened salmon with salsa(See recipe in the recipes section)

BREAKFAST

1. BUDDHA BOWL

Preparation Time: 4 minutes
Cooking Time: 5minutes, 59 seconds
Total Time: 10 Minutes

Prep Time: 10 min.
Total Time: 25 min.
Makes: 2 servings

INGREDIENTS

- 2 pastured eggs, poached
- 2 Paleo sausages, precooked (we used a spicy lamb sausage)
- 1 cup cauliflower rice
- Grass-fed ghee for cooking
- 1 avocado, sliced
- 1/4 cucumber, sliced
- 2 tbsp organic leafy greens (lightly steamed)
- Garnish with fresh herbs, sliced chilli, sliced spring onions, a wedge of lemon, and salt and pepper to taste.

DIRECTIONS

1. Preheat a frying pan on low.
2. Enable 1-2 tablespoons of ghee to melt in the tub. Cook until the cauliflower rice is done to your liking.
3. Place the leafy greens on a plate or in a big mixing cup.
4. Place the cauliflower rice alongside the leafy greens until it's set.
5. Reheat the sausages in the same frying pan.
6. Meanwhile, arrange the avocado, cucumber slices, and poached eggs on top of the cauliflower rice and leafy greens as desired.
7. When the sausages are cooked, add them to the bowl with the rest of the ingredients.
8. Garnish with your garnishes, then serve and enjoy!

Nutrition Fact: Calories Per Serving 323: Total Fat 40.5g: Cholesterol 0mg: Sodium 223mg: Total Carbohydrate 258.1g: Dietary Fiber 26.1g: Sugars 20.8g: Protein 25.8g

2. KETO COCONUT FLOUR PANCAKES

Preparation Time: 4 minutes
Cooking Time: 5minutes, 59 seconds
Total Time: 10 Minutes

Start to Finish: 15 minutes

INGREDIENTS:

- 1/2 cup (50g) coconut flour
- 1/2 tsp baking soda
- 2 tablespoons coconut oil, melted
- 4 organic, pasture raised eggs, room temperature
- 1 tsp vanilla
- 1/2 tsp Ceylon cinnamon
- 1/2 cup coconut cream (the thick part of canned coconut cream, unsweetened)
- 1/2 cup almond milk, unsweetened
- 1/4 tsp Himalayan salt
- Grass-fed Ghee or coconut oil for cooking

DIRECTIONS:

1. Add all ingredients except ghee to a high-powered blender and blend until smooth, scraping down the sides if desired.
2. Add enough ghee to brush the bottom of a medium skillet over medium flame. Pour about 1/2 cup of batter into the skillet until it has heated up. Cook until golden brown on one side, then turn and cook until golden brown on the other side (note: Thicker pancakes will take longer to cook). Set aside and continue to cook until there is no more batter.
3. Hot coconut flour pancakes with grass-fed ghee, fruit, or other keto-friendly toppings

Nutrition Fact: Calories Per Serving 244**:** Fat: 23g : Saturated Fat: 19.1g : Cholesterol: 123mg : Salt: 296mg : Carbs: 4.9g: Fiber: 2.7g : Sugar: 1.5g : Net Carbs: 2.2g : Protein: 5.5g

3. BERRY MATCHA SMOOTHIE

Preparation Time: 4 minutes
Cooking Time: 5minutes, 59 seconds
Total Time: 10 Minutes

INGREDIENTS:

- 1 coconut milk cup
- 1 cup purified water
- 1-1.5 cup organic frozen berries
- a half avocado
- Brain Octane C8 MCT Oil 1 tbsp
- 1 heaping tablespoon Invincible Full Daily Energy Collagen Protein Vanilla Bean
- 1 heaping tablespoon InnerFuel Prebiotic is impenetrable.
- 1 tsp matcha powder
- 1 tsp vanilla extract
- Optional: To taste, ice and sweetener of choice.

DIRECTIONS:

1. In a blender, combine all of the ingredients and mix until absolutely smooth.
2. Taste and make the required adjustments.
3. Pour into two glasses and serve right away.

Nutrition Fact: Calories: 496 : Fat: 40.9g : Saturated Fat: 30.4g : Cholesterol: 0mg: Salt: 56mg :Carbs: 30g : Fiber: 10g :Sugar: 7.5g : Protein: 10.7g

4. KETO BREAKFAST PIZZA (DAIRY-FREE)

Preparation Time: 4 minutes
Cooking Time: 5minutes, 59 seconds
Total Time: 10 Minutes

INGREDIENTS:

- 2 cups cauliflower, grated
- 2 tbsp coconut flour
- 4 eggs, 1/2 tsp salt
- 1 tbsp powdered psyllium husk
- Smoked salmon, coconut, spices, spinach, and olive oil

DIRECTIONS:

1. Preheat oven to 350 degrees Fahrenheit. Use parchment paper to line a pizza tray or a sheet plate.
2. Combine all ingredients (except toppings) in a mixing bowl and stir to combine. Enable coconut flour and psyllium husk to absorb liquid and thicken for 5 minutes before serving.
3. Pour the breakfast pizza base into the pan with care. Form it into a round, including pizza crust with your hands.
4. Bake for 15 minutes, or until completely cooked and golden brown.
5. Remove the breakfast pizza from the oven and finish with your preferred toppings. Heat the dish before serving.

Nutrition Fact: Calories: 454 : Fat: 31g : Saturated Fat: 75g : Cholesterol: 348mg : Carbs: 26g : Fiber: 17.2g : Sugar: 4.4g : Net Carbs: 8.8g : Protein: 22g

5. COLLAGEN BREAKFAST COOKIES

Preparation Time: 4 minutes
Cooking Time: 5minutes, 59 seconds
Total Time: 10 Minutes

Start to Finish: 25 minutes

INGREDIENTS:

- 2 eggs
- 1/2 cup almond flour
- 1/2 cup shredded coconut
- 1/2 cup sliced almonds
- 1/2 cup pecans
- 1/3 cup roasted almond butter
- 1/3 cup birchwood xylitol
- 1/2 cup pumpkin seeds
- 2 Tbsp. ground flax meal
  - Tbsp. Bulletproof Vanilla Collagen Protein
- 2-3 tsp. cinnamon
- 2-3 tsp. ginger powder
- 1 tsp. vanilla extract

Optional: 1/2 cup of quality chocolate, chopped (or sugar-free chocolate chips)

DIRECTIONS:
1. Preheat the oven to 350 degrees Fahrenheit (175 degrees Celsius).
2. Preheat oven to 350°F. Line two baking trays with parchment paper.

3. In a mixing cup, combine all cookie ingredients.
4. Roll the mixture into balls with your hands oiled with coconut oil. Place the cookies on the prepared baking trays and press them smooth and even.
5. Preheat the oven to 350°F and bake the tray for 20 minutes, or until golden and baked through.
6. Remove the cookies from the oven and set them aside to cool.
7. Serve with a steaming cup of Bulletproof Coffee.

Nutrition Fact : Calories: 329 : Fat: 27.9g : Saturated Fat: 4.3g Cholesterol: 15mg : Salt: 59mg : Carbs: 14g : Fiber: 5.4g : Sugar: 2.2g Protein: 10.7g

6. BREAKFAST SALAD

Preparation Time: 4 minutes
Cooking Time: 5minutes, 59 seconds
Total Time: 10 Minutes

INGREDIENTS:
- 2 eggs from a pasture
- 1 pound nitrate-free bacon
- a 1/2 of an avocado
- 1 cup sweet potato diced
- 1 tsp avocado oil
- 1 tsp kosher salt
- 3 cups greens (mixed)
- 1 sprig fresh dill

DIRECTIONS:
1. Preheat oven to 325 degrees Fahrenheit.
2. 2 quarts water, brought to a rolling boil
3. Toss a few drops of vinegar into the water.
4. Break the eggs into tiny bowls and gently drop each one into the water.
5. Cook for 3 minutes with the lid on the oven.
6. Remove with a slotted spoon and set aside for a couple of minutes to cool.
7. Bacon can be minced and cooked on low heat until it is no longer translucent.
8. In a cup, toss sweet potatoes with salt and avocado oil, then move to a parchment-lined baking sheet and bake for 40 minutes (Do this step the night before if you want to increase resistant starch.)

9. Toss in the vegetables, eggs, bacon, avocado, and potatoes, and top with dill.

Nutrition Fact: Calories: 455: Protein: 19g: Carbs: 34g: Fiber: 9g : Sugar:7g : Fat: 28g: Saturated Fat: 6g : Polyunsaturated: 4g : Monounsaturated: 15g : Cholesterol: 380mg

7. SMOKED SALMON AND GARLIC SPINACH BREAKFAST SANDWICH

Preparation Time: 4 minutes
Cooking Time: 5minutes, 59 seconds
Total Time: 10 Minutes

INGREDIENTS:
- Four tablespoons coconut oil
- Eight slices of your favorite sandwich vessel
- Smoked salmon, 4 oz.
- Nine ounces new spinach
- Two whole pasture-raised eggs or 4 tbsp raw powdered eggs
- 4 tablespoons water
- Two garlic cloves or 1/2 tsp garlic powder
- About a lemon

DIRECTIONS:
1. If you're using dried eggs, make sure to rehydrate them in water first. Allow to sit for 5 minutes after stirring.
2. In the meantime, heat the burner to low. 2 tbsp coconut oil in a jar
3. All sides of the sandwich bread should be toasted. Mince the garlic cloves when the bread is toasting.
4. Add the remaining 2 tbsp. coconut oil to the pan once all of the slices have been toasted. Garlic should be cooked for 1-2 minutes. Cook for 2-3 minutes, or until spinach is wilted.
5. Toss in the eggs. Stir gently to scramble the eggs and cook for 2-3 minutes, or until set. Add a squeeze of lemon to finish.
6. On bread, layer smoked salmon and garlic spinach scramble. Consume!
7. Approximately 2-4 servings

Nutrition Fact : Calories: 329 : Fat: 27.9g : Saturated Fat: 4.3g Cholesterol: 15mg : Salt: 59mg : Carbs: 14g : Fiber: 5.4g : Sugar: 2.2g Protein: 10.7g

8. POACHED EGGS AND BACON ON TOAST

Preparation Time: 4 minutes
Cooking Time: 5minutes, 59 seconds
Total Time: 10 Minutes

The gentle sizzle of bacon on a skillet is the ideal way to start every day. Imagine the meaty, savory aroma that lingers in the air even after it has passed through your stomach; how could anyone be angry after that? Cover the toast with eggs for a more filling meal, and you'll never have to hear about a grumbling stomach at an 11 a.m. meeting again.

INGREDIENTS:

- 2 slices bacon
- 2 medium eggs
- 200 grams baby leaf spinach
- Salmon (optional)
- 1 slice of toast
- Sea salt
- Black pepper

DIRECTION:

1. Get a big pot of water to a low boil.
2. Gently swirl the water before cracking the eggs into it; poach for 4 minutes or until the whites are just set.
3. Meanwhile, prepare a deep frying pan over high heat, add a splash of water, and toss in the spinach. Cook for 2 minutes, or until the spinach has wilted.
4. Remove the spinach from the pan and place it on a tray. Cook the bacon in a skillet until golden brown.
5. Season the spinach (as well as the salmon) on the toast with salt and pepper.
6. Add the poached eggs and bacon to round it off.

Nutrition Fact: Calories Per Serving 219: Total Fat 16.5g: Cholesterol 0mg: Sodium 602mg: Total Carbohydrate 78.1g: Dietary Fiber 26.1g: Sugars 20.8g: Protein 14.8g

9. BULLETPROOF COFFEE

Preparation Time: 2 minutes
Cooking Time: 5 minutes
Total Time: 7 Minutes

Basic Bulletproof Coffee includes all of the required ingredients as well as instructions for making your own breakfast in a cup. Intermittent fasting is a powerful dietary technique that can help you lose weight and recover energy.

INGREDIENTS

- 1 12 oz. cup hot decaf or daily coffee
- 1 tbsp grass-fed unsalted butter or ghee (1 tbsp MCT oil or coconut oil)

DIRECTIONS

1. In a mixer, combine the hot coffee and the sugar.
2. MCT oil and unsalted butter are added. Place the cover on the blender.
3. When mixing hot liquids, use caution. Begin at the slowest possible tempo.
4. Increase the pace to medium after 12 seconds of blending.
5. Serve the food.

Nutrition Fact: Calories Per Serving 214: Total Fat 25.5g: Cholesterol 0mg: Sodium 602mg: Total Carbohydrate 1.1g: Dietary Fiber 26.1g: Sugars 20.8g: Protein 11.8g

10. MELON AND PARMA HAM RECIPE

Preparation Time: 3 minutes
Cooking Time: 7 minutes
Total Time: 10 Minutes
Serves 4

A lovely combination of two delicate flavors: soft and juicy melon and smoky Parma ham slices. This is an excellent appetizer for a dinner party. Directions are available here.

INGREDIENTS

- 1 honeydew melon
- 2 x 88g (2oz) packs of parma ham, torn
- 50g (2oz) wild rocket
- pinch ground black pepper
- 4 tsp rapeseed oil

DIRECTIONS

1. Remove the skin and any pips from the melon before slicing it into thick slices. After that, cut the meat into big portions.
2. Place the melon on four plates and top with the parma ham.
3. Season with black pepper and drizzle with rapeseed oil before scattering with a little rocket.

Nutrition Fact: Calories Per Serving 200: Total Fat 16.5g: Cholesterol 40mg: Sodium 602mg: Total Carbohydrate

78.1g: Dietary Fiber 26.1g: Sugars 20.8g: Protein 14.8g

11. BOILED EGGS & ASPARAGUS SOLDIERS

Preparation Time: 4 minutes
Cooking Time: 15minutes
Total Time: 10 Minutes

"An advanced version of the ultimate boiled egg. The super-charged asparagus soldiers are a brilliant way to up your veg consumption while still enriching the body with a delicious, balanced combination of egg and whole meal toast." What a wonderful time!

INGREDIENTS
- 1 large bunch of asparagus , (16 spears)
- 8 slices of higher-welfare pancetta
- 4 large free-range eggs
- 4 slices of wholemeal bread , (50g each)

DIRECTIONS
1. To heat up a griddle pan, position it over high heat.
2. Remove and compost the woody ends of the asparagus.
3. Fill a medium saucepan three-quarters full of water, add a pinch of sea salt, and bring to a rapid boil over high heat.
4. Break the pancetta in half in the middle on a chopping board to make 16 pieces, then gently roll each one out.
5. Wrap each asparagus spear in a slice of pancetta and put on a hot griddle, rotating regularly, for 5 minutes, or until the asparagus is tender and the pancetta is crisp.
6. Place the eggs on a spoon one at a time, then slowly dip them in and out of the boiling water a couple times to reduce the temperature shock to prevent cracking, then gently lower into the pan.
7. Set a timer for 512 minutes to ensure the eggs are runny enough for dunking.
8. Remove the eggs from the water with care and put them in egg cups on a tray, then divide the asparagus.
9. Meanwhile, toast the bread for 30 seconds on either side on the griddle. Remove the pan from the heat, split the meat into soldiers on a cutting board, and divide among the dishes.

10. Remove the tops of each egg with a light touch, season with black pepper, and tuck in.

Nutrition Fact: Calories 240 : Fat 10.6g : Saturates 2.9g : Sugars 3.1g: Salt 1g : Protein 15.7g

12. PORRIDGE WITH APPLE AND CINNAMON

Preparation Time: 4 minutes
Cooking Time: 5minutes, 59 seconds
Total Time: 10 Minutes

INGREDIENTS
- 100g porridge oats
- 200ml milk
- 1tbsp honey
- 1 apple, peeled, cored and chopped
- ½tsp of cinnamon

DIRECTIONS
1. Heat the milk in a saucepan until it starts to bubble. Cook for 5 minutes, or until the milk has been consumed, before adding the oats.

2. Enable the honey and apple to soften and caramelize for a few minutes in a separate pan over low heat.
3. Place the apples on top of the porridge in two cups. Serve with a dash of extra cinnamon on top.

Nutation Fact: Calories 294 kCal : Fat 6.1g : Saturates 1.8g : Carbohydrates 54.8g : Sugars 19.2g : Protein 9.4g : Salt 0.11g

13. PORRIDGE WITH BLUEBERRY COMPOTE

Preparation Time: 5 minutes
Cooking Time: 5minutes
Total Time: 10 Minutes

To make this filling snack, top high-fiber porridge oats with smooth Greek yogurt and organic blueberries – buy frozen to save money.

INGREDIENTS
- 6 tbsp porridge oats

- just under ½ x 200ml tub 0% fat Greek-style yogurt
- ½ x 350g pack frozen blueberries
- 1 tsp honey (optional)

DIRECTIONS

1. STEP 1 Combine the oats and 400ml water in a nonstick pan and simmer over medium heat, stirring periodically, for around 2 minutes, or until thickened. Take the pan off the heat and stir in a third of the yogurt.
2. STEP 2 In the meantime, gently poach the blueberries in a pan with 1 tbsp water and the sugar, if using, until they have thawed and are tender but still retain their form.
3. STEP 3 Divide the porridge among bowls, top with the remaining yogurt, and scatter the blueberries on top.

Nutrition Fact: Calories Per Serving 214: Total Fat 4.5g: Cholesterol 0mg: Sodium 602mg: Total Carbohydrate 35.1g: Dietary Fiber 7.1g: Sugars 20.8g: Protein 13.8g

14. SCRAMBLED EGG BREAKFAST TOAST WITH TOMATO AND CHIVE GOAT CHEESE

Preparation Time: 5 minutes

Cooking Time: 5minutes
Total Time: 10 Minutes

INGREDIENTS

- 2 eggs
- Splash of water about 2 tbsp
- Fresh cut chives desired amount
- 1 tomato thinly sliced
- goat cheese spread about 2 ounces but adjust to taste
- Salt and pepper to taste
- 1/2 - 1 tbsp butter or olive oil

DIRECTIONS

1. In a mixing cup, whisk together two shells.
2. Whisk in the water once more.
3. In a medium-low-heat pan, melt butter or olive oil. (After the butter has melted, pour in the eggs and cook them slowly.)
4. To account for carryover frying, remove the eggs from the heat until they're finished. They can always be a little loose and runny.
5. 2 slices of bread, toasted

6. Combine goat cheese and chopped chives in a mixing bowl.
7. On the bread, spread the cheese and finish with tomato, eggs, and more chives.

Nutrition Fact: Calories 240 : Fat 10.6g : Saturates 2.9g : Sugars 3.1g: Salt 1g : Protein 15.7g

15. TOMATO, SPINACH & FETA OMELET

Preparation Time: 4 minutes
Cooking Time: 5minutes, 59 seconds
Total Time: 10 Minutes

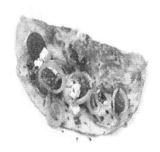

INGREDIENTS
- 4 Large Eggland's Best eggs
- 1 cup baby Spinach, chopped
- ½ tsp dried Oregano
- ¼ tsp Salt
- 1 plum Tomato, sliced
- 2 tablespoons Feta Cheese, crumbled
- ¼ red Onion, thinly sliced (optional)

DIRECTIONS
1. Step 1
2. In a medium mixing dish, whisk together the eggs, spinach, oregano, and salt. Blend until it is well combined. Cover a 9-inch nonstick skillet lightly with cooking spray and heat on low. Fill the skillet with the egg mixture. Cook for 5-6 minutes, or until the bottom is gently browned and solid. Flip the omelet on the other side with a spatula and cook for another 3 minutes. Place the omelet on a serving platter. On one hand, spread tomatoes and cheese (along with onions if desired) and fold over the other half to protect. Allow 1 minute for the tomatoes and cheese to warm up. Slice in two. Vegetarian diet Just 15 minutes, you'll have your meal ready.

Nutrition Fact: Per Serving: Calories 176; Fat 10g (2% calories from fat); Protein 14g; Carbohydrate 4g; Dietary Fiber 1g; Cholesterol 358mg; Sodium 512mg.

16. TZATZIKI WITH CRUDITES

Preparation Time: 5 minutes
Cooking Time: 1 Hour

Total Time: 1hour 5 Minutes

INGREDIENTS

- 4 cups lowfat yogurt
- 1/2 cucumber, seeded and chopped
- 1/4 cup fresh mint leaves
- 1 garlic clove
- 2 1/2 tsps hot sauce
- Juice and zest of 1/2 a lemon
- salt and freshly ground black pepper
- Crudites platter

DIRECTIONS

1. Within a fine mesh strainer, put a sheet of towels and the strainer in a tub. Pour the yogurt into the strainer, cover with plastic wrap, and let drain overnight in the refrigerator. The yogurt should have doubled in thickness with a very dense consistency.
2. In a food processor, combine the yogurt, cucumber, mint, garlic, hot sauce, lemon juice, and zest and process until smooth. Season with salt and pepper to taste. Place in a mixing dish. Serve on a crudites platter after chilling for at least one hour.
3. Fold and dampen a towel and put it underneath the bowl you are serving the Sauce on the platter with crudites while serving the Sauce on a platter with crudites.

This will save the cup from overflowing.

Nutrition Fact: Calories Per Serving 320: Total Fat 16.5g: Cholesterol 0mg: Sodium 602mg: Total Carbohydrate 78.1g: Dietary Fiber 26.1g: Sugars 20.8g: Protein 14.8g

17. MAPLE, PECAN AND CRANBERRY GRANOLA

Preparation Time: 15 minutes
Cooking Time: 30 minutes
Total Time: 45 Minutes

INGREDIENTS

- 125ml/4fl oz maple syrup
- 25g/1oz caster sugar
- 25ml/1fl oz sunflower oil
- ½ tsp vanilla extract
- 500g/1lb 2oz jumbo rolled oats
- 175g/6oz mixed seeds (like pumpkin, sunflower, sesame or linseeds)

- 150g/5oz pecans (or walnuts)
- 50g/2oz whole almonds
- 25g/1oz flaked almonds
- 75g/2¾oz desiccated coconut
- pinch of salt (optional)
- 2 tsp cinnamon (optional)
- 150g/5½oz dried cranberries

DIRECTIONS

1. Preheat the oven to 170 degrees Celsius (325 degrees Fahrenheit)/325 degrees Fahrenheit/325 degrees Fahrenheit/325 degrees Fahrenheit/325 degrees Fahren Set aside two big roasting trays lined with parchment paper.
2. In a big mixing cup, combine the maple syrup, sugar, grease, and vanilla extract. Then add the peas, blended beans, pecans (or walnuts), whole almonds, flaked almonds, coconut, salt, and cinnamon and combine well (if using). Give it a good stir, and get your hands in there and hold it up, allowing it to fall down and brush and moisten it thoroughly.
3. Fill the roasting trays halfway with the mixture and spread it out thinly. Bake for 15 minutes, giving it a nice swirl halfway through before switching them around on their shelves.
4. When baked, the granola should be golden brown. Remove from the heat and set aside to cool entirely before stirring in the cranberries. For up to a month, store in an airtight bag..

Nutrition Fact: Calories Per Serving 330: Total Fat 27.5g: Cholesterol 0mg: Sodium 602mg: Total Carbohydrate 78.1g: Dietary Fiber 26.1g: Sugars 20.8g: Protein 14.8g

18. ONE-PAN EGG & VEG BRUNCH

Preparation Time: 5 minutes
Cooking Time: 25minutes
Total Time: 30 Minutes

INGREDIENTS
- 300g baby new potatoes , halved
- ½ tbsp rapeseed oil
- 1 knob of butter
- 1 courgette , cut into small chunks

- 1 yellow pepper , cut into small chunks
- 1 red pepper , cut into small chunks
- 2 spring onions , finely sliced
- 1 garlic clove , crushed
- 1 sprig thyme , leaves picked
- 4 eggs
- Toast , to serve

DIRECTIONS

1. STEP 1: Cook the fresh potatoes for 8 minutes before draining them.
2. STEP 2 In a big nonstick frying pan, heat the oil and butter, then add the courgette, peppers, potatoes, and a pinch of salt and pepper. Cook for 10 minutes, stirring sometimes, before it begins to tan. Cook for another 2 minutes after adding the spring onions, garlic, and thyme.
3. STEP 3 Smash the eggs into four spaces in the jar. Cook for about 4 minutes, or until the eggs are cooked, covered with foil or a lid (with the yolks soft for dipping into). If desired, top with additional thyme leaves and freshly ground black pepper. Serve with toasted bread.

Nutrition Fact: Calories Per Serving 270: Total Fat 16.5g: Cholesterol 0mg: Sodium 602mg: Total Carbohydrate 68.1g: Dietary Fiber 26.1g: Sugars 28.8g: Protein 14.8g

19. MASALA OMELETTE MUFFINS

Preparation Time: 10 minutes
Cooking Time: 25minutes
Total Time: 35 Minutes

INGREDIENTS

- Rapeseed oil , for greasing
- 2 medium courgettes , coarsely grated
- 6 large eggs
- 2 large or 4 small garlic cloves , finely grated
- 1 red chilli , deseeded and finely chopped
- 1 tsp chilli powder
- 1 tsp ground cumin
- 1 tsp ground coriander

81

- Handful fresh coriander , chopped
- 125g frozen peas
- 40g feta

DIRECTIONS

1. STEP 1 Preheat the oven to 220°C/200°C fan/gas 7 and gently grease four 200ml ramekins. Grate the courgettes and press them as much as you can to extract as much liquid as possible. In a big jug, combine all of the ingredients except the feta and stir thoroughly.
2. STEP 2
3. Pour into the ramekins, top with feta, and bake for 20-25 minutes, or until risen and placed on a baking sheet. The muffins may be served hot or cold with lettuce, slaw, or fried vegetables..

Nutrition Fact: Calories Per Serving 179: Total Fat 10.5g: Cholesterol 0mg: Sodium 602mg: Total Carbohydrate 5.1g: Dietary Fiber 26.1g: Sugars 20.8g: Protein 15.8g

20. PEA & BROAD BEAN SHAKSHUKA

Preparation Time: 20 minutes
Cooking Time: 30 minutes
Total Time: 30 Minutes

INGREDIENTS

- 1 bunch asparagus spears
- 200g sprouting broccoli
- 2 tbsp olive oil
- 2 spring onions , finely sliced
- 2 tsp cumin seeds
- large pinch cayenne pepper , plus extra to serve
- 4 ripe tomatoes , chopped
- 1 small pack parsley , finely chopped
- 50g shelled peas
- 50g podded broad beans
- 4 large eggs
- 50g pea shoots
- Greek yogurt and flatbreads, to serve

DIRECTIONS

1. *STEP ONE*
2. Trim or snap the asparagus' woody ends and thinly slice the spears, leaving the tips and about 2cm at the top intact. In the same way, finely dice the broccoli, leaving the heads and about 2cm of stalk

intact. In a frying pan, heat the gasoline. Fry gently until the spring onions, sliced asparagus, and sliced broccoli soften a bit, then whisk in the cumin seeds, cayenne, tomatoes (with juices), parsley, and plenty of seasoning. To make a base sauce, cover and cook for 5 minutes, then add the asparagus spears, broccoli heads, peas, and large beans, cover again, and cook for 2 minutes.

3. *STEP 2*
4. Dip four times into the mixture. Break an egg into each dip, top with half of the pea shoots, season well, cover, and cook until the egg whites are just set. Serve with the remaining pea shoots, a spoonful of yogurt, and some flatbreads, and a pinch of cayenne pepper, if desired.

Nutrition Fact: Calories Per Serving 199**:** Total Fat 12.5g**:** Cholesterol 0mg**:** Sodium 602mg**:** Total Carbohydrate 7.1g**:** Dietary Fiber 26.1g**:** Sugars 20.8g**:** Protein 13.8g

21. ROASTED SPICED CAULIFLOWER

Preparation Time: 10minutes
Cooking Time: 1 Hour
Total Time: 1hour, 10 Minutes

INGREDIENTS

- 1 tsp ras el hanout
- ¼ tsp cinnamon
- ½ tsp smoked paprika
- 1 garlic clove , crushed
- 1 tsp olive oil
- 170g pot greek yogurt
- 1 small cauliflower
- 2 tbsp tahini
- Juice 2 lemons
- 400g can chickpeas , drained
- To serve
- 2 wholemeal pitta breads (or gluten-free alternative)
- 110g pack pomegranate seeds (or seeds from 1 small pomegranate)
- 2 tbsp sunflower seeds , toasted
- Small handful flat-leaf parsley , leaves only, chopped
- Small handful mint , leaves only, chopped

DIRECTIONS

1. Preheat the oven to 180°C/160°C fan/gas mark 1 4. Combine the ras

el hanout, cinnamon, paprika, garlic, oil, and yogurt in a shallow dish. Remove the outer leaves and the base of the stalk from the cauliflower so that it can lie flat in a large roasting tin. Pour 100ml water into the roasting pan around the base of the cauliflower and rub the spiced yogurt mixture all over it. Cover with foil and roast for 45 minutes in the oven.

2. In the meantime, whisk together the tahini and lemon juice in a mixing bowl until smooth – it should be the consistency of single milk. Refrigerate until desired.

3. Break the foil and add the cauliflower to the oven for another 10-15 minutes after it has cooked. Cook the chickpeas with 50ml water in a saucepan over medium heat until piping hot. Season, then mash with a potato masher – some should be smooth, while others should be slightly smashed. 1 tsp tahini sauce, stirred in

4. Remove the cauliflower from the oven and warm the pita bread for 2-3 minutes while cutting the cauliflower into 8 wedges.

5. To serve, start with a warmed pita bread on each dish, then top with crushed chickpeas and cauliflower wedges. Sprinkle the pomegranate seeds, sunflower seeds, and herbs with the remaining tahini sauce. Serve

Nutrition Fact: Calories Per Serving 194: Total Fat 8.5g: Cholesterol 0mg: Sodium 602mg: Total Carbohydrate 13.1g: Dietary Fiber 6.1g: Sugars 20.8g: Protein 13.8g

22. POTATO SALAD WITH ANCHOVY & QUAIL'S EGGS

Preparation Time: 10 minutes
Cooking Time: 20 minutes
Total Time: 30 Minutes

INGREDIENTS
- Four quail eggs
- Green beans (100g)
- 100g fresh potatoes, halved or quartered if big
- 1 finely chopped anchovy

- 1 tablespoon chopped parsley
- 1 tablespoon chives juice
- 0.5 tsp lemon

DIRECTIONS

1. Bring a medium saucepan of water to a low boil. Cook for 2 minutes after lowering the quail eggs into the water. With a slotted spoon, remove the eggs and place them in a bowl of cold water. Add the beans to the pan and cook for 4 minutes, or until tender. Remove with a slotted spoon and place in a bowl of cold water.

2. Boil the potatoes for 10-15 minutes, or until they are tender. In a colander, drain the potatoes and set them aside to cool. Peel and cut the eggs in half while the potatoes are cooking. Toss the potatoes and beans with the diced anchovies, spices, and lemon juice in a large mixing bowl. To eat, top with quail eggs.

Nutrition Fact: Calories Per Serving 174**:** Total Fat 5.5g**:** Cholesterol 0mg**:** Sodium 602mg**:** Total Carbohydrate 20.1g**:** Dietary Fiber 5.1g**:** Sugars 4.8g**:** Protein 9.8g

23. MUSHROOM & BASIL OMELETTE WITH SMASHED TOMATO

Preparation Time: 5 minutes
Cooking Time: 15minutes
Total Time: 25 Minutes

INGREDIENTS

- 2 tomatoes , halved
- 3 medium eggs
- 1 tbsp snipped chive
- 300g chestnut mushroom , sliced
- 1 tsp unsalted butter
- 2 tbsp low-fat cream cheese
- 1 tbsp finely chopped basil leaves

DIRECTIONS

1. Preheat the grill to high and put the tomatoes on a square of foil underneath, rotating periodically to avoid burning. Remove the tomatoes from the grill as they are partially scorched, squashing them slightly to expel the juices.

2. In a mixing cup, crack the eggs and whisk them together with a fork.

Mix with a tiny amount of water. Add the chives and a pinch of black pepper, and continue to beat. When you're preparing the mushrooms, set aside.

3. Heat the butter in a nonstick frying pan over medium heat until it foams. Cook, stirring sometimes, for 5-8 minutes, or until the mushrooms are tender. Remove the item and set it aside.

4. Stir the egg mixture vigorously, then pour it into the hot pan (tilting it to cover the entire base) and cook for 10 seconds or before it starts to set. Gently stir the egg with a fork here and there to ensure that every unset mixture is fried.

5. Spoon the mushroom mixture into one side of the omelette while the egg mixture is still slightly loose, then finish with cream cheese and basil leaves. If desired, flip the omelette over to cover the other side. Cook for an additional minute, then break in half and place each half on a tray. Serve promptly with a side of tomatoes.

Nutrition Fact: Calories Per Serving 196: Total Fat 14.5g: Cholesterol 0mg: Sodium 602mg: Total Carbohydrate 4.1g: Dietary Fiber 26.1g: Sugars 20.8g: Protein 14.8g

24. BOOM BANG-A-BANG CHICKEN CUPS

Preparation Time: 30 minutes
Cooking Time: 5minutes
Total Time: 35 Minutes

INGREDIENTS

- 100g peanut butter, smooth
- 140g full-fat coconut yogurt or homemade yogurt combined with 2 tablespoons desiccated coconut
- 2 tablespoons sweet chili sauce
- 2 tablespoons soy sauce
- 2-3 finely shredded spring onions
- Three shredded baked skinless chicken breasts
- Two baby gem lettuces, with large leaves divided
- 12 cucumber, halved lengthwise, seeds scraped out with a tsp, matchsticks
- Toasted sesame seeds

DIRECTIONS

1. Gently warm the peanut butter, yogurt, 3 tbsp water, sweet chilli, and soy sauce in your smallest pan

until combined into a smooth sauce. Enable to cool before serving.

2. Season the sauce with the spring onions and chicken. Holding the lettuce leaves and cucumber under damp kitchen paper before the group.

3. To assemble, place a cucumber bundle and a spoonful of the chicken mixture in each lettuce leaf cup. Serve on a large platter of sesame seeds for everybody to dive into. Alternatively, serve a pile of lettuce leaves alongside chicken and cucumber dishes.

Nutrition Fact: Calories Per Serving 176: Total Fat 10.5g: Cholesterol 0mg: Sodium 602mg: Total Carbohydrate 6.1g: Dietary Fiber 1.1g: Sugars 20.8g: Protein 16.8g

25. CHIPOTLE BLACK BEAN SOUP WITH LIME-PICKLED ONIONS

Preparation Time: 10 minutes
Cooking Time: 25 minutes
Total Time: 35 Minutes

INGREDIENTS

- Juice 2 limes
- 2 small red onions, thinly sliced
- ½ tbsp olive oil
- 2 garlic cloves, finely chopped
- ½ tbsp ground cumin
- ½ tbsp smoked paprika
- ½ tbsp chipotle paste , or tabasco, to taste
- 400g can black bean , drained and rinsed
- 400ml vegetable stock
- Half-fat soured cream , to serve
- Coriander leaves, to serve
- Crisp tortilla chips , to serve

DIRECTIONS

1. To produce the lime-pickled onions, season a small bowl with 12 tablespoons lime juice and 12 tablespoons onions. Allow 30 minutes for pickling.

2. Meanwhile, in a saucepan over medium-high heat, heat the olive oil. Season with salt and pepper after adding the garlic and remaining onions. Cook until the onions are transparent, around 8

minutes. Cook for 1 minute after adding the spices and chipotle purée, then add the beans, stock, and remaining lime juice. Simmer for 15 minutes before blending.

3. To reheat the soup, pour it into a clean tub. Serve with tortillas on the side and a little of the drained pickled onions served with a little drizzle of soured cream and some coriander..

Nutrition Fact: Calories Per Serving 190: Total Fat 5.5g: Cholesterol 0mg: Sodium 602mg: Total Carbohydrate 78.1g: Dietary Fiber 26.1g: Sugars 6.8g: Protein 9.8g

26. CREAMY TOMATO SOUP

Preparation Time: 30 minutes
Cooking Time: 45 minutes
Total Time: 75 Minutes

INGREDIENTS

- 3 tbsp olive oil
- 2 onions, chopped
- 2 celery sticks, chopped
- 300g carrot, chopped
- 500g potato, diced
- 4 bay leaves
- 5 tbsp tomato purée
- 2 tbsp sugar
- 2 tbsp red or white wine vinegar
- 4 x 400g cans chopped tomatoes
- 500g passata
- 3 vegetable stock cubes
- 400ml whole milk

DIRECTIONS

1. In a large casserole dish or two saucepans, combine the oil, onions, celery, carrots, potatoes, and bay leaves. Cook, stirring sometimes, until the onions are softened, around 10-15 minutes. Fill the kettle with water and bring it to a boil.

2. Toss in the tomato purée, cinnamon, vinegar, sliced tomatoes, and passata, then add the stock cubes crumbled. Bring 1 litre of boiling water to a low simmer. Cover and cook for 15 minutes, or until the potato is tender. Remove the bay leaves before serving. Purée until very smooth with a stick blender (or ladle into a blender in batches). Season to

taste, and if necessary, apply a pinch of sugar. The soup can now be refrigerated for up to two days or frozen for up to three months.

3. Reheat the soup before serving, stirring in the milk and being careful not to let it boil. Serve with cheese sausage rolls in small bowls for the kids, then in bowls for the adults as Hot Bloody Mary soup.

Nutrition Fact: Calories Per Serving 180: Total Fat 6.5g: Cholesterol 0mg: Sodium 602mg: Total Carbohydrate 78.1g: Dietary Fiber 26.1g: Sugars 20.8g: Protein 6.8g

27. COURGETTE, PEA & PESTO SOUP

Preparation Time: 10 minutes
Cooking Time: 15minutes
Total Time: 25 Minutes

INGREDIENTS
- 1 tbsp olive oil
- 1 garlic clove , sliced
- 500g courgettes quartered lengthways and chopped
- 200g frozen peas
- 400g can cannellini beans ,drained and rinsed
- 1l hot vegetable stock
- 2 tbsp basil pesto ,or vegetarian alternative

DIRECTIONS
1. In a big saucepan, heat the oil. Cook for a few seconds after adding the garlic, then add the courgettes and cook for 3 minutes, or before they begin to soften. Cook for another 3 minutes after adding the peas and cannellini beans, as well as the hot stock.
2. Toss the pesto into the soup with a pinch of salt and pepper, then ladle into bowls and top with crusty brown bread, if desired. Alternatively, pour into a flask to take to work.

Nutrition Fact: Calories Per Serving 206: Total Fat 8.5g: Cholesterol 0mg: Sodium 602mg: Total Carbohydrate 19.1g: Dietary Fiber 9.1g: Sugars 7.8g: Protein 10.8g

28. CHINESE STEAMED BASS WITH CABBAGE

Preparation Time: 10minutes
Cooking Time: 10 minutes
Total Time: 20 Minutes

INGREDIENTS
- 2 sea bass , or other white fish fillets
- One green or red chilli , finely chopped
- 1 tsp fresh root ginger
- 300g green cabbage , finely shredded
- 2 tsp sunflower oil
- 1 tsp sesame oil
- 2 garlic cloves , thinly sliced
- 2 tsp low salt soy sauce

DIRECTIONS
1. Chilli, ginger, and a pinch of salt should be sprinkled over the fish. 5 minutes of steaming cabbage Place the fish on top of the cabbage and steam for another 5 minutes, or until completely cooked.
2. Meanwhile, in a small pan, heat the oils, add the garlic, and quickly fry, stirring constantly, until lightly browned. Place the cabbage and fish on serving plates, top with 1 tsp soy sauce, and drizzle with the garlicky oil.

Nutrition Fact: Calories Per Serving 188: Total Fat 8.5g: Cholesterol 0mg: Sodium 602mg: Total Carbohydrate 78.1g: Dietary Fiber 26.1g: Sugars 20.8g: Protein 23.8g

29. THAI SPICED TURKEY PATTIES WITH NOODLE SALAD

Preparation Time: 15 minutes
Cooking Time: 10minutes
Total Time: 25 Minutes

INGREDIENTS
- 400g turkey breast or fillet, roughly chopped
- 1 lemongrass stalk, finely chopped
- 2 garlic cloves , crushed

- Zest and juice 1 lime
- 3 tbsp low-sodium soy sauce
- Small bunch coriander , chopped
- 1 red chilli , deseeded and chopped
- 2 nests medium wheat noodles
- 300g pack mixed peppers stir-fry vegetables
- Sweet chilli sauce , to serve (optional)

DIRECTIONS

1. Preheat the grill to medium-high heat. Pulse the turkey until it is minced in a food processor. Pulse in the lemongrass, garlic, and lime zest, as well as half of the soy sauce, coriander, and chili, until well mixed. Place the mixture in a bowl and season with black pepper. Form into 8 patties, then move to a nonstick baking tray and grill for 3-4 minutes on either side, or until thoroughly fried.
2. Meanwhile, soak the noodles as directed on the package, then drain and combine with the vegetables, remaining soy sauce, and lime juice. Toss thoroughly, split among plates, and top with the remaining coriander and chilli. Serve with the turkey patties and, if desired, some warm chilli sauce for dipping.

Nutrition Fact: Calories Per Serving 173: Total Fat 2.5g: Cholesterol 0mg: Sodium 602mg: Total Carbohydrate 78.1g: Dietary Fiber 2.1g: Sugars 5.8g: Protein 27.8g

30. CRAB & SWEETCORN CHOWDE

Preparation Time: 5 minutes
Cooking Time: 30minutes
Total Time: 40 Minutes

INGREDIENTS
- 1 finely chopped onion
- 1 leek, divided and cut into green and white pieces
- 1 litre/1.5 pints - 1.75 pints low-sodium chicken or vegetable stock 2 carrots, diced 850ml
- 1 big diced potato 175g/ 6oz frozen sweetcorn
- 170g drained may white crabmeat
- 4 tablespoons soft crème fraîche
- 1 tablespoon chopped chives

DIRECTIONS

1. In a big skillet, combine the onion, white part of the leek, and carrots with a few tablespoons of stock. Cook, stirring occasionally, for around 10 minutes over medium heat, or until tender. If the vegetables begin to adhere, add a splash more stock.

2. Simmer for 10-15 minutes, until the potato is tender, with the green leek and the majority of the stock. Cook for another 1-2 minutes after adding the sweetcorn and crab meat. Remove the pan from the fire and mix in the crème fraîche and a pinch of salt and pepper. If the soup is too thick, add the remaining stock. If desired, garnish with chives and serve with brown bread.

Nutrition Fact: Calories Per Serving 191: Total Fat 5.5g: Cholesterol 0mg: Sodium 602mg: Total Carbohydrate 25.1g: Dietary Fiber 3.1g: Sugars 7.8g: Protein 13.8g

31. GREEN CUCUMBER & MINT GAZPACHO

Preparation Time: 4 minutes
Cooking Time: 5minutes, 59 seconds
Total Time: 10 Minutes

INGREDIENTS
- One cucumber, halved lengthwise, deseeded, and chopped
- One deseeded and finely diced yellow pepper
- Two ground garlic cloves
- One tiny avocado, diced
- a bunch of diced spring onions
- Mint, chopped in a little bunch.
- Natural fat-free yogurt in a 150ml jar.
- 2 tablespoons white wine vinegar
- Green Tabasco sauce, a few shakes
- To serve, snipped chives

DIRECTIONS
1. Blitz all of the ingredients in a food processor or blender until creamy, reserving half of the mint and yogurt. Add more vinegar, Tabasco, and seasoning to taste, then thin with a splash of water if desired.

2. Refrigerate until very cold, then top with a dollop of yogurt, mint, chives, and a few ice cubes if desired. The soup can be refrigerated for up to two days; just

giving it a good swirl before eating.

Nutrition Fact: Calories Per Serving 186: Total Fat 11.5g: Cholesterol 0mg: Sodium 602mg: Total Carbohydrate 15.1g: Dietary Fiber 5.1g: Sugars 14.8g: Protein 14.8g

32. BAKED COURGETTES STUFFED WITH SPICED LAMB & TOMATO SAUCE

Preparation Time: 15 minutes
Cooking Time: 1 Hour
Total Time: 1Hour 15 Minutes

INGREDIENTS
- 4 big courgettes, cut in half lengthwise
- 1 tablespoon olive oil
- coriander flowers, a small handful
- 500g lean minced lamb 2 tsp per ground cumin, coriander, and cinnamon for stuffing
- 1 tablespoon cayenne pepper
- To make the tomato sauce
- 1 tablespoon olive oil
- 4 crushed garlic cloves
- 1 tsp per cayenne pepper, cinnamon, coriander, and cumin
- 2 cans sliced tomatoes (400g)
- 2 tsps sugar

DIRECTIONS
1. Preheat the oven to 220°C/200°C fan/gas mark 1 7. In a medium pan, heat the oil and fried the garlic for 2-3 minutes, or until tender, before adding the spices and frying for 1 minute more. Add the tomatoes and sugar and cook for 20 minutes, or until thickened, with half a tin of water. It's the time of year.
2. Meanwhile, scoop out and discard some of the flesh from the courgettes and place them in 1 large or 2 small roasting trays, drizzle with oil, and bake for 15 minutes, until golden and slightly softened.
3. To make the stuffing, combine the lamb, herbs, and salt in a mixing bowl. Instead of squeezing it together, lightly swirl it with your palms until it's all mixed. When the courgettes are over, stuff the lamb into the cavities and pour the sauce over them. Bake for 15-20 minutes, or until the sauce has

thickened and is bubbling. Serve with a garnish of coriander.

Nutrition Fact: Calories Per Serving 200: Total Fat 12.5g: Cholesterol 0mg: Sodium 602mg: Total Carbohydrate 8.1g: Dietary Fiber 26.1g: Sugars 5.8g: Protein 16.8g

33. GUJARATI CABBAGE WITH COCONUT & POTATO

Preparation Time: 10 minutes
Cooking Time: 20 minutes
Total Time: 30 Minutes

INGREDIENTS
- 500g Charlotte or other fresh potato, peeled and cut in half
- 2 tablespoons sunflower oil
- 1 tsp asafetida
- 1 tablespoon black mustard seeds
- 1 tsp cumin seeds
- Two dry red peppers
- One deseeded and thinly sliced fresh red or green chili
- 1 finely shredded pointed (sweetheart) cabbage
- 12 lemon juice
- 2 tbsp toasted desiccated or shaved fresh coconut
- Coriander bunch, finely chopped

DIRECTIONS
1. Cook potatoes for 10 minutes in salted boiling water until tender. Return to the pan after draining well. Crush lightly with the back of a fork to break apart rather than mash.
2. In a big frying pan, heat the oil and then add the asafoetida, cloves, and dried chilies. Cook for a few minutes, until the herbs are fragrant and the chillies have darkened in color.
3. Stir in the new chilli, cabbage, and a pinch of salt for 3-4 minutes. Cook for another 2-3 minutes, or until the cabbage is soft but still has some crunch, adding the warm potatoes to the pan. Serve with the lemon juice, coconut, and coriander.

Nutrition Fact: Calories Per Serving 199: Total Fat 10.5g: Cholesterol 0mg: Sodium 602mg: Total Carbohydrate 25.1g: Dietary Fiber 4.1g: Sugars 20.8g: Protein 4.8g

34. EASY RATATOUILLE WITH POACHED EGGS

Preparation Time: 15 minutes
Cooking Time: 50 minutes
Total Time: 1 Hour 5 Minutes

INGREDIENTS

- 1 tablespoon olive oil
- 1 big chopped onion
- One deseeded and thinly sliced red or orange pepper
- Two finely chopped garlic cloves
- 1 tbsp rosemary, chopped
- One sliced aubergine
- Two minced courgettes
- 400g sliced tomatoes from a can
- 1 tsp balsamic vinegar
- Four big eggs
- A handful of basil leaves

DIRECTIONS

1. In a big frying pan, heat the oil. Cook for 5 minutes, stirring regularly, until the onion has softened, adding the onion, pepper, garlic, and rosemary. Cook for another 2 minutes after adding the aubergine and courgettes.
2. Fill the can halfway with water, swirl it up, and tip it into the pan with the tomatoes. Bring to a boil, cover, and cook for 40 minutes, uncovering after 20 minutes, until the liquid has reduced and become pulpy.
3. Create four spaces for the eggs in the ratatouille after adding the vinegar. In each hole, crack an egg and season with black pepper. Cover and cook for 2-5 minutes, or until gently or securely set as desired. Serve with crusty bread to mop up the juices and a sprinkle of basil.

Nutrition Fact: Calories Per Serving 398: Total Fat 16.5g: Cholesterol 0mg: Sodium 602mg: Total Carbohydrate 13.1g: Dietary Fiber 5.1g: Sugars 10.8g: Protein 14.8g

35. JAPANESE SALAD WITH GINGER SOY DRESSING

Preparation Time: 20 minutes
Cooking Time: 30 minutes

INGREDIENTS

- 4 baby gem lettuces , halved lengthways
- 200g frozen shelled edamame (soy) beans, defrosted
- 4 carrots , cut into long matchsticks
- 140g radish , thinly sliced
- For the dressing
- 2 tbsp rice wine vinegar
- 2 tbsp reduced-salt soy sauce
- 2 tbsp caster sugar
- ½ small onion , chopped
- 2 tsp chopped ginger
- 1 tbsp tomato purée
- 2 tbsp vegetable oil

DIRECTIONS

1. In a mixer or food processor, combine all of the dressing ingredients and 1 tablespoon of water. Blend until fully smooth. On 4 plates or 1 large platter, arrange the halved spinach, edamame, carrots, and radishes.

Drizzle the dressing on top until about to eat.

Nutrition Fact: Calories Per Serving 318: Total Fat 16.5g: Cholesterol 0mg: Sodium 602mg: Total Carbohydrate 78.1g: Dietary Fiber 26.1g: Sugars 20.8g: Protein 14.8g

36. BANANA PANCAKES

Preparation Time: 5minutes
Cooking Time: 5minutes
Total Time: 10 Minutes

INGREDIENTS

- 1 large banana
- 2 medium eggs, beaten
- pinch of baking powder (gluten-free if coeliac)
- splash of vanilla extract
- 1 tsp oil
- 25g pecans, roughly chopped
- 125g raspberries

DIRECTIONS

2. 1 big banana, mashed with a fork in a bowl until it resembles a thick purée

3. 2 pounded eggs, a sprinkle of baking powder (gluten-free if coeliac), and a dash of vanilla extract are combined in a mixing bowl.

4. Brush a big nonstick frying pan or pancake pan with 12 tsp oil and heat over low heat.

5. Spoon two pancakes into the pan with half the flour, cook for 1-2 minutes on either side, then transfer to a tray. Repeat the procedure with the remaining batter and 12 tsp gasoline.

6. 25g pecans, finely sliced, and 125g raspberries on top of the pancakes.

Nutrition Fact: Calories Per Serving 243: Total Fat 16.5g: Cholesterol 0mg: Sodium 602mg: Total Carbohydrate 78.1g: Dietary Fiber 26.1g: Sugars 14.8g: Protein 9.8g

37. CARDAMOM & PEACH QUINOA PORRIDGE

Preparation Time: 3 minutes
Cooking Time: 20minutes
Total Time: 23 Minutes

INGREDIENTS

75g quinoa
25g porridge oats
4 cardamom pods
250ml unsweetened almond milk
2 ripe peaches , cut into slices
1 tsp maple syrup

DIRECTIONS

1. In a shallow saucepan, combine the quinoa, peas, and cardamom pods with 250mL water and 100mL almond milk. Bring to a boil, then reduce to a low heat and cook for 15 minutes, stirring periodically.

2. Cook for another 5 minutes, or until the almond milk is creamy.

3. Remove the cardamom pods, then spoon the peaches and maple syrup into bowls or pots.

Nutrition Fact: Calories Per Serving 231: Total Fat 4.5g: Cholesterol 0mg: Sodium 602mg: Total Carbohydrate 78.1g: Dietary Fiber 26.1g: Sugars 20.8g: Protein 8.8g

38. KALE, TOMATO & POACHED EGG ON TOAST

Preparation Time: 2 minutes
Cooking Time: 7minutes
Total Time: 9 Minutes

INGREDIENTS

- 2 tsp oil
- 100g ready-chopped kale
- 1 garlic clove , crushed
- ½ tsp chilli flakes
- 2 large eggs
- 2slices multigrain bread
- 50g cherry tomatoes , halved
- 15g feta , crumbled

DIRECTIONS

1. A big pot of water should be brought to a boil. In a frying pan over medium pressure, heat the oil and add the kale, garlic, and chilli flakes. Cook for 4 minutes, stirring regularly, until the kale starts to crisp and wilt to half its original scale. Remove from the equation.

2. Poach the eggs for 2 minutes after bringing the water to a rolling boil. Toast the bread in the meantime.

3. With a slotted spoon, remove the poached eggs and cover each slice of toast with half of the kale, an egg, cherry tomatoes, and feta.

Nutrition Fact: Calories Per Serving 251: Total Fat 12.5g: Cholesterol 0mg: Sodium 602mg: Total Carbohydrate 78.1g: Dietary Fiber 3.1g: Sugars 2.8g: Protein 15.8g

39. PISTACHIO NUT & SPICED APPLE BIRCHER MUESLI

Preparation Time: 10 minutes
Cooking Time: 15minutes
Total Time: 25 Minutes

INGREDIENTS

- For the base ingredients
- 50g jumbo porridge oat
- 50ml apple juice
- Large pinch cinnamon
- Large pinch nutmeg
- 1 medium apple , cored and grated

- 2 tbsp low-fat natural yogurt
- For the topping
- 25g chopped pistachio
- 3 tbsp pomegranate seeds or mixed berries

DIRECTIONS

1. Allow all of the base ingredients, except the yogurt, to soak in 150ml water for at least 20 minutes, or overnight if possible. Stir in the yogurt until the oats have softened, then split the mixture into two cups. Serve with half of the topping on top of each dish.

Nutrition Fact: Calories Per Serving 229: Total Fat 8.5g: Cholesterol 0mg: Sodium 602mg: Total Carbohydrate 29.1g: Dietary Fiber 26.1g: Sugars 14.8g: Protein 8.8g

INGREDIENTS

- 2 medium eggs
- 2 tbsp orange juice
- 2 slices spelt bread, halved
- 50g low-fat cottage cheese
- 1 tsp orange zest
- 1 tsp rapeseed oil
- 50g raspberries
- Clear honey , to serve (optional)

40. EGGY SPELT BREAD WITH ORANGE CHEESE & RASPBERRIES

Preparation Time: 5minutes
Cooking Time: 5minutes
Total Time: 10 Minutes

DIRECTIONS

2. In a bowl large enough to hold the bread, whisk together the eggs and orange juice. Soak the bread for about 2 minutes in the eggs and milk, turning halfway through.

3. Meanwhile, combine the cheese and orange zest in a shallow dish. In a nonstick frying pan over high pressure, heat the rapeseed oil. When the pan is warmed, toss in the eggy bread. Allow to cook for a few minutes without disturbing it, then flip and cook for another 1-2 minutes on the other side.

4. Divide the bread into two plates and cover with the cheese, raspberries, and honey, if desired.

Nutrition Fact: Calories Per Serving 197: Total Fat 10.5g: Cholesterol 0mg: Sodium 602mg: Total Carbohydrate 12.1g: Dietary Fiber 2.1g: Sugars 4.8g: Protein 14.8g

41. CREAMY MUSTARD MUSHROOMS ON TOAST WITH A GLASS OF JUICE

Preparation Time: 5minutes
Cooking Time: 5minutes
Total Time: 10 Minutes

INGREDIENTS

- 1 slice wholemeal bread
- 1 ½ tbsp light cream cheese
- 1 tsp rapeseed oil
- Three cut tiny flat mushrooms, 3 tbsp.
- 2 tbsp. skim milk
- 1/4 tsp wholegrain mustard
- 1 tablespoon snipped chives
- 150ml orange juice, either newly squeezed or from a carton

DIRECTIONS

1. Toast the bread and sprinkle it with a small amount of cheese (no butter).
2. Meanwhile, heat the oil in a nonstick pan and cook the mushrooms until softened, stirring regularly. In a mixing bowl, combine the cream, leftover cheese, and mustard. Stir until it is evenly coated. Serve with the juice and a sprinkling of chives on top of the toast.

Nutrition Fact: Calories Per Serving 231: Total Fat 16.5g: Cholesterol 0mg: Sodium 602mg: Total Carbohydrate 78.1g: Dietary Fiber 26.1g: Sugars 20.8g: Protein 18.8g

42. HAM, MUSHROOM & SPINACH FRITTATA

Preparation Time: 4 minutes
Cooking Time: 9minutes
Total Time: 13 Minutes

INGREDIENTS

- 1 tsp oil
- 80g chestnut mushrooms , sliced
- 50g ham , diced
- 80g bag spinach
- 4 medium eggs , beaten
- 1 tbsp grated cheddar

DIRECTIONS

1. Raise the temperature of the grill to its highest setting. In an ovenproof frying pan, heat the oil over medium-high heat. Add the mushrooms and cook for 2 minutes, or until they are mostly softened. Cook for 1 minute longer, or until the spinach has wilted, after adding the ham and spinach. Season with a pinch of salt and black pepper.

2. Reduce the heat to low and dump the mixture over the eggs. Cook for 3 minutes, stirring occasionally, until the eggs are almost set. Sprinkle the cheese on top and cook for 2 minutes under the grill. Serve warm or chilled.

Nutrition Fact: Calories Per Serving 188: Total Fat 12.5g: Cholesterol 0mg: Sodium 602mg: Total Carbohydrate 78.1g: Dietary Fiber 27.1g: Sugars 20.8g: Protein 18g

43. VEGGIE BREAKFAST BAKES

Preparation Time: 15 minutes
Cooking Time: 30minutes
Total Time: 45 Minutes

INGREDIENTS

- 4 large field mushrooms
- 8 tomatoes , halved
- 1 garlic clove , thinly sliced
- 2 tsp olive oil
- 200g bag spinach
- 4 eggs

DIRECTIONS

1. Preheat the oven to 200 degrees Fahrenheit/180 degrees Fahrenheit fan/gas 6. In four ovenproof pots, combine the mushrooms and tomatoes. Divide the garlic between the pans, drizzle with oil and season with salt and pepper, and bake for 10 minutes.

2. Meanwhile, wilt the spinach by placing it in a big colander and pouring boiling water over it.

Squeeze the extra water out of the spinach before adding it to the plates. Make a little space between the vegetables and crack an egg into each of the dishes. Return to the oven for another 8-10 minutes, or until the egg is fried to your preference.

Nutrition Fact: Calories Per Serving 269: Total Fat 12.5g: Cholesterol 0mg: Sodium 602mg: Total Carbohydrate 78.1g: Dietary Fiber 20.1g: Sugars 20.8g: Protein 9.8g

44. SPICED FRUIT LOAF

Preparation Time: 30 minutes
Cooking Time: 20minutes
Total Time: 50 Minutes

INGREDIENTS

For the dough
- 450g strong white flour , plus extra for dusting
- 2 x 7g sachets easy-blend yeast
- 50g caster sugar
- 150ml warm milk
- 1 egg , beaten
- 50g unsalted butter , melted, plus extra for greasing
- Oil , for greasing
- For the spices
- 1½ tsp ground cinnamon
- 1 tsp ground ginger
- For the dried fruit
- 50g dried apricot , chopped
- 50g dried fig , chopped
- 50g pitted date , chopped
- 50g sultana
- 50g glacé cherry , chopped
- Juice 1 orange

DIRECTIONS

1. Soak the dried fruits in the orange juice for about 30 minutes, then strain the juice and set aside.
2. In a big mixing cup, combine the starch, yeast, caster sugar, and 1 tsp salt, along with the spices and soaked fruit. In the center of the bowl, make a well and pour in the warm milk, reserved orange juice, beaten egg, and melted butter. To make a dough, begin with a wooden spoon and work your way to the end with your hands. Add a little more warm water if the dough is too dry; if it's too wet, add more flour.

3. Knead the dough in the tub or on a floured surface until smooth and springy. Cover loosely with a clean, moist tea towel and transfer to a clean, gently greased tub. Allow to grow in a warm place until it has approximately doubled in size – this would take around 1 hour based on the temperature of the room.

4. Knead the dough for a few seconds to get it back to life. 2 x 2 pound loaf tins, floured Cut the dough in half. Shape each half into a smooth oval with a little flour, then place them in the muffin tins. Cover all loosely with a clean, damp tea towel and set aside to prove for about 20 minutes in a warm spot. Preheat the oven to 180°C/160°C fan/gas 4 in the meantime.

5. Cook for 20 minutes in the oven, then cool fully in the tins before turning out.

Nutrition Fact: Calories Per Serving 190: Total Fat 4.5g: Cholesterol 0mg: Sodium 602mg: Total Carbohydrate 36.1g: Dietary Fiber 2.1g: Sugars 14.8g: Protein 5.8g

45. CRANBERRY & RASPBERRY SMOOTHIE

Preparation Time: 10 minutes
Cooking Time: 15minutes

Total Time: 25 Minutes

INGREDIENTS
- 200ml cranberry juice
- 175g frozen raspberry , defrosted
- 100ml milk
- 200ml natural yogurt
- 1 tbsp caster sugar , or to taste
- Mint sprigs, to serve

DIRECTIONS
1. In a blender, combine all of the ingredients and process until creamy. Pour into glasses and garnish with new mint leaves.

Nutrition Fact: Calories Per Serving 100: Total Fat 2.5g: Cholesterol 0mg: Sodium 602mg: Total Carbohydrate 78.1g: Dietary Fiber 26.1g: Sugars 20.8g: Protein 4.8g

46. ASPARAGUS SOLDIERS WITH A SOFT-BOILED EGG

Preparation Time: 10 minutes
Cooking Time: 10 minutes
Total Time: 20 Minutes

INGREDIENTS

- 1 tbsp olive oil
- 50g fine dry breadcrumbs
- Pinch each chilli and paprika
- 16-20 asparagus spears
- 4 eggs

DIRECTIONS

2. In a skillet, heat the oil, then add the breadcrumbs and fry until golden and crisp. Allow to cool after seasoning with the spices and flaky sea salt. In a big pot of hot salted water, cook the asparagus for 3-5 minutes, or until tender. Boil the eggs for 3-4 minutes at the same time. On a tray, place each egg in an egg cup. Drain and split the asparagus between plates. Serve with a sprinkling of crumbs.

Nutrition Fact: Calories Per Serving 186: Total Fat 10.5g: Cholesterol 0mg: Sodium 602mg: Total Carbohydrate 12.1g: Dietary Fiber 26.1g: Sugars 20.8g: Protein 12.8g

47. HONEY NUT CRUNCH PEARS

Preparation Time: 5 minutes
Cooking Time: 10 minutes
Total Time: 15 Minutes

INGREDIENTS

- 4 ripe pears
- knob of butter
- ½ tsp mixed spice
- 2 tbsp clear honey
- 50g cornflake
- 25g toasted flaked almond

DIRECTIONS

1. Preheat oven to 200°C/180°C fan forced/gas 6 Round the pears in half lengthwise, remove the center (see tip to the left), and finish with a little knob of butter and a sprinkling of mixed seasoning. Place the pears in a shallow baking dish and bake for 5 minutes, or

until they begin to soften. Meanwhile, in a big microwave-safe tub, heat the honey and another knob of butter for 30 seconds. Combine the cornflakes and nuts in a mixing bowl.

2. Remove the pears from the oven and sprinkle with the cornflake mixture. Cook for 5 minutes more, or until the cornflakes have turned a dark golden color. Allow to cool for a few minutes (the cornflakes will crunch up) before serving warm with ice cream.

Nutrition Fact: Calories Per Serving 179: Total Fat 16.5g: Cholesterol 0mg: Sodium 602mg: Total Carbohydrate 31.1g: Dietary Fiber 26.1g: Sugars 20.8g: Protein 3.8g

48. HASH BROWNS WITH MUSTARD & SMOKED SALMON

Preparation Time: 10 minutes
Cooking Time: 10 minutes
Total Time: 20 Minutes

INGREDIENTS

- 1 large potato (about350g/12oz), washed
- 1 tbsp plain flour
- 1 tbsp wholegrain mustard or horseradish sauce
- Knob of butter
- 1 tbsp sunflower oil
- 4 slices smoked salmon
- Soured cream or crème fraîche , to serve
- Chives , to serve

DIRECTIONS

1. Using a spare tea towel, grate the unpeeled potato. Bring the towel's edges up over the sink and pinch to drain any remaining water from the potatoes. Combine the rice, mustard, and horseradish in a mixing cup. Season to taste and combine.

2. Make 8 balls out of the mixture and flatten them between your palms.

Heat the butter and oil in a big frying pan before adding the potatoes. Cook for 2-3 minutes on each hand, until golden brown, over a medium heat.

3. To eat, pile a pair of hash browns on each plate and finish with a slice of smoked salmon, a dollop of soured cream or crème fraîche, and some chives.

Nutrition Fact: Calories Per Serving 153: Total Fat 6.5g: Cholesterol 0mg: Sodium 602mg: Total Carbohydrate 18.1g: Dietary Fiber 1.1g: Sugars 20.8g: Protein 9.8g

49. BREAKFAST SMOOTHIE

Preparation Time: 5 minutes
Cooking Time: 15 minutes
Total Time: 25 Minutes

INGREDIENTS
- 1 small ripe banana

- About 140g blackberries, blueberries, raspberries or strawberries (or use a mix), plus extra to serve
- Apple juice or mineral water, optional
- Runny honey , to serve

DIRECTIONS
1. Connect the berries of your choosing to your blender or food processor after slicing the banana. Blend until fully smooth. Pour in juice or water as the blades are spinning to achieve the desired consistency. Serve with a few extra fruits and honey drizzled on top.

Nutrition Fact: Calories Per Serving 124: Total Fat 1.5g: Cholesterol 0mg: Sodium 602mg: Total Carbohydrate 25.1g: Dietary Fiber 26.1g: Sugars 20.8g: Protein 14.8g

50. PERFECT PORRIDGE

Preparation Time: 5 minutes
Cooking Time: 15 minutes
Total Time: 25 Minutes

INGREDIENTS
- 50g oat porridge
- 350ml milk or water to serve, or a combination of the two Greek

yogurts thinned with a little milk and clear honey

DIRECTIONS

2. In a saucepan, combine 50g porridge oats, 350ml milk or water, and a pinch of salt. Bring to a boil, then reduce to a low heat and cook for 4-5 minutes, stirring occasionally and making sure it doesn't stick to the bottom of the pan.
3. You should even do it in the oven. In a big microwaveproof dish, combine the porridge oats, milk or water, and a pinch of salt, then microwave on High for 5 minutes, stirring halfway through. Allow 2 minutes to stand before feeding.
4. Pour into cups, fill with Greek yogurt thinned with a little sugar, and drizzle with honey to serve.

NUTRITION

Nutrition Fact: Calories Per Serving 175: Total Fat 5.5g: Cholesterol 0mg: Sodium 602mg: Total Carbohydrate 25.1g: Dietary Fiber 26.1g: Sugars 20.8g: Protein 10.8g

51. HIGH-FIBRE MUESLI

Preparation Time: 5 minutes
Cooking Time: 15 minutes
Total Time: 25 Minutes

INGREDIENTS

- 300g jumbo oats
- 100g All-Bran
- 25g wheatgerm
- 100g dark raisins
- 140g ready-to-eat apricots , snipped into chunks
- 50g golden linseed

DIRECTIONS

1. In a big mixing cup, combine all of the ingredients. In an airtight bag, you can keep this for up to 2 months. Pour a large amount of chilled milk over the top when about to eat and let it soak for a few minutes.

Nutrition Fact: Calories Per Serving 124: Total Fat 3.5g: Cholesterol 0mg: Sodium 602mg: Total Carbohydrate 78.1g: Dietary Fiber 26.1g: Sugars 20.8g: Protein 4.8g

52. SKINNY PEPPER, TOMATO & HAM OMELETTE

Preparation Time: 15 minutes
Cooking Time: 10 minutes
Total Time: 25 Minutes

INGREDIENTS

- 3 egg whites and 2 entire eggs
- 1 tablespoon olive oil
- One deseeded and finely chopped red pepper
- Two spring onions, finely sliced, white and green sections kept apart.
- a few wafer-thin extra-lean ham slices, shredded
- 25g mature reduced-fat cheddar
- To eat, wholemeal toast.
- To serve, add 1-2 chopped fresh tomatoes.

DIRECTIONS

1. Place aside the eggs and egg whites, along with some seasoning. In a medium nonstick frying pan, heat the oil and cook the pepper for 3-4 minutes. Cook for 1 minute more after adding the white bits of the spring onions. Pour in the eggs and cook, stirring sometimes, until almost set.

2. Continue to cook until the ham and cheese are only set in the middle, or if you like it well baked, flash it under a hot grill. Serve immediately from the plate, garnished with the green portion of the spring onion, chopped tomato, and wholemeal toast.

Nutrition Fact: Calories Per Serving 206: Total Fat 12.5g: Cholesterol 0mg: Sodium 602mg: Total Carbohydrate 78.1g: Dietary Fiber 26.1g: Sugars 5.8g: Protein 21.8g

53. THE ULTIMATE MAKEOVER: BLUEBERRY MUFFINS

Preparation Time: 15 minutes
Cooking Time: 25 minutes
Total Time: 40 Minutes

INGREDIENTS

- Five tablespoons rapeseed oil
- 225 grams self-rising flour

- Wholemeal flour (115g)
- Two tsp baking powder
- 12 lemon zest and 1 tsp juice
- 85g caster sugar, golden
- 50g muscovado sugar, light
- One small black-skinned banana, very ripe.
- ONE EGG
- 284ml buttermilk pot
- 225g blueberries, fresh

DIRECTIONS

1. Preheat oven to 200°C/180°C fan/gas mark 6. 6. Lightly grease a 12-hole muffin tray with 1 tsp oil (or use paper cases). Combine all flours, baking powder, and lemon zest in a mixing bowl. 1 tbsp caster sugar set aside, then mix the rest of the sugar into the flour with the muscovado.
2. Well mash the banana. In a separate dish, whisk together the egg, banana, buttermilk, and oil. Lightly stir through the flour mixture with a big metal spoon, only to blend. Overmixing can result in difficult muffins. Toss in the blueberries and gently stir them in with a spoon, being careful not to crush them.
3. Fill each hole in the tin to the brim with the mixture. Bake for 20-25 minutes, or until golden.
4. Combine the lemon juice and the reserved caster sugar. Remove the muffins from the oven when they're finished and clean them with the sugar and lemon mixture while they're still sweet. With a knife, gently loosen the edges of each muffin, then leave in the tin for 15 minutes to cool slightly because they're very fragile when heated. Place on a wire rack to cool. It's best eaten the day it's made, but it can last up to two days in the fridge.

Nutrition Fact: Calories Per Serving 206: Total Fat 18.5g: Cholesterol 0mg: Sodium 602mg: Total Carbohydrate 78.1g: Dietary Fiber 26.1g: Sugars 20.8g: Protein 16.8g

54. BANANA YOGURT POTS

Preparation Time: 5 minutes
Cooking Time: 15 minutes
Total Time: 20 Minutes

INGREDIENTS

- 1 x tub thick yogurt
- 3-4 bananas cut into chunks
- 4 tbsp sort dark brown sugar
- 25g walnuts , toasted and chopped

DIRECTIONS

1 tbsp yogurt, poured into the bottoms of 4 shallow glasses Place a layer of banana on top, followed by another layer of yogurt. Continue layering until the glasses are fully filled. Sprinkle the sugar and nuts on top, then chill for 20 minutes, or until the sugar has melted.

Nutrition Fact: Calories Per Serving 230: Total Fat 6.5g: Cholesterol 0mg: Sodium 602mg: Total Carbohydrate 40.1g: Dietary Fiber 26.1g: Sugars 20.8g: Protein 7.8g

55. BAKED EGGS BRUNCH

Preparation Time: 10 minutes
Cooking Time: 30minutes
Total Time: 40 Minutes

INGREDIENTS

- 2 tbsp olive oil
- 2 leeks , thinly sliced
- 2 onions , thinly sliced
- 2 x 100g bags baby spinach leaves
- Handful fresh wholemeal breadcrumbs
- 25g parmesan (or vegetarian alternative), finely grated
- 4 sundried tomatoes , chopped
- 4 medium eggs

DIRECTIONS

1. Preheat the oven to 200 degrees Fahrenheit/180 degrees Fahrenheit fan/gas 6. In a skillet, heat the oil and add the leeks, onions, and seasoning. Cook for 15-20 minutes, or until tender and caramelizing.

2. In the meantime, strain the spinach in a colander over a pot of hot water. Squeeze out as much moisture as you can until it's cold enough to touch. Combine the breadcrumbs and cheese in a mixing bowl.

3. Divide the leek and onion mixture among four ovenproof pots, then top with the spinach and sundried tomato bits. In the center of each dish, make a well and crack an egg into it. Season with salt and pepper, then top with cheese crumbs. Cook for 12-15 minutes, before the whites are set and the

yolks are fried to your taste, on a baking tray.

Nutrition Fact: Calories Per Serving 210: Total Fat 13.5g: Cholesterol 0mg: Sodium 602mg: Total Carbohydrate 78.1g: Dietary Fiber 26.1g: Sugars 7.8g: Protein 12.8g

56. CREAMY YOGURT PORRIDGE

Preparation Time: 1 minutes
Cooking Time: 3 minutes
Total Time: 10 Minutes

INGREDIENTS

- 3 tbsp (25g) porridge oat
- 150g pot 0% fat probiotic yogurt

DIRECTIONS

In a shallow non-stick pan, pour 200ml water and stir in porridge oats.

Cook, stirring sometimes, until the sauce has thickened and is bubbling. Use a deep jar to avoid spillage so the mixture can climb as it heats in the microwave, and steam for 3 minutes on High.

Stir in the yogurt, or whisk half of it in and then top with the rest. Serve simple or with a variety of toppings.

Nutrition Fact: Calories Per Serving 184: Total Fat 2.5g: Cholesterol 0mg: Sodium 602mg: Total Carbohydrate 78.1g: Dietary Fiber 26.1g: Sugars 20.8g: Protein 13.g

57. SPICY MOROCCAN EGGS

Preparation Time: 10 minutes
Cooking Time: 15minutes
Total Time: 25 Minutes

INGREDIENTS

- 2 tsp rapeseed oil
- 1 large onion , halved and thinly sliced
- 3 garlic cloves , sliced
- 1 tbsp rose harissa
- 1 tsp ground coriander
- 150ml vegetable stock

- 400g can chickpea
- 2 x 400g cans cherry tomatoes
- 2 courgettes , finely diced
- 200g bag baby spinach
- 4 tbsp chopped coriander
- 4 large eggs

DIRECTIONS

1. In a big, deep frying pan, heat the oil and fry the onion and garlic for about 8 minutes, stirring occasionally, until golden. Stir in the harissa and ground coriander, then add the stock and chickpeas, along with their liquid. Cover and cook for 5 minutes, then mash one-third of the chickpeas to thicken the supply.
2. Cook for 10 minutes, until the courgettes are soft, with the tomatoes and courgettes in the pan. Fold the spinach into the pan such that it wilts.
3. Stir in the chopped coriander, then crack the eggs into four hollows in the mixture. Cover and simmer for 2 minutes, then remove from heat and set aside for 2 minutes before serving.

Nutrition Fact: Calories Per Serving 242: Total Fat 10.5g: Cholesterol 0mg: Sodium 602mg: Total Carbohydrate 78.1g: Dietary Fiber 8.1g: Sugars 20.8g: Protein 16.8g

58. FIG, NUT & SEED BREAD WITH RICOTTA & FRUIT

Preparation Time: 15 minutes
Cooking Time: 1 hour and 15 minutes
Total Time: 1 Hour and 30 Minutes

INGREDIENTS

- 400ml hot strong black tea
- 100g dried fig , hard stalks removed, thinly sliced
- 140g sultana
- 50g porridge oat
- 200g self-raising wholemeal flour
- 1 tsp baking powder
- 100g mixed nuts (almonds, walnuts, Brazils, hazelnuts), plus 50g for the topping
- 1 tbsp golden linseed
- 1 tbsp sesame seed , plus 2 tsp to sprinkle
- 25g pumpkin seed
- 1 large egg

- 25g ricotta per person
- 1 orange or green apple, thickly sliced, per person

DIRECTIONS

1. Preheat oven to 170 degrees Celsius/150 degrees Celsius fan/gas 312. In a big mixing cup, combine the tea, figs, sultanas, and oats. Allow to soak for a while.

2. Meanwhile, cover a 1kg loaf tray with baking parchment on the bottom and sides. Combine the rice, baking powder, almonds, and seeds in a mixing bowl. After beating the egg into the cooled fruit mixture, stir in the dry ingredients. Fill the tin halfway with the batter, and level the top and top with the remaining nuts and sesame seeds.

3. Bake for 1 hour, then cover with foil and bake for another 15 minutes, or until a skewer inserted into the center comes out clean. Remove the cake from the tin to cool, but keep the parchment on until it is fully cool. Serve with fruit after cutting into slices and spreading with ricotta. It can stay for a month in the fridge or can be frozen in slices.

Nutrition Fact: Calories Per Serving 249: Total Fat 10.5g: Cholesterol 0mg: Sodium 602mg: Total Carbohydrate 30.1g: Dietary Fiber 26.1g: Sugars 20.8g: Protein 10.8g

59. BAKED SALMON & EGGS

Preparation Time: 5 minutes
Cooking Time: 15minutes
Total Time: 25 Minutes

INGREDIENTS

- 6 crusty white rolls (poppy seed ones look lovely)
- 25g butter , melted
- 6 slices smoked salmon or gravadlax
- 6 medium eggs
- A few snipped chives

DIRECTIONS

1. Preheat oven to 180°C/160°C fan/gas 4 (180°C/160°C fan/gas 4). Slice off the top of each roll, then carefully cut the bread inside until a hole wide enough to fit a slice of

salmon and an egg remains. Place the rolls on a baking sheet, with the tops set aside. (You should whizz the middles into crumbs and freeze them for another recipe.)

2. Brush the inside and sides of the rolls with melted butter, then stuff each one with a slice of salmon. Season with salt and pepper and crack an egg into each. Bake for 10-15 minutes, or until the eggs are completely cooked. Sprinkle with chives that have been snipped. Toast the tops, then clean them with the remaining butter before cutting them into soldiers to dip into the shells.

Nutrition Fact: Calories Per Serving 238: Total Fat 10.5g: Cholesterol 0mg: Sodium 602mg: Total Carbohydrate 78.1g: Dietary Fiber 4.1g: Sugars 20.8g: Protein 17.8g

60. EGG SCRAMBLE WITH SWEET POTATOES

Preparation Time: 10 minutes
Cooking Time: 15 minutes

INGREDIENTS:

- 1 (8-oz) sweet potato, diced
- ½ cup chopped onion
- 2 tsp chopped rosemary
- Salt
- Pepper
- 4 large eggs
- 4 large egg whites
- 2 tbsp chopped chive

DIRECTIONS:

1. Preheat the oven to 425 degrees Fahrenheit. Toss the sweet potato, cabbage, rosemary, and salt and pepper on a baking dish. Cook until crispy, about 20 minutes, after spraying with cooking spray.
2. Meanwhile, whisk together the eggs, egg whites, and a touch of salt and pepper in a medium mixing dish. Scramble the eggs in a skillet sprayed with cooking spray for around 5 minutes on low.

3. Serve with the spuds and a sprinkling of chopped chives.

Nutrition Fact: Calories Per Serving 571: Total Fat 16.5g: Cholesterol 0mg: Sodium 602mg: Total Carbohydrate 78.1g: Dietary Fiber 29.1g: Sugars 20.8g: Protein 44.8g

LUNCH

1. KETO BLT SANDWICH

Preparation Time: 5 minutes
Cooking Time: 15minutes
Total Time: 20 Minutes

INGREDIENTS:

- Paleo Coconut Bread (1/2 loaf) (sliced in half again to make 2 squares)
- 2 cups spinach leaves, raw
- 1 ripe tomato, peeled and sliced (optional)
- 2 or 3 strips pasture-raised bacon
- 1/2 tbsp. butter or ghee (for frying)
- Season with salt to taste
- 1 cut tiny avocado
- Herbs include parsley, cilantro, rosemary, oregano, or thyme
- Optional extras: Avocado oil mayonnaise, vinegar, or pickles made from scratch

DIRECTIONS:

1. Preheat the oven to 350°F and a big frying pan to medium heat. When the pan is hot, add the bacon and cook until golden brown.
2. Remove the fried bacon to a plate and set aside the drippings.
3. In the same skillet, easily saute the spinach in the bacon fat. Remove the spinach and place it in a bowl with the bacon.
4. Swirl butter or ghee into the frying pan to cover the whole surface. Fry the bread squares until golden brown.
5. Assemble an open-faced sandwich by combining the following ingredients: Cover with sauteed spinach, sliced tomatoes, avocado, crispy bacon, remaining add-ins, new herbs, and a pinch of salt to taste.

Nutrition Fact: Calories Per Serving 306: Total Fat 10.5g: Cholesterol 0mg: Sodium 602mg: Total Carbohydrate 78.1g: Dietary Fiber 26.1g: Sugars 20.8g: Protein 21.8g

2. LAMB KETO TACOS WITH CAULIFLOWER TORTILLAS

Preparation Time: 10 minutes
Cooking Time: 30minutes
Total Time: 40 Minutes

KETO TACOS INGREDIENTS:

- Two pounds lamb stew meat or 1 inch pieces lamb shoulder
- Three cup chicken broth
- One thyme bunch
- 2 tbsp avocado oil (or ghee)
- Season with salt to taste

INGREDIENTS:

- 1 head of cauliflower, broken into florets
- 2 eggs
- Generous pinch of salt
- Avocado oil for greasing
- Radishes to garnish, sliced thinly
- Chopped cilantro to garnish

DIRECTIONS:

1. In a big heavy-bottomed jar, heat avocado oil over medium-high heat. Season the lamb generously with salt and pepper before searing it for 1-2 minutes on either hand.
2. Bring the liquid to a light boil with the chicken stock and thyme. Cover and steam for 2 hours, or until fork tender, until it has reached a simmer.
3. Prepare the cauliflower tortillas while the lamb is cooking. Preheat the oven to 375 degrees Fahrenheit. Roughly chop cauliflower florets and pulse in a food processor until fine crumbles form, operating in batches.
4. Using a thin coating of oil, gently grease a baking dish. Bake for 10 minutes, or until cauliflower is thoroughly baked, after spreading it out on the baking sheet.
5. When the cauliflower is cold enough to touch, wring out any extra moisture with a clean, dry kitchen towel (be careful not to burn yourself). The cauliflower should resemble masa dough in appearance. Combine in a mixing dish with the eggs and salt.
6. Using the back of a spoon, spread 1/4 cup of the dough in a circle onto a parchment-lined baking dish. Rep until there is no more dough.
7. Toasted tortillas can be baked for 25 minutes, turning once every 10 minutes.
8. Lightly shred the lamb and put it on a cauliflower tortilla with some of the cooking juices, sliced radishes, and cilantro to eat keto tacos.

Nutrition Fact: Calories Per Serving 398: Total Fat 16.5g: Cholesterol 0mg: Sodium 602mg: Total Carbohydrate 78.1g: Dietary Fiber 26.1g: Sugars 20.8g: Protein 14.8g

3. LOW-CARB THAI SALAD WITH GRILLED STEAK

Preparation Time: 15 minutes
Cooking Time: 25minutes
Total Time: 40 Minutes

INGREDIENTS:

- 1 tbsp coconut oil or ghee (grass-fed)
- 1 bok choy head, cut lengthwise into quarters
- a quarter of a medium red cabbage, finely shredded
- 1 medium spiralized carrot
- 2 oz. top sirloin or hanger steaks (approximately 3/4-inch thick)
- Alternate: To garnish, use fresh cilantro, sliced radishes, fresh lime juice, or chopped green onions.

MARINADE INGREDIENTS:

- 2 tbsp of coconut aminos
- 1/2 tsp ground ginger 1/2 tsp ground coriander
- 1 tsp unrefined honey
- 1 tsp new lime juice
- A half tsp of salt

DIRECTIONS:

1. Whisk together the marinade ingredients in a mixing cup. Toss the steaks in the cup with the marinade. Cover and set aside for 20 minutes to marinate. (If you want to marinate the steaks for longer, put them in the fridge.)
2. Bring 1 inch of water to a boil in a pan with a steamer basket. Reduce to a low heat and steam the bok choy for around 6 minutes, or until tender. Remove the item and set it aside.
3. Sauté the red cabbage in coconut oil in a saucepan over medium heat until tender. Remove the cabbage and return the carrots to the pan, cooking for another 2-3 minutes.
4. Warm a cast iron griddle pan over medium-high pressure. Attach the steaks and cook for 3 minutes once the pan is heated. Cook for another 2 minutes after flipping the steaks.
5. Allow your steaks to rest for 3-5 minutes before slicing against the grain.
6. Assemble the Thai salad as follows: Arrange the vegetables on the plate and top with the steak. If necessary, add garnishes.

Nutrition Fact: Calories Per Serving 438: Total Fat 24.5g: Cholesterol 0mg: Sodium 602mg: Total Carbohydrate 78.1g: Dietary Fiber 26.1g: Sugars 20.8g: Protein 30.8g

4. PALEO CAULIFLOWER FRITTERS

Preparation Time: 5 minutes
Cooking Time: 25minutes
Total Time: 40 Minutes

INGREDIENTS:

- 1 large cauliflower head, broken into florets
- 1/3 cup collagen protein
- 1/3 cup coconut flour
- 2 pasture-raised eggs
- 1 tsp baking soda
- 1/2 tsp ground turmeric
- 1/2 tsp ground ginger
- 1/2 tsp ground cinnamon
- 1 tablespoon grass-fed ghee
- Fresh cilantro to garnish
- Salt to taste

DIRECTIONS:

1. Steam cauliflower florets until tender in a steamer basket filled with 1 inch boiling water. Enable to cool on a plate while you prepare the remaining ingredients.
2. Add cauliflower to a blender and pulse until it develops a rice-like texture. Pour into a clean kitchen towel and suck out as much water as possible.
3. Add the remaining ingredients, minus the cilantro, to the cauliflower in a mixing cup. Mix thoroughly so all is well blended.
4. Ghee can be melted around the pan in a skillet over medium heat.
5. Shape the cauliflower mixture into 6 fritters with your fingertips. Cook for 4-5 minutes with the fritters in the skillet. Cook for an extra 4-5 minutes after flipping.
6. Cauliflower fritters should be served warm, with salt and cilantro to taste.

Nutrition Fact: Calories Per Serving 165: Total Fat 7.5g: Cholesterol 0mg: Sodium 602mg: Total Carbohydrate 11.1g: Dietary Fiber 26.1g: Sugars 20.8g: Protein 19.8g

5. TOFU SCRAMBLE

Preparation Time: 5 minutes
Cooking Time: 10 minutes

INGREDIENTS

- 8 ounces firm tofu (225 g)
- 1/4 tsp salt, see notes
- 1/4 tsp turmeric powder, see notes
- 1/8 tsp ground black pepper

DIRECTIONS

1. Chop the tofu and crumble it with a fork into bite-sized bits.
2. In a frying pan, heat some oil and then add the tofu and the remaining ingredients (salt, turmeric powder, and ground black pepper). Cook for 5 to 10 minutes over medium-high heat, stirring constantly. Stir once in a while.
3. Serve instantly with fresh strawberries, vegan bacon, or vegan sausages as part of a vegan brunch (I served my tofu scramble over some toasted bread and topped it with fresh parsley). It's also delicious with vegan pancakes and a cup of coffee or milk.
4. Refrigerate leftovers for up to 1 week in an airtight bag. You can also prepare the tofu ahead of time and store it in the freezer for up to 5 months.

Notes

1. You can use any salt you want, but I prefer Kala Namak salt (also known as Himalayan black salt) because it tastes like real eggs.
2. If you're not a fan of turmeric or aren't used to its flavor, start with 1/8 tsp turmeric powder, then taste the scramble and add more if necessary.
3. Spices, vegetables, and other foods to taste.
4. If you don't want to use gasoline, just use water or vegetable stock instead.

NUTRITION

Calories: 80Sugar: 0.7 gSodium: 248 mgFat: 4.7g; Saturated Fat: 1 gCarbohydrates: 2.1 gFiber: 1.1 gProtein: 9.3 g

6. PHILADELPHIA PROTEIN PACKED RYVITA

Preparation Time: 5minutes
Cooking Time: 10minutes
Total Time: 15 Minutes

INGREDIENTS

- 30 g   Philadelphia Light
- 30 g   wafer thin ham
- 0.5 x   avocado
- 0.5 x   lemon
- 1 x   free range egg, at room temperature
- cracked black pepper
- 1-2 sprigs flat leaf parsley
- 2 x slices   Ryvita 'Chia Seed & Buckwheat' Protein
- 1 x   handful mixed salad leaves, to serve
- 1 tsp   olive oil, to serve

DIRECTION

1. Place the egg in a shallow pan with at least 3 cm of cold water and a big pinch of salt to make a great hardboiled egg.

2. Place the pan over high heat and, as soon as the water begins to boil, reduce to medium and continue to cook for 8 minutes.

3. Using a slotted spoon, separate the fish from the water and put it in a bowl of ice water. Remove the egg from the bath and tap it all over on a rough surface until it has cooled. To make peeling easier, gently remove the shell while keeping it under a cold running tap. Cut into 4 thick slices and set aside.

4. To save the avocado from discoloring, cut it into 4-5 slices with a little lemon juice squeezed over it.

5. To put it together, spread Philadelphia on both Ryvita slices. Then, in a pattern, laid a slice of ham, an egg, and an avocado, alternating with each. Serve with a mixed leaf salad drizzled with olive oil and a splash of lemon juice, and a sprinkle of finely chopped parsley on top.

Nutrition Fact: Calories Per Serving 498: Total Fat 28.5g: Cholesterol 0mg: Sodium 602mg: Total Carbohydrate 78.1g: Dietary Fiber 26.1g: Sugars 20.8g: Protein 21.8g

7. EGG AND PARMA HAM SALAD WITH PINE NUTS

Preparation Time: 5 minutes
Cooking Time: 5minutes
Total Time: 10 Minutes

INGREDIENTS

- 1 medium egg
- 3 cherry tomatoes
- 2 slices Parma ham
- 80g mixed leaf salad
- 1 tbsp pine nuts
- 1 tbsp fat free dressing

DIRECTIONS

1. Allow the egg to cool after it has been hardboiled.
2. Toast the pine nuts for 1-2 minutes in a frying pan over medium heat (optional)
3. In a tub, arrange the salad leaves.
4. Cut the tomatoes in half, dice the egg, and toss everything into the salad bowl.
5. Place the Parma ham on top and tear it up.
6. Drizzle the salad dressing on top (and mix to coat, if you prefer)
7. Enjoy with a sprinkling of (toasted) pine nuts!

Nutrition Fact: Calories Per Serving 209: Total Fat 16.5g: Cholesterol 0mg: Sodium 602mg: Total Carbohydrate 5.1g: Dietary Fiber 8.1g: Sugars 20.8g: Protein 15.8g

8. HADDOCK PARCELS AND COCONUT RICE

Preparation Time: 15 minutes
Cooking Time: 25minutes
Total Time: 40 Minutes

INGREDIENTS

- 4 haddock fillets, about 150g/5½ oz each
- 4 tbsp chopped fresh coriander
- 1 red chilli, chopped
- 1 shallot, thinly sliced
- 1 lime, sliced, plus extra lime halves to serve
- 2 lemongrass stalks, 1 roughly chopped and 1 bashed

- 300g/10½oz basmati rice
- 2 fresh or dried kaffir lime leaves
- 50ml/2fl oz reduced-fat coconut milk

DIRECTIONS

1. Preheat the oven to 180 degrees Celsius/160 degrees Celsius fan/Gas 4.
2. Cut four 30cm/12in squares of nonstick baking material. Place a haddock fillet in the center of each piece and equally distribute the coriander, chili, shallot, lime, and chopped lemongrass stalk. Make tidy parcels out of them. Bake for 20 minutes after transferring the parcels to a baking sheet.
3. Fill a lidded saucepan halfway with water and bring to a boil. Cook for 10 minutes with the lid on, or until the rice is fluffy. Stir in the coconut milk after the rice has been cooked and the water has been absorbed.
4. Serve with rice and extra lime halves alongside the haddock parcels.

Nutrition Fact: Calories 403 kcal, 34.4g protein, 57.5g carbohydrate (of which 0.4g sugars), 2.2g fat (of which 0.9g saturates), 0.1g fibre and 0.3g salt per portion.

9. ITALIAN BROCCOLI AND EGG SALAD

Preparation Time: 10minutes
Cooking Time: 30minutes
Total Time: 40 Minutes

INGREDIENTS

- 4 free-range eggs
- 300g/10½oz broccoli, cut in to florets
- 2 small leeks, about 300g/10½oz in total, trimmed, slit and thickly sliced
- 4 tbsp lemon juice
- 2 tbsp olive oil
- 2 tbsp clear honey
- 1 tbsp capers, well drained
- 2 tbsp chopped tarragon
- Salt and freshly ground pepper

DIRECTIONS

1. In a big kettle, crack the eggs, cover with cold water, and bring to a boil. Cook for another 7-10 minutes after the water has reached a boil. When the eggs are finished,

place them in ice cold water for 1 minute before removing them and setting them aside.

2. Meanwhile, steam the broccoli for 3 minutes in the top of a steamer. Cook for another 2 minutes after adding the leeks.

3. In a salad bowl, combine the lemon juice, oil, sugar, capers, and tarragon for the dressing. Salt and freshly ground black pepper to taste.

4. The eggs should be shelled and finely chopped.

5. Toss together the broccoli and leeks with the dressing. Serve with a sprinkling of chopped eggs.

Nutrition Fact: Calories 192 kcal, 12.1g protein, 6.6g carbohydrate (of which 5.8g sugars), 13.2g fat (of which 2.8g saturates), 4.8g fibre and 0.2g salt per portion.

10. BAKE-IN-A-BAG FISH

Preparation Time: 20 minutes
Cooking Time: 30 minutes
Total Time: 50 Minutes

INGREDIENTS
2 tbsp olive oil
¼ fennel bulb, finely sliced
½ onion, finely sliced
salt and freshly ground black pepper
1 medium tomato, sliced
2 fish fillets, about 175g/6oz each, such as cod, sea bass or trout
olive oil, drizzle
squeeze lemon juice
1 tbsp chopped dill (optional)
1 tsp capers (optional)
2-3 tbsp white wine (optional)

DIRECTIONS
Preheat the oven to 200°C/180°C fan/Gas 6 degrees Celsius. Cut two squares of baking paper (40cm/16in square) and two squares of tin foil (40cm/16in square) to the same size. On top of each sheet of foil, place a square of baking paper.

In a frying pan, heat the oil and cook the fennel and onion, seasoning with salt and pepper, for 2-3 minutes, until softened. Divide the fennel and onions between the two baking paper squares, sprinkle on the sliced tomatoes, and cover each heap with a fish fillet. Season with salt and freshly ground black pepper, drizzled with olive oil and a splash of lemon juice. If used, garnish with minced dill and a few capers. Fold the foil and paper over the fish and double-fold each edge to close the package, leaving an opening at the top for a few tsps of white wine (if using). Fill the parcel of wine, and fully seal it, but not too tightly, so it will spread in the oven when it heats.

Bake the parcels for 12-14 minutes, or until the fish is only opaque and cooked through, on a baking tray. The packets can be served on each plate so that they can be opened at the table.

Nutrition Fact

Calories 370 kcal, 34g protein, 2.5g carbohydrate (of which 1.8g sugars), 23g fat (of which 2.5g saturates), 1.2g fibre and 0.3g salt per portion.

11. SWEET POTATO BREAKFAST HASH

Preparation Time: 5 minutes
Cooking Time: 20minutes
Total Time: 25 Minutes

INGREDIENTS

- 2 sweet potatoes large, peeled and diced small
- 3 tablespoons olive oil
- 1/2 tsp kosher salt
- 1/4 tsp ground white pepper
- 1 tablespoon apple cider vinegar
- 2 garlic cloves minced
- 1 tsp honey
- 1/4 cup yellow onion diced small
- 1/4 cup green bell pepper diced small
- 8 ounces ham low-sodium, sulfate-free, diced small
- 1 tablespoon lemon juice
- 1 avocado peeled, pit removed and diced small

DIRECTIONS

1. Preheat the oven to 450 degrees Fahrenheit. Using tape, line a baking dish.

2. Toss the sliced sweet potatoes with 1/2 tablespoon olive oil, salt, and pepper and spread out on the baking sheet in an even layer. Bake for 15 minutes, or until the potatoes are soft and lightly browned.

3. In a shallow cup, combine the apple cider vinegar, garlic, and honey. 1 tablespoon extra virgin olive oil, whisked constantly Whisk all together until it's smooth. Remove from the equation.

4. Heat the remaining olive oil in a big skillet over medium heat. Add the onion and green pepper until the pan is heated. Add the ham and fried potatoes after the onions have softened somewhat. Cook until the ham has started to brown. Take the

pan off the heat and add the apple cider vinegar sauce.

5. Combine the avocado and lemon juice in a mixing bowl. Stir gently into the hash. Serve immediately!

6. Notes OPTIONAL TIP: For more protein and a complete meal, top with a poached egg.

NUTRITION

Serving: 0.5cup | Calories: 186kcal | Carbohydrates: 14g | Protein: 8g | Fat: 11g | Saturated Fat: 2g | Cholesterol: 22mg | Sodium: 457mg | Fiber: 4g | Sugar: 2g | Smart Points (Freestyle): 6

12. SPICY BLACK BEAN AND SHRIMP SALAD

Preparation Time: 5 minutes
Cooking Time: 20minutes
Total Time: 30 Minutes

INGREDIENTS

- 1/2 pound raw, peeled, and deveined big shrimp 1/4 tsp crushed red pepper 1 tsp chili powder

- smoked paprika, 1 tsp
- 1 tsp cumin powder
- a half tsp kosher salt
- 2 tsps olive oil
- 1 cup kernels of corn
- 1/4 cup thin diced red onion
- 1 tsp lime juice
- 15 ounces rinsed and dried black beans
- 2 cups shredded or finely minced kale
- 2 cup shredded or finely diced romaine lettuce
- 1 cup halved grape tomatoes
- 1 avocado, peeled, pitted, and sliced
- 2 tbsp. new, chopped cilantro

DIRECTIONS

1. Combine the lobster, red pepper, chili powder, paprika, cumin, and salt in a shallow dish. Toss the shrimp in the seasonings thoroughly.

2. In a big skillet, heat 1 tablespoon of olive oil. Add the seasoned shrimp until the pan is warmed. Cook for 5 to 6 minutes, or until the meat is pink and solid. Keep the shrimp warm by removing them from the skillet.

3. Return the shrimp to the plate with the remaining tablespoon of olive oil. Set on high and add the corn

and onion once the pan is warmed. Cook, stirring sometimes, until the corn starts to char and the onions are tender, around 5 minutes. Combine the lime juice, black beans, and fried shrimp in a mixing bowl. Cook for just a few minutes, or until the beans are sweet.

4. Toss the kale and romaine together in a big salad dish. Add the shrimp mixture, onion, and avocado to the top. Serve with a sprinkling of cilantro on top.

Nutrition Fact: Serving: 2cups | Calories: 357kcal | Carbohydrates: 36g | Protein: 22g | Fat: 16g

13. SPINACH PARMESAN BAKED EGGS

Preparation Time: 4 minutes
Cooking Time: 5minutes, 59 seconds
Total Time: 10 Minutes

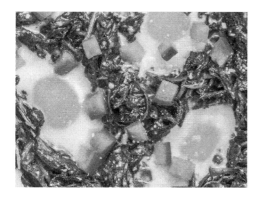

INGREDIENTS

- 2 tsps olive oil
- 2 garlic cloves minced
- 4 cups baby spinach
- 1/2 cup parmesan cheese fat-free, grated
- 4 eggs
- 1 tomato small, diced small

DIRECTIONS

1. Preheat the oven to 350 degrees Fahrenheit. Using nonstick oil, coat an 8-inch x 8-inch casserole dish.
2. Heat the olive oil in a big skillet over medium heat. Add the spinach and garlic until the pan is warmed. Cook until the spinach is almost wilted. Remove the pan from the heat and drain any remaining oil. Stir in the parmesan cheese, then spoon the mixture into the casserole dish in an even layer.
3. For the chickens, make four little divots in the spinach. In each divot, crack an egg. Bake for 15 to 20 minutes, or until the egg whites are almost fully set. Remove from the oven and set aside to cool for 5 minutes before adding the tomato. Serve and have fun!

Nutrition Fact: Serving: 1egg with 1/2 cup spinach mixture | Calories: 149kcal | Carbohydrates: 3g | Protein: 12g | Fat: 10g

| Saturated Fat: 4g | Cholesterol: 170mg | Sodium: 280mg | Fiber: 1g | Sugar: 1g | SmartPoints (Freestyle): 3

14. OVEN-CRISP FISH TACOS

Preparation Time: 10 minutes
Cooking Time: 25minutes
Total Time: 35 Minutes

INGREDIENTS

- 1 to 1 1/2 pounds fish filets I prefer wild-caught flounder or tilapia, cut into 2 inch wide strips (3 or 4 strips per fillet)
- 1/4 cup white whole-wheat flour
- 2 egg whites
- 1/4 cup cornmeal
- 1/4 cup whole-wheat bread crumbs
- 2 tablespoons lime juice freshly squeezed, 1 medium lime
- 2 tablespoons taco seasoning recipe for homemade Taco Seasoning
- 8 corn tortillas 6 inches or whole-wheat flour tortillas
- 1 cup lettuce or cabbage shredded
- 1 cup salsa no sugar added or 1 medium tomato, diced
- 1 cup Greek yogurt nonfat, optional nonfat sour cream

DIRECTIONS

1. Preheat oven to 450 degrees Fahrenheit.
2. Using tape, line a baking dish. Spray a cooling rack with olive oil or canola oil cooking spray and place it on top of the baking sheet.
3. In a small dish, combine breadcrumbs, cornmeal, and taco seasoning.
4. Whisk the egg whites and lime juice together in a separate shallow bowl until frothy.
5. In a small dish, sift the rice.
6. To finely coat all sides of the fish strips, gently dip them into the flour. Dip the fish parts in the egg whites, allowing excess to run off, before pressing them onto the seasoned cornmeal and breadcrumbs on both sides.
7. Cook the breaded fish strips for 10 to 12 minutes on the prepared rack, until the outside is golden crisp and the fish is opaque and flakes easily with a fork.
8. Coat a griddle or a saute pan with cooking oil. Heat the tortillas on both sides over medium heat for 30 seconds to 1 minute, or until

thoroughly cooked. When ready to eat, keep tortillas warm in a clean kitchen towel.

9. Cover each tortilla with 2 strips of tuna, shredded romaine, salsa or tomato, and a dollop of yogurt.

Nutrition Fact: Serving: 1taco | Calories: 198kcal | Carbohydrates: 24g | Protein: 18g | Fat: 4g | Saturated Fat: 1g | Cholesterol: 33mg | Sodium: 285mg | Fiber: 3g | Sugar: 3g | SmartPoints (Freestyle): 5

15. EASY TURKEY BURRITO SKILLET

Preparation Time: 4 minutes
Cooking Time: 5minutes, 59 seconds
Total Time: 10 Minutes

INGREDIENTS
- 1 pound turkey field
- 1 tsp chili powder
- 1 tsp cumin, 1 tablespoon lime juice
- a half tsp kosher salt
- 1/4 tsp ground black pepper (or crushed red pepper flakes if you like it hot!)
- 1 cup of water
- 1 cup salsa chunky no artificial sugar
- 15 ounces black beans, rinsed and washed
- 4 whole-wheat flour tortillas, 6 inches long, sliced into 1 inch strips
- 1 cup low-fat cheddar cheese
- 1/2 cup pure Greek yogurt
- 1/4 cup chopped new cilantro

DIRECTIONS
1. Cook the ground turkey in a big skillet until it is cooked through, breaking it up into small pieces as it heats. Chili powder, cumin, lime juice, salt, pepper, water, salsa, and beans can all be mixed together. Bring to a boil, then lower to a low heat. Cook, stirring sometimes, for 3 to 5 minutes, or until the sauce thickens.

2. Remove the pan from the heat and add the tortilla strips, followed by the melted cheese. Cover and keep warm until the cheese has melted. Serve with a dollop of Greek yogurt and a sprig of fresh cilantro on top of each serving. Serve and have fun!

Nutrition Fact: Serving: 1cup | Calories: 379kcal | Carbohydrates: 31g | Protein: 30g | Fat: 15g.

16. WILD CAUGHT COD WITH MOROCCAN COUSCOUS

Preparation Time: 20 minutes
Cooking Time: 25 minutes
Total Time: 40 Minutes

This cod and couscous meal is filling, healthy, and delicious; you won't be disappointed.

INGREDIENTS

- 1/2 cup fat-free, low-sodium chicken broth 14 1 pound sliced tomatoes with green chilies
- 1 tbsp. plus 2 tsp. extra virgin olive oil
- 3/4 cup Moroccan couscous optional whole-wheat couscous to taste kosher or sea salt
- 16 ounces thawed wild-caught cod fillets, black pepper to taste (4 fillets)
- 1 tbsp newly squeezed lemon juice

DIRECTIONS

1. Add chicken broth, 2 tsps extra-virgin olive oil, and diced tomatoes with juice to a medium cup. Bring to a boil over medium-high heat, then add the couscous and season with salt and pepper. Remove from heat, stir, and cover saucepan. Allow the couscous to sit while you prepare the cod.

2. Season the cod with a pinch of salt and a grind of black pepper. In a large nonstick skillet, heat 1 tablespoon oil over medium-high heat and cook the filets until they flake with a fork, around 2-3 minutes per hand. Take the pan off the fire and serve with couscous. Pour lemon juice over the fillets.

Nutrition Fact: Serving: 1fillet and 1/2 cup couscous | Calories: 279kcal | Carbohydrates: 31g | Protein: 26g | Fat: 5g.

17. HONEY GARLIC SHRIMP STIR-FRY

Preparation Time: 4 minutes
Cooking Time: 5minutes, 59 seconds
Total Time: 10 Minutes

INGREDIENTS

- 1 tablespoon coconut oil
- 1 pound shrimp raw, peeled and deveined
- 2 garlic cloves minced
- 1 tablespoon ginger fresh, minced
- 1 yellow onion small, cut into thin strips
- 1 red bell pepper small, cut into thin strips
- 1 cup peas
- 1/2 tsp kosher salt
- 2 tablespoons honey
- 1 tablespoon soy sauce
- 1 tablespoon orange zest
- 2 cups brown rice cooked

DIRECTIONS

1. Heat the coconut oil in a big skillet over high heat. Add the shrimp, half of the garlic, and half of the ginger once the pan is heated. Cook until the shrimp are solid, stirring continuously. Remove the shrimp from the pan and set them aside.

2. Add the cabbage, bell pepper, snap peas, and the leftover garlic and ginger to the same pan where the shrimp are fried. Cook on high heat, stirring continuously, until the vegetables tend to soften.

3. Return the shrimp to the pan, add the sugar, soy sauce, and orange zest, and season with salt. Cook until all of the ingredients are heated and well-coated in the sauce. Serve with brown rice and eat up!

Nutrition Fact: Serving: 1cup stir-fry with 1/2 cup rice | Calories: 316kcal | Carbohydrates: 41g | Protein: 28g | Fat: 5g | Saturated Fat: 3g | Cholesterol: 183mg | Sodium: 595mg | Fiber: 5g | Sugar: 12g | SmartPoints (Freestyle): 7

18. HAM AND EGG BREAKFAST CUPS

Preparation Time: 10 minutes
Cooking Time: 20minutes,
Total Time: 30 Minutes

INGREDIENTS

- 12 slices ham low-sodium, all-natural
- 3 eggs
- 3 egg whites
- 1/2 cup skim milk
- 2 green onions chopped

DIRECTIONS

1. Preheat the oven to 350 degrees Fahrenheit.
2. Using non-stick oil, lightly coat a muffin tin. Each ham slice should be pressed into a cup shape in the muffin pan.
3. Whisk together the egg, egg whites, and milk in a mixing cup. Add the green onion and fill the ham cups to about 3/4 capacity.
4. Bake for about 20 minutes, or until the eggs are fully fixed. Remove from the oven and set aside to cool slightly before eating. Have fun!

Nutrition Fact: Serving: 2ham and egg cups | Calories: 92kcal | Carbohydrates: 3g | Protein: 10g | Fat: 5g | Saturated Fat: 2g | Cholesterol: 96mg | Sodium: 384mg | Sugar: 1g | SmartPoints (Freestyle): 2

19. SWEET POTATO AND TURKEY SKILLET

Preparation Time: 5 minutes
Cooking Time: 25 minutes
Total Time: 30 Minutes

This skillet dish is high in protein and low in calories, making it a delicious and healthy meal.

INGREDIENTS

- 1 tablespoon extra virgin olive oil
- 1 onion medium, minced
- 1 pound lean ground turkey
- 2 sweet potatoes medium, diced into small cubes
- 1 tsp cumin
- 2 sage leaves fresh, roughly chopped
- 1/2 tsp kosher or sea salt
- 1/4 tsp pepper
- 1/2 cup mozzarella cheese part-skim, grated

DIRECTIONS

1. Sauté the onion in a big saucepan with extra virgin olive oil over medium-low heat until soft, around 4 minutes. Cook until the turkey is no longer green, breaking it up with a fork. Remove all excess fat. Combine the sweet potatoes, cumin, sage, salt, and pepper in a large mixing bowl. Cook, stirring occasionally, until potatoes are tender but not falling apart, around 5 to 10 minutes.

2. Sprinkle the mozzarella on top of the sweet potatoes when they're soft, cover, and turn off the oven.

3. Until eating, wait until the cheese has melted.

Nutrition Fact: Calories: 211kcal | Carbohydrates: 11g | Protein: 17g | Fat: 11g | Saturated Fat: 3g | Cholesterol: 64mg | Sodium: 338mg | Fiber: 2g | Sugar: 3g | SmartPoints (Freestyle): 6

20. SAVORY LEMON WHITE FISH FILLETS

Preparation Time: 15 minutes
Cooking Time: 20minutes
Total Time: 35 Minutes

This fish recipe is a simple and fast way to make a delicious and nutritious meal that only needs five ingredients.

INGREDIENTS

- 16 to 24 ounces cod fillets halibut or flounder for substitute (4 fillets)
- 3 tablespoons olive oil divided
- 1/4 tsp kosher or sea salt
- 1/4 tsp black pepper freshly ground
- 2 lemons one cut in halves, one cut in wedges

DIRECTIONS

1. Enable the fish to rest for 10 to 15 minutes in a tank at room temperature.

2. On both sides of each fillet, rub one tablespoon olive oil and season with salt and pepper. Add two tsps of olive oil to a skillet or sauté pan over medium heat. After around one minute, when the oil is hot and shimmering but not smoking, add the fish. Cook for two to three minutes on either side, until the fish is golden brown and cooked through.

3. Remove the fish from the heat by squeezing both lemon halves over it. If there is some remaining lemon juice in the pan, drizzle it over the fish before serving. Serve with lemon wedges on the side.

Notes

Tip: Serve as a side salad by tossing arugula, baby kale, or other lettuce greens with lemon juice, olive oil, salt, and pepper.

Nutrition Fact: Serving: 1fillet | Calories: 197kcal | Carbohydrates: 1g | Protein: 21g | Fat: 12g | Saturated Fat: 2g | Cholesterol: 56mg | Sodium: 223mg | SmartPoints (Freestyle): 5

21. NO-BAKE OATMEAL RAISIN ENERGY BITES

Preparation Time: 10 minutes
Refrigerate Time: 30minutes
Total Time: 40 Minutes

Try these incredibly tasty and super nutritious Oatmeal Raisin Energy Bites for on-the-go nutrition.

INGREDIENTS
- 1 cup dry oats
- 1/4 cup peanut butter
- 2 tablespoons honey
- 1/4 cup semisweet mini chocolate chips
- 1/4 cup raisins
- 1/4 cup peanuts chopped
- 1/2 tsp ground cinnamon
- 1 tablespoon vanilla protein powder

DIRECTIONS
1. Combine all ingredients in a large mixing bowl and stir until well combined and moist.
2. Roll into 1 inch balls and put on a baking sheet lined with parchment paper. Refrigerate for about 30 minutes, or until solid. Store in an airtight jar, sealed and refrigerated.

Nutrition Fact: Serving: 2bites | Calories: 152kcal | Carbohydrates: 20g | Protein: 6g | Fat: 6g | Saturated Fat: 2g | Cholesterol: 1mg | Sodium: 5mg | Fiber: 2g | Sugar: 9g | SmartPoints (Freestyle): 7

22. SKINNY SALMON, KALE, AND CASHEW BOWL

Preparation Time: 10 minutes
Cooking Time: 15minutes
Total Time: 25 Minutes

This dish is a delightful powerhouse of healthy-eating, with omega-3 fatty acids and other vital nutrients.

INGREDIENTS

- 12 ounces salmon skinless
- 2 tablespoons olive oil
- 1/2 tsp kosher salt
- 1/4 tsp ground black pepper
- 2 garlic cloves minced
- 4 cups kale stems removed and chopped
- 1/2 cup carrots shredded
- 2 cups quinoa cooked according to package
- 1/4 cup cashews chopped
- Optional Lemon Yogurt Sauce
- 3/4 cup Greek yogurt
- 1 tsp lemon juice
- 1 garlic clove finely grated or minced
- 1/2 tsp lemon zest
- 1/4 tsp kosher salt

DIRECTIONS

1. Preheat the oven to 400 degrees Fahrenheit and prepare a baking sheet with parchment paper. Spread the salmon fillets out on the baking sheet. Season the salmon with salt and pepper after brushing it with 1 tablespoon of the oil (reserve the other tablespoon for later). Preheat oven to 350°F and bake for 15 minutes, or until firm and flaky.
2. Meanwhile, in a pan, heat the remaining gasoline. Add the garlic, kale, and carrot once the pan is warmed. Cook until the kale is wilted and tender, stirring often. Combine the quinoa and cashews in a mixing bowl. Cook, stirring constantly, until the mixture is sweet.
3. Fill a serving cup halfway with the kale and quinoa mixture. Place the salmon on top of the kale after it has been removed from the oven. Serve and have fun.
4. Yogurt Sauce (optional)
5. Combine all ingredients in a small bowl and stir well. Allow for a 10-minute rest period. Drizzle the sauce over the grilled salmon and eat!

Nutrition Fact: Serving: 1bowl | Calories: 429kcal | Carbohydrates: 42g | Protein: 22g | Fat: 20g | Saturated Fat: 4g | Cholesterol: 31mg | Sodium: 206mg | Fiber: 5g | Sugar: 1g | SmartPoints (Freestyle): 12

23. Cucumber Quinoa Salad with Ground Turkey, Olives, Feta

Preparation Time: 10 minutes
Cooking Time: 20 minutes
Total Time: 30 Minutes
INGREDIENTS

- 1/2 pound ground turkey sausage
- 3 cucumbers large, sliced into 1/4 inch half circles
- 1 red onion small, sliced thin
- 1 cup grape tomatoes sliced in half
- 1/2 cup kalamata olives
- 1/2 cup feta cheese crumbles fat-free
- 1 1/2 cup quinoa cooked
- 2 tablespoons mint fresh, chopped
- 2 garlic cloves minced
- 1 tablespoon oregano fresh, chopped
- 1 tablespoon lemon juice

DIRECTIONS

1. Heat the turkey sausage in a big skillet. As the sausage cooks, break it up into little bits. Drain any remaining liquid and allow to cool fully.
2. Combine the turkey sausage with the remaining ingredients until it has coolcd. Until eating, thoroughly combine all ingredients and relax. Have fun!

Nutrition Fact: Serving: 0.5cup | Calories: 97kcal | Carbohydrates: 10g | Protein: 6g | Fat: 4g | Saturated Fat: 1g | Cholesterol: 20mg | Sodium: 211mg | Fiber: 2g | Sugar: 2g | SmartPoints (Freestyle): 2

24. Baked Chicken and Vegetable Spring Rolls

Preparation Time: 20 minutes
Cooking Time: 40 minutes
Total Time: 1 Hour

These delectable rolls are packed with fresh and nutritious ingredients and taste incredible.

INGREDIENTS

- 3 tablespoons extra virgin olive oil divided
- 1 garlic clove finely chopped
- 1 onion small, finely chopped
- 4 ounces boneless and skinless chicken breasts diced small
- 1 cup carrots julienned

- 1 cup string beans or flat beans, ends taken away and sliced diagonally
- 1 cup cabbage julienned
- 3 tablespoons soy sauce low salt
- 1/4 tsp salt
- 1/4 tsp ground pepper
- 8 spring roll wrappers or 4 phyllo (filo) pastry sheets (layer 2 sheets at a time and cut into 4 squares with kitchen scissors)

DIRECTIONS

1. Preheat oven to 400 degrees Fahrenheit.
2. Sauté the garlic and onion in a big saucepan with 2 tsps extra virgin olive oil over medium heat for 1 minute.
3. Cook for about 5 minutes after adding the chicken.
4. Toss in all of the vegetables and cook for about 15 minutes.
5. Toss for 1 minute with the soy sauce, salt, and pepper. Remove from the equation.
6. Lay out 2 filo squares (1 square will quickly break) or 1 spring roll wrapper on the work surface to make the rolls. Place a portion of sautéed chicken and vegetables nearest to you. Roll, tuck in the ends, and continue rolling until you reach the edge. Wet your fingers with water and gently dab

the filo ends to cover them. Continue to work on the remaining spring rolls.

7. Place the spring rolls on a baking tray lined with parchment paper.
8. Brush the remaining 1 tablespoon extra virgin olive oil over each spring roll.
9. Preheat oven to 350°F and bake for 15 to 20 minutes, or until golden brown.
10. Serve with a sweet and sour sauce or some other dipping sauce of your choice.

Nutrition Fact: Serving: 1spring roll | Calories: 127kcal | Carbohydrates: 12g | Protein: 4g | Fat: 7g | Saturated Fat: 1g | Cholesterol: 11mg | Sodium: 368mg | Fiber: 1g | Sugar: 2g | SmartPoints (Freestyle): 3

25. SKINNY TURKEY MEATLOAF

Preparation Time: 5 minutes
Cooking Time: 45 minutes
Total Time: 50 Minutes

This simple meatloaf is a delicious and healthy family favorite.

INGREDIENTS

- 1 pound lean ground turkey recommend 93% lean
- 1 egg lightly whipped with a fork
- 1/3 cup rolled oats uncooked

- 1/3 cup chunky salsa no sugar added
- 1/2 cup onion diced
- 1/2 tsp black pepper
- 1/4 tsp salt
- 1/3 cup ketchup

DIRECTIONS

1. Preheat the oven to 375 degrees Fahrenheit.
2. In a mixing cup, combine all ingredients except the ketchup. Fill a 5 x 7-inch loaf pan halfway with the mixture and press to shape a loaf. Wrap and bake for 35 minutes.
3. Remove the pan from the oven and generously layer the ketchup on top. Bake for another 10 minutes.
4. Allow for a 5-minute rest period. Remove the whole loaf from the pan and put it on a serving platter, or split the loaf first.

Nutrition Fact: Serving: 1slice | Calories: 124kcal | Carbohydrates: 7g | Protein: 12g | Fat: 6g | Saturated Fat: 1g | Cholesterol: 62mg | Sodium: 224mg | Fiber: 1g | Sugar: 3g | SmartPoints (Freestyle): 3

26. KETO LOW CARB EGG DROP SOUP

Preparation Time: 10 minutes

Cooking Time: 20minutes
Total Time: 30 Minutes

INGREDIENTS

- 4 1/4 cups chicken stock
- 1/2 cup chopped green onion
- 2 Tablespoons coconut aminos
- 1/2 tsp salt
- 1/2 tsp black pepper
- 1/4 tsp ground ginger
- 2 whole eggs
- 1 egg yolk
- 2 tsps xanthan gum (OPTIONAL) coconut flour or arrowroot flour works as well)

DIRECTIONS

- Bring 4 cups broth, green onion, coconut aminos, salt, pepper, and ginger to a boil in a large stock pot.
- In a shallow mixing cup, whisk together the eggs and egg yolk. Pour the egg slowly into the boiling broth while whisking constantly to build the egg strands.
- 1/4 cup residual stock and 2 tablespoons arrowroot powder in a

shallow mixing bowl Slowly pour in the slurry mixture into the broth. Cook for a further 2-3 minutes, or before the soup thickens. Serve right away.

Nutrition Fact: Calories Per Serving 243: Total Fat 88.5g: Cholesterol 0mg: Sodium 602mg: Total Carbohydrate 78.1g: Dietary Fiber 26.1g: Sugars 20.8g: Protein 41.8g

27. HONEY LIME RAINBOW FRUIT SALAD

Preparation Time: 20 minutes
Cooking Time: 20 minutes
Total Time: 40 Minutes

INGREDIENTS
- 1 lb fresh strawberries, chopped
- 1 lb chopped fresh pineapple,
- 12 oz fresh blueberries
- 12 oz red grapes, sliced into halves
- 4 kiwis, peeled and chopped
- 3 mandarin oranges*
- 2 bananas, sliced (optional)
- Honey Lime Dressing

- 1/4 cup honey
- 2 tsp lime zest (zest of 2 medium limes)
- 1 1/2 Tbsp fresh lime juice

DIRECTIONS
1. In a big mixing cup, combine all of the berries.
2. Whisk together the sugar, lime zest, and lime juice in a shallow mixing cup.
3. Pour over the fruit and toss to cover evenly; serve right away.
4. 1 (15 oz) may mandarin oranges in juice or light syrup, drained properly, can also be used in this recipe (which was what was previously listed, I just now prefer the fresh).
5. Fruit can be sliced a day ahead of time (except banana), and the dressing can be made a day ahead of time and held separate and chilled; toss just before eating.
6. The recipe was first published in June 2014, and the photographs have been revised.

Nutrition Fact: Calories Per Serving 165: Total Fat 18.5g: Cholesterol 0mg: Sodium 602mg: Total Carbohydrate 28.1g: Dietary Fiber 26.1g: Sugars 20.8g: Protein 31.8g

28. KETO LOW CARB VEGETABLE SOUP RECIPE

Preparation Time: 5 minutes
Cooking Time: 30 minutes
Total Time: 35 Minutes

INGREDIENTS

- 2 tbsp Olive oil
- 1 large Onion (diced)
- 2 large Bell peppers (diced, the same size as onions)
- 4 cloves Garlic (minced)
- 1 medium head Cauliflower (cut into 1-inch florets)
- 2 cups Green beans (trimmed, cut into 1-inch pieces)
- 2 14.5-oz cans Diced tomatoes
- 8 cups Chicken broth (or vegetable broth for vegetarian/vegan)
- 1 tbsp Italian seasoning
- 2 Dried bay leaves (optional)
- Sea salt (optional, to taste)
- Black pepper (optional, to taste)

DIRECTIONS

1. In a pot or dutch oven, melt the olive oil over low heat.
2. Combine the onions and bell peppers in a large mixing bowl. Cook, stirring occasionally, for 7 to 10 minutes, or until onions are translucent and browned.
3. Add the garlic, minced. Cook, stirring sometimes, for about a minute, or until fragrant.
4. Cauliflower, green beans, diced tomatoes, broth, and Italian seasoning are added to the pan. Toss in a pinch of sea salt and a pinch of black pepper to taste. For using, add the bay leaves.
5. Toss the soup in a pot with enough water to cover it and bring to a boil. Cook for 10 to 20 minutes, covered, on medium low heat, until vegetables are tender.

Nutrition Fact: Calories Per Serving 98: Total Fat 8.5g: Cholesterol 0mg: Sodium 602mg: Total Carbohydrate 78.1g: Dietary Fiber 26.1g: Sugars 20.8g: Protein 13.8g

29. BAKED SALMON IN FOIL

Preparation Time: 15 minutes
Cooking Time: 15minutes
Total Time: 30 Minutes
SERVINGS: 6 servings

INGREDIENTS

- Two pound boneless side of salmon (skin on or off, based on preference), wild caught if possible.
- Five sprigs fresh rosemary or other fresh herbs of your choice; no dried herbs.
- 2 small lemons, split, plus extra to serve as desired
- 2 tbsp. extra virgin olive oil
- 1 tsp of kosher salt
- 1/4 tsp black pepper, ground
- Four garlic cloves, peeled and finely sliced
- New herbs such as basil, thyme, parsley, dill, or green onion, chopped (optional).

DIRECTIONS

1. Remove the salmon from the refrigerator and set aside for 10 minutes to come to room temperature while you prepare the other ingredients. Preheat the oven to 375 degrees Fahrenheit. Using a big strip of aluminum foil, line a large baking dish or rimmed baking sheet.

2. Cover the foil lightly with baking spray, then place two rosemary sprigs down the middle. Cut one of the lemons into thin slices and place half of them with the rosemary down the middle. On top of that, position the salmon.

3. Drizzle the olive oil over the salmon and season with salt and pepper. After rubbing to coat, sprinkle the garlic cloves on top. On top of the salmon, scatter the leftover rosemary and lemon slices. The second lemon should be juiced and then poured.

4. Fold the aluminum foil sides up and over the top of the salmon to fully enclose it. Place a second piece of foil on top and fold the edges under to form a sealed packet if your first piece isn't big enough. Allow a small amount of space inside the foil for air to flow.

5. Bake for 15-20 minutes, or until the thickest portion of the salmon is almost entirely cooked through. Depending on the thickness of the salmon, the cooking time can vary. Check few minutes early if your side is thinner (around 1-inch thick) to ensure your salmon does not overcook. It can take longer if the piece is really thick (12 inches or more).

6. Remove the salmon from the oven and gently open the foil to expose the whole surface of the fish (be careful of hot steam). Return the fish to the oven and broil for 3 minutes, or until the salmon and

garlic are slightly golden and the fish is cooked through. Keep an eye on the salmon as it broils to make sure it doesn't overcook or the garlic burns. Let the salmon out of the microwave. If it still looks underdone, tie the foil around it again and set it aside for a few minutes. Allow it to sit for a short time—salmon will easily go from "not done" to "over done." As soon as it flakes quickly with a fuck, it's ready to eat.

7. Break the salmon into pieces to eat. As required, top with additional fresh herbs or a squeeze of lemon.

8. Notes: This recipe is best eaten the day it is prepared, as reheated salmon can dry out. See the blog post linked above for reheating ideas.

9. Even then, there are plenty of delicious ways to use extra salmon! Serve it room temperature the next day over a sandwich, mix it with spaghetti, or flake it and scramble it with eggs.

Nutrition Fact: Calories Per Serving 568: Total Fat 67.5g: Cholesterol 60mg: Sodium 602mg: Total Carbohydrate 78.1g: Dietary Fiber 26.1g: Sugars 20.8g: Protein 41.8g

30. HOMEMADE MARGHERITA PIZZA RECIPE

Preparation Time: 10 minutes
Cooking Time: 10 minutes
Total Time: 20 Minutes

INGREDIENTS

- 1 cup self-rising flour
- 1 cup nonfat Greek yogurt
- 1/4 cup canned San Marzano tomatoes blended until saucy like a tomato sauce
- 2 slices fresh mozzarella pat dry and cut into 1/2-inch (1.25 cm) pieces
- 10 fresh basil leaves either whole or thinly cut into strips

DIRECTIONS

1. Preheat the oven to its highest setting. Mine reaches a maximum temperature of 550 degrees Fahrenheit (290 degrees Celsius). In the middle rack, place a pizza block, cast-iron skillet, inverted baking sheet, or pizza pan. Allow

for at least 30 minutes of heating time.

2. In the meantime, cook the no yeast pizza dough and the toppings for the pizza. When the crust is finished, transfer it to a pizza pan or a big plate that can be used to slip the pizza onto the preheated oven top.

3. Spread a thin coat of tomato sauce on both ends, leaving a 12-inch (1.25 cm) border. Distribute the basil, as well as the cheese, equally.

4. Slide the pizza onto the preheated stone, skillet, or pan and bake for 10 minutes, or until the crust is golden brown and the cheese is bubbling and caramelized. Bake for 15 minutes at 500 degrees Fahrenheit (260 degrees Celsius).

5. To take the pizza out of the oven, wear gloves. If required, transfer to a cutting board and drizzle with extra-virgin olive oil. Serve immediately with the remaining new basil on top. Assemble and bake the second pizza if you have extra crust.

NOTES

You should keep leftovers in the fridge for up to 2 days in a sealable plastic container. The dough, flattened into a disk and covered in plastic wrap, can be frozen for up to 2 months. Allow 10 minutes for it to come to room temperature before applying the toppings and baking.

4 WAYS TO GET A CRISPY CRUST

1. Preheat the oven to the maximum possible setting. Set the oven's optimum temperature to wherever it can do.

2. Preheat for at least 30 minutes a pizza plate, inverted baking dish, pizza pan, or cast-iron skillet..

3. When it goes into the oven, the pizza crust must be very thin. To achieve crisp pizza, keep in mind that the middle of the crust must be thin enough to allow any light to pass through (although the edges can be thick).

4. Top with a thin layer of sauce to resemble a typical Margherita pizza but still preventing the sauce from penetrating the crust and becoming soggy.

Nutrition Fact: Calories: 102kcal | Carbohydrates: 15g | Protein: 6g | Fat: 2g | Saturated Fat: 1g | Cholesterol: 7mg | Sodium: 64mg | Potassium: 61mg | Sugar: 4g | Vitamin A: 83IU | Vitamin C: 1mg | Calcium: 40mg

31. STUFFED MARROW BAKE

Preparation Time: 4 minutes
Cooking Time: 5minutes, 59 seconds
Total Time: 10 Minutes

INGREDIENTS

- 1 tbsp olive oil
- 1 onion, chopped
- 1 garlic clove, crushed
- 1 tbsp dried mixed herbs
- 500g pack turkey mince
- 2 x 400g cans chopped tomatoes
- 1 marrow, cut into 4cm thick slices
- 4 tbsp breadcrumbs
- 3 tbsp grated parmesan

DIRECTIONS

1. Preheat oven to 200°C/180°C fan/gas mark 6. 6. In a big frying pan, heat the oil and cook the onion, garlic, and 2 tsp herbs for 3 minutes, or until they begin to soften. Brown the turkey all over, then add the tomatoes and simmer for another 5 minutes.

2. Scoop out the marrow's center and recycle (or cook, then freeze for later – try it mashed with potatoes). In a baking bowl, arrange the slices. Spoon half of the mince into the center of each marrow piece, then top with the remaining mince. Bake for 30 minutes, covered in foil.

3. Meanwhile, combine the remaining spices, breadcrumbs, and Parmesan cheese in a mixing bowl. Take the marrow out of the oven, open it, and scatter the crumbs on top. Return to the oven for another 10 minutes, or until finished.

Nutrition Fact: Calories Per Serving 198: Total Fat 58.5g: Cholesterol 56mg: Sodium 602mg: Total Carbohydrate 78.1g: Dietary Fiber 26.1g: Sugars 20.8g: Protein 31.8g

32. CREAMY INSTANT POT TOMATO SOUP

Preparation Time: 5 minutes
Cooking Time: 5minutes
Total Time: 10 Minutes

INGREDIENTS

- 5cups (828ml) vegetable broth stock
- 4 green onions scallions / spring onions, chopped
- 1 tsp minced garlic
- 1 tsp dried oregano
- ½ tsp smoked paprika
- 6 basil leaves
- salt
- black pepper
- 45 ounces 3 x 15oz (400g) cans of diced or crushed tomatoes with juice
- 2-3 tbsp almond butter optional

- toasted almonds for topping optional

DIRECTIONS

INSTANT POT DIRECTIONS:

1. In the Instant Pot insert, combine all of the ingredients.
2. Place the lid on the Instant Pot, lock it, and set the valve to seal.
3. Set to Manual (or Pressure Cook) for 5 minutes at high pressure.
4. Enable for a complete natural pressure release until you've done (NPR).
5. Allow time for the soup to cool.
6. Then, either stir and eat as is, or mix the soup with an immersion blender or in a blender if you want a cleaner soup.
7. To eat, divide the mixture into bowls and finish with toasted nuts (if desired).

STOVETOP DIRECTIONS:

1. In a big kettle, combine all of the ingredients.
2. Bring to a boil, then reduce to a low heat and cook for about 20 minutes, or until the sauce has thickened.
3. Serve immediately or puree in a blender with an immersion blender or a regular blender.

4. Serve by dividing into bowls and topping with toasted nuts (if desired).

Nutrition Fact: Calories: 60kcal | Carbohydrates: 9g | Protein: 2g | Fat: 2g | Sodium: 640mg | Potassium: 346mg | Fiber: 2g | Sugar: 5g | Vitamin A: 545IU | Vitamin C: 16.1mg | Calcium: 70mg | Iron: 1.9mg

33. WHITE BEAN AVOCADO TOAST

This delicious toast is packed with superfood goodness and can be eaten at any time of day.

Preparation Time: 10 minutes
Cooking Time: 10minutes
Total Time: 20 Minutes

INGREDIENTS

- 1/2 cup canned white beans, drained and rinsed
- 2 tbsp. tahini paste 2 tbsp. lemon juice
- a half tsp kosher salt
- 1/2 avocado (peeled and pitted)
- 4 toasted slices whole-grain bread or your choice bread
- 1/2 cup grape tomatoes, halved

145

DIRECTIONS

1. Combine the rice, tahini, half of the lemon juice, and half of the salt in a shallow cup. Mash all together well.
2. Combine the avocado, remaining lemon juice, and remaining salt in a second dish. Using a fork, lightly mash the potatoes.
3. On the toast, spread the mashed beans. Add the avocado and tomatoes to the end of the beans. Serve and have fun!

Nutrition Fact: Calories Per Serving 348: Total Fat 68.5g: Cholesterol 0mg: Sodium 602mg: Total Carbohydrate 78.1g: Dietary Fiber 26.1g: Sugars 20.8g: Protein 16.8g

34. CABBAGE AND SAUSAGE SKILLET

Preparation Time: 15 minutes
Cooking Time: 15minutes
Total Time: 30 Minutes

INGREDIENTS

- 2 Tbsp olive oil
- 3 Tbsp butter
- 1 lb andouille (or spicy) sausage
- 1 head cabbage, coarsely chopped
- 1 sweet onion, chopped
- 1 cup chicken stock
- Salt and pepper to taste

DIRECTIONS

1. Obtain a big cutting board as well as a knife. Set aside the onion, which you can chop into tiny bits.
2. After washing the cabbage, cut up the whole head. These can be coarsely chopped, with chunks that aren't too thin.
3. Using a sharp knife, cut the sausage into strips. Every slice should be halved to make bite-sized bits.
4. Preheat a big skillet to medium-high. Heat the butter and oil before the butter is molten.
5. In a pan, combine the tomatoes, ham, cabbage, and chicken stock.
6. Cook, covered, for about five minutes, or until the cabbage has softened slightly.
7. Remove the cap and season to taste with salt and pepper.
8. Cook until the sausage is finished, around 5 to 10 minutes depending on the thickness of the sausage and your preference. Serve immediately and enjoy!

Nutrition Fact: Calories: 171total fat: 11gsaturated fat: 4gtrans fat: 0gunsaturated fat: 6gcholesterol: 16mgsodium: 173mgcarbohydrates: 17gfiber: 5gsugar: 9gprotein: 4g

35. MOROCCAN BAKED EGGS

Preparation Time: 30 minutes
Cooking Time: 20inutes
Total Time: 50 Minutes

INGREDIENTS

- ½ tbsp olive oil
- ½ onion, chopped
- 1 garlic clove, sliced
- ½ tsp ras-el-hanout
- pinch ground cinnamon
- ½ tsp ground coriander
- 400g/14oz cherry tomatoes, chopped
- 2 tbsp chopped coriander
- 2 free-range eggs
- salt and freshly ground black pepper

DIRECTIONS

1. Preheat the oven to 220 degrees Celsius/200 degrees Celsius fan/Gas 7.
2. In a frying pan, heat the oil and cook the onion and garlic for 6-7 minutes, or until tender. Stir in the spices and simmer for another minute, stirring constantly.
3. Season the tomatoes with salt and pepper, then cook for 8-10 minutes on low heat.
4. 1 tablespoon coriander strewn on top, then split the tomato mixture into two ovenproof pans. In each dish, crack an egg.
5. Bake for 8-10 minutes, or until the egg whites are firm but the yolks are still runny. If you want the eggs to be completely cooked, cook for another 2-3 minutes.
6. Serve with the remaining coriander on top.

Nutrition Fact: Calories 170 kcal per portion. If eating it as part of a daily Intermittent diet menu, also enjoy 200ml skimmed milk (70 calories).

36. RED LENTIL & SWEET POTATO PÂTÉ

Preparation Time: 10 minutes
Cooking Time: 30minutes
Total Time: 40 Minutes

INGREDIENTS

- 1 tablespoon olive oil, and more for drizzling
- 12 finely chopped onion
- 1 tsp smoked paprika, with a pinch more
- 1 tiny peeled and diced sweet potato
- 140g lentils red
- 3 thyme sprigs, chopped flowers, and a little more to garnish (optional)
- 500ml vegetable stock (low sodium) (choose a vegan brand, if desired)
- 1 tablespoon red wine vinegar (choose a vegan brand, if desired)
- To serve, pita bread and vegetable sticks

DIRECTIONS

1. In a large skillet, heat the oil, then add the onion and fry, stirring occasionally, until soft and golden. Cook for another 2 minutes with the paprika before adding the sweet potato, lentils, thyme, and stock. Bring to a low boil, then reduce to a low heat and cook for 20 minutes, or until the potato and lentils are tender.

2. Add the vinegar and a pinch of salt and pepper, and mash the mixture until it has a shape you like. After 1 hour of chilling, drizzle with olive oil, brush with extra paprika, and top with thyme sprigs, if desired. With pita bread and vegetable sticks, serve.

Nutrition Fact: Calories Per Serving 278: Total Fat 19.5g: Cholesterol 6mg: Sodium 602mg: Total Carbohydrate 78.1g: Dietary Fiber 26.1g: Sugars 20.8g: Protein 21.8g

37. EGG NIÇOISE SALAD

Preparation Time: 410 minutes
Cooking Time: 10 minutes
Total Time: 20 Minutes

INGREDIENTS

- To make the dressing

- 2 tablespoons rapeseed oil
- 1 lemon, juiced
- 1 tablespoon balsamic vinegar
- 1 grated garlic clove
- 1/3 little packs basil, chopped
- Three pitted, rinsed, and diced black Kalamata olives
- To make the salad.
- two nests
- 250g thickly cut fresh potatoes
- 200g green beans, good
- 1/2 red onion, finely chopped
- 14 halved cherry tomatoes
- Six romaine lettuce leaves, shredded into bite-size pieces
- Six pitted, rinsed, and halved black Kalamata olives

DIRECTIONS

1. In a small tub, whisk together the dressing ingredients with 1 tablespoon of water.
2. Meanwhile, boil the potatoes for 7 minutes, then add the beans and cook for another 5 minutes, or until both are only tender. 2 eggs, boiled for 8 minutes, then shelled and halved
3. In a big mixing bowl, combine the bcans, ricc, and rcmaining salad ingredients (except the eggs) with half of the dressing. Place the eggs on top and pour the remaining dressing over them.

Nutrition Fact: Calories Per Serving 498**:** Total Fat 28.5g**:** Cholesterol 0mg**:** Sodium 602mg**:** Total Carbohydrate 78.1g**:** Dietary Fiber 26.1g**:** Sugars 20.8g**:** Protein 51.8g

38. TURKEY & SPRING ONION WRAPS

Preparation Time: 5 minutes
Cooking Time: 15minutes
Total Time: 25 Minutes

INGREDIENTS
- 2 tbsp reduced-fat mayonnaise
- 2 tbsp pesto
- 4 curly lettuce leaves
- 250g cooked turkey , shredded
- 6 spring onions , shredded
- 12cm chunk cucumber ,shredded
- 4 flour tortillas

DIRECTIONS
1. Combine the mayonnaise and pesto in a mixing bowl. Between

the tortillas, divide the lettuce leaves, turkey, spring onions, and cucumber. Drizzle the pesto dressing on top, then curl up and enjoy.

Nutrition Fact: Calories Per Serving 276: Total Fat 28.5g: Cholesterol 0mg: Sodium 602mg: Total Carbohydrate 78.1g: Dietary Fiber 26.1g: Sugars 20.8g: Protein 31.8g

39. FAVOURITE PASTA SALAD

Preparation Time: 10 minutes
Cooking Time: 12 minutes
Total Time: 22 Minutes

INGREDIENTS

- 250g pasta shapes (use vegan-friendly dried pasta)
- 140g frozen peas
- pack parsley , chopped
- small pack chives , snipped
- zest and juice 1 lemon
- 2 tbsp olive oil

DIRECTIONS

2. Cook the pasta for the last 2 minutes of cooking time, then add the peas. Drain, then rinse with cold water to cool before draining once more. Combine the sliced spices, lemon zest and juice, olive oil, and plenty of seasoning in a

mixing bowl and stir well. Cover and chill until ready to serve, spooning out portions as needed. If you're doing this for only one guy, you'll need to add a little olive oil or something smooth on days 3 and 4 to loosen the pasta.

Nutrition Fact: Calories Per Serving 498: Total Fat 28.5g: Cholesterol 0mg: Sodium 602mg: Total Carbohydrate 78.1g: Dietary Fiber 26.1g: Sugars 20.8g: Protein 21.8g

40. SMOKY BEEF STEW

Preparation Time: 10 minutes
Cooking Time: 40 Minutes
Total Time: 50 Minutes

INGREDIENTS

- 1 pound stew beef, cut into large chunks
- 2 onions, finely chopped
- Tomatoes, chopped, 800g (2 cans)
- 2 tsp sweet paprika, cumin, and mild chilli powder

- 2 tbsp wine vinegar (red or white)
- caster sugar, 2 tbsp
- Butter beans, 400g can, rinsed and drained

DIRECTIONS

3. Preheat oven to 160 degrees Fahrenheit/140 degrees Fahrenheit fan/gas 3 (preheat oven to 160 degrees Fahrenheit/140 degrees Fahrenheit fan/gas 3). Combine the meat, carrots, tomatoes, vegetables, vinegar, and sugar in a casserole dish. Bake for 212 hours, covered in foil. Bake for another 30 minutes, or until the beef is tender, stirring in the beans (with the cover off if the casserole is a little wet or the lid on if the consistency is good).

4. Allow to cool completely before freezing in 6-8 sections in small food bags or plastic cups. Warm in the morning and transfer to a thermos jar, or warm in the oven for lunch.

Nutrition Fact: Calories Per Serving 498: Total Fat 28.5g: Cholesterol 0mg: Sodium 602mg: Total Carbohydrate 78.1g: Dietary Fiber 26.1g: Sugars 20.8g: Protein 21.8g

41. QUICK QUORN LUNCH BOWL

Preparation Time: 10 minutes
Cooking Time: 10 Minutes
Total Time: 20 Minutes

INGREDIENTS

- 350 mL (12 oz) frozen chicken or vegetable stock, homemade or store-bought
- 2 tbsp soy sauce or Thai fish sauce
- 1 tablespoon mirin (rice wine).
- 2 tsp ginger, freshly grated or frozen prepared
- 1 tsp of brown sugar
- 2 Quorn fillets, cut into thin strips from frozen (taken from a 312g pack of 6 frozen fillets).
- Frozen green beans, cut into short strips, 100g (312oz).
- 2-3 trimmed and chopped spring onions
- Basmati rice, pre-cooked, 180g sachet (taken from 720g pack of 4 sachets).
- Frozen leaf spinach, 60g (2oz) (4 chunks).
- 1 tablespoon frozen coriander, chopped
- 1 lime's juice
- Garlic bread is ready to be served.

DIRECTION

1. In a pan, combine the stock, fish or soy sauce, mirin, ginger, and sugar. Bring to a boil and cook for a few minutes. Combine the Quorn strips and beans in a mixing bowl. Return to a low simmer for another 4 minutes.

2. Cook for a few minutes more after adding the spring onions, rice, and spinach. Toss in the coriander and a squeeze of lime, to taste. Serve with garlic bread; if using frozen garlic bread, bake or grill as directed on the package. Alternatively, toast frozen bread and spread garlic butter on top.

Nutrition Fact: Calories Per Serving 498**:** Total Fat 28.5g**:** Cholesterol 0mg**:** Sodium 602mg**:** Total Carbohydrate 78.1g**:** Dietary Fiber 26.1g**:** Sugars 20.8g**:** Protein 21.8g

42. STEAK, CHICORY AND ORANGE SALAD

Preparation Time: 10 minutes
Cooking Time: 30 Hours
Total Time: 40 Minutes

INGREDIENTS
- 6 tablespoons olive oil
- 2 sirloin steaks (thick) (about 150g).
- 1 orange juiced, 1 orange segmented
- 2 tablespoons sherry vinegar
- 1 tsp Dijon mustard, rounded
- Black pepper, salt, and freshly ground black pepper
- 1 red onion, peeled and cut into eight wedges
- 2 heads white chicory, sliced lengthwise into 4 pieces
- 1 red chicory or radicchio head
- Wild rocket, a good handful

DIRECTION
1. Preheat a frying pan to medium-high heat. 1 tsp oil, rubbed over each steak Season them and cook them for 112-2 minutes on each side. Wrap the foil around the chicken and set it aside.

2. In a saucepan, bring the orange juice to a boil until it becomes syrupy and has been reduced by half. Remove the pan from the heat and whisk in the vinegar, mustard, 1 tsp oil, and seasoning.

3. In the remaining oil, toss the red onion and white chicory. Griddle them for a few minutes, or until

they're golden brown and tender. Thinly slice the steaks.

4. Combine all of the warm ingredients, including the orange segments and the dressing, in a mixing bowl. Serve with red chicory and rocket on plates.

Nutrition Fact: Calories Per Serving 498: Total Fat 28.5g: Cholesterol 0mg: Sodium 602mg: Total Carbohydrate 78.1g: Dietary Fiber 26.1g: Sugars 20.8g: Protein 21.8g

43. HOMEMADE SPRING VEGETABLE SOUP

Preparation Time: 10 minutes
Cooking Time: 20 Minutes
Total Time: 30 Minutes

INGREDIENTS
- 1 litre hot chicken or vegetable stock
- 1 peeled and finely chopped small onion
- trimmed and halved lengthways 100g Chantenay or baby carrots
- 1 celery stick, finely sliced
- 4 trimmed and chopped baby leeks
- 2 garlic cloves, peeled and finely sliced
- 250g quartered baby new potatoes
- 100g peas, fresh or frozen
- 3-4 baby pak choi heads or spring greens
- Approximately 12 mint leaves

DIRECTION
1. In a large pot, bring the stock to a boil for your vegetable soup. Combine the onion, carrots, celery, leeks, and garlic in a large mixing bowl. Bring the water back to a boil, then add the potatoes. Simmer for 12-15 minutes, or until the vegetables are just tender.
2. Simmer for another 5 minutes with the peas on top and the pak choi just below the level of the stock.
3. Garnish with roughly chopped mint and serve in warm bowls.

Nutrition Fact: Calories Per Serving 498: Total Fat 28.5g: Cholesterol 0mg: Sodium 602mg: Total Carbohydrate 78.1g: Dietary Fiber 26.1g: Sugars 20.8g: Protein 21.8g

44. CHICKEN PITTAS

Preparation Time: 10 minutes
Cooking Time: 15 Hours
Total Time: 25 Minutes

INGREDIENTS

- 2 tbsp natural low-fat yoghurt
- 2 tablespoons tomato puree
- 2 tsp curry paste (tikka masala).
- 150 g uncooked skinless chicken thigh or breast, cut into strips
- 1 tsp of vegetable oil
- 2 pita breads (wholegrain).
- Lettuce shredded and cherry tomatoes

DIRECTION

1. Combine the yoghurt, tomato puree, and curry paste in a mixing bowl to make this chicken breast recipe. Toss in the chicken to coat it. Refrigerate for 15 minutes after covering.
2. Preheat a nonstick frying pan to medium-high heat. Pour in the oil.
3. Place the marinated chicken pieces in a hot pan and stir-fry until cooked but still juicy, about 5 minutes (about 5-8 minutes).
4. Warm the pita breads and split them open, then stuff them with shredded lettuce. Serve with

cherry tomatoes after adding the cooked chicken.

Nutrition Fact: Calories Per Serving 498: Total Fat 28.5g: Cholesterol 0mg: Sodium 602mg: Total Carbohydrate 78.1g: Dietary Fiber 26.1g: Sugars 20.8g: Protein 21.8g

45. CRUSHED NEW POTATOES AND SHOOTS

Preparation Time: 10 minutes
Cooking Time: 3 Hours
Total Time: 3Hours, 10 Minutes
Prep: 15 minCooking: 22 min

INGREDIENTS

- 500 grams of new potatoes
- 100 g asparagus spears
- extra virgin olive oil, 3 tbsp
- 1 lemon, half-zest and half-juice
- 2-4 trimmed and finely chopped spring onions
- Black pepper, salt, and freshly ground black pepper
- 100g freshly cooked petit pois
- 8 hard-boiled quail eggs
- a couple of handfuls of pea shoots
- mustard and cress, 1 punnet

DIRECTION

1. In a pan of boiling salted water, cook the potatoes for 15-20 minutes, or until almost tender. For 2 minutes, add the asparagus to the pan. Remove the spears and rinse them in cold water. Drain the potatoes and set aside for 5 minutes in a colander.

2. As you place the potatoes in a bowl, cut them in half and gently squash them with a fork. In a jar, combine the oil, lemon zest, and juice. Pour half of the dressing over the potatoes, toss in the spring onion, and season to taste.

3. Cook the quail eggs for 2 1/2 to 3 minutes in boiling salted water, then refresh under cold water and remove the shells.

4. Arrange the asparagus on plates in a pleasing manner. Top with the potato mixture. Add the peas, followed by the egg halves and pea shoots. Drizzle more dressing around the plate's edge and scatter mustard and cress around it.

Nutrition Fact: Calories Per Serving 498: Total Fat 28.5g: Cholesterol 0mg: Sodium 602mg: Total Carbohydrate 78.1g: Dietary Fiber 26.1g: Sugars 20.8g: Protein 21.8g

46. CREAMED CORN SALAD

INGREDIENTS

- 2 of corn on the cob
- 25 g of butter
- 1 shallot, thinly sliced
- 340g sweetcorn can, drained
- 5 tbsp cream (single).
- 3 tablespoons pumpkin seeds

DIRECTION

1. Dry fry the corn on the cobs in a large frying pan until they're lightly charred on all sides. Allow to cool slightly after removing from the pan. The kernels should then be cut off with a sharp knife.

2. Meanwhile, soften the butter with the shallot over low heat. Warm the canned sweetcorn and cream together in a saucepan. Remove from the heat and whizz until coarse with a hand blender. Season with salt and pepper to taste, and keep warm.

3. Cook the pumpkin seeds in the frying pan until they are crisp. Top

the creamed corn with charred kernels and toasted pumpkin seeds before serving.

Nutrition Fact: Calories Per Serving 498: Total Fat 28.5g: Cholesterol 0mg: Sodium 602mg: Total Carbohydrate 78.1g: Dietary Fiber 26.1g: Sugars 20.8g: Protein 21.8g

47. WARM RAINBOW CABBAGE SALAD

Preparation Time: 15 minutes
Cooking Time: 5 Hours
Total Time: 20 Minutes

INGREDIENTS

- 1 tablespoon sunflower oil
- 1 sliced red onion
- Optional: 1 small fennel bulb, finely sliced
- 12 cup finely shredded red cabbage (about 350g).
- Shredded half of a Sweetheart or Pointed cabbage (approximately 250g).
- 1 medium peeled and grated carrot
- 3 tablespoons lightly toasted pumpkin seeds
- Flat-leaf parsley, a handful
- 2 tsp mustard (wholegrain or Dijon)
- a generous pinch of light brown sugar
- balsamic vinegar, 2 tbsp
- 4 tbsp extra virgin olive oil

DIRECTION

1. In a frying pan, heat the oil and cook the onion and fennel (if using) for 1-2 minutes. Cook for another 2-3 minutes after adding the red cabbage. Place the mixture in a large serving bowl. Add the green cabbage and carrots, both raw.

2. To make the dressing, combine all of the ingredients in a mixing bowl and season to taste. Pour over the salad and toss to combine. Serve warm with a sprinkle of pumpkin seeds and flatleaf parsley on top.

Nutrition Fact: Calories Per Serving 498: Total Fat 28.5g: Cholesterol 0mg: Sodium 602mg: Total Carbohydrate 78.1g: Dietary Fiber 26.1g: Sugars 20.8g: Protein 21.8g

48. LEEK AND POTATO SOUP WITH PEAS

Preparation Time: 10 minutes
Cooking Time: 30 Minutes
Total Time: 40Minutes

INGREDIENTS

- 2 large washed leeks (approximately 500g)
- 1 peeled and chopped onion
- 30 g of butter
- 2 cubes or pots of vegetable stock
- 1 large peeled and chopped potato (approximately 250g)
- Peas, 100g

To make the garnish, combine the following ingredients in a mixing bowl.

1. 1 large egg white
2. Saffron threads, a pinch
3. 1 tablespoon plain flourOil, for frying

DIRECTION

1. Set aside a 10-cm leek piece for garnish. Cook the remaining leek slices in butter in a large pan with the onion until softened, about 10 minutes. Add 1 liter of water and the stock pots/cubes. Bring to a boil, then reduce to a low heat and cook for 10 minutes. Cook for another 10 minutes after adding the peas.

2. In the meantime, infuse the egg white with the saffron strands in a small bowl. Cut the reserved leek into rings and place them in cold water. To make a smooth batter, whisk together the egg white, flour, and seasoning.

3. In a food processor, puree the soup until smooth (or keep it lumpy if you prefer). If necessary, season and reheat.

4. In a small pan, heat some oil, then drain and dry the leek rings before dipping them in batter and frying them until golden and crunchy. Drain on paper towels. Pour the soup into a bowl and season with crispy leek rings and salt and pepper.

Nutrition Fact: Calories Per Serving 498: Total Fat 28.5g: Cholesterol 0mg: Sodium 602mg: Total Carbohydrate 78.1g: Dietary Fiber 26.1g: Sugars 20.8g: Protein 21.8g

49. FRUITY PRAWN COCKTAIL

Preparation Time: 10 minutes
Cooking Time: 10 Minute
Total Time: 20 Minutes

INGREDIENTS

- 350g tiger prawns, cooked
- 1 cored and chopped apple
- 2 celery sticks, sliced
- 150g seedless black or red grapes, halved
- 2 tablespoons fresh dill, plus sprigs for garnish
- 250g fromage frais sans gras
- 2-3 Little Gem lettuce rings, sliced
- For garnish, 3-4 cooked prawns with shells on

DIRECTIONS

1. Season the fromage frais to taste with salt and pepper and add the prawns, apple, celery, grapes, and dill.
2. Serve the lettuce on plates with the prawn mixture on top, garnished with a prawn and a sprig of dill.

Nutrition Fact: Calories Per Serving 498: Total Fat 28.5g: Cholesterol 0mg: Sodium 602mg: Total Carbohydrate 78.1g: Dietary Fiber 26.1g: Sugars 20.8g: Protein 21.8g

50. BEAN AND PEPPER SALAD

Preparation Time: 35 minutes
Cooking Time: 15 Minute
Total Time: 50 Minutes

INGREDIENTS

- 2 halved and deseeded red peppers
- 2 halved and deseeded yellow or orange peppers
- Green beans, 350-500g
- Salad leaves, 140-200g bag

Dressing Ingredients:

6 tablespoons olive oil
balsamic vinegar, 2 tbsp
1 tsp caster sugar
1 tbsp ginger, freshly grated

DIRECTIONS

1. Preheat the oven to 200°C/400°F/Gas mark 6 (200°C/400°F/Gas mark 6).
2. Place the peppers on a baking tray, cut-side down, and roast for 20-30 minutes, or until the skins begin to

char. Place the peppers in a freezer bag after removing them from the oven. Allow time for them to cool. Remove the skins and chop coarsely.

3. Cook the beans for 4-5 minutes in boiling water, or until they're just tender. Drain them and rinse them under cold running water to quickly cool them, then drain them thoroughly.

4. In a large mixing bowl, combine all of the vegetables.

5. To make the dressing, combine all of the ingredients in a mixing bowl and pour over the vegetables. Toss to combine and coat in dressing. Rather than being served chilled, this salad is best served at room temperature.

Nutrition Fact: Calories Per Serving 498: Total Fat 28.5g: Cholesterol 0mg: Sodium 602mg: Total Carbohydrate 78.1g: Dietary Fiber 26.1g: Sugars 20.8g: Protein 21.8g

51. SPANISH TORTILLA WITH ARTICHOKES

Preparation Time: 10 minutes
Cooking Time: 15 Minute
Total Time: 25 Minutes

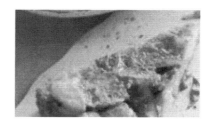

INGREDIENTS

- 280g jar artichoke hearts in oil, quartered
- 500g large peeled potatoes, roughly chopped into 1.5cm cubes
- 1 peeled and chopped small onion
- A dozen large eggs
- A large handful of parsley, roughly chopped

DIRECTION

1. Remove 2 tablespoons of the oil from the artichoke jar and place it in the pan over medium heat. Add the potato, onion, and a pinch of salt, then cover and cook for 10-12 minutes, stirring occasionally, until the potatoes are just tender.

2. Meanwhile, in a large mixing bowl, whisk together the eggs and season generously with salt and pepper. Stir the artichoke hearts and parsley into the onion and potato mixture in the eggs. When the pan is hot, add another tablespoon of oil and pour the egg and potato mixture back in, lightly pressing it down. Cook over medium heat, scraping the edges

with a spatula as needed, until the edges are set but the center is still a little runny.

3. Invert the tortilla by placing a large flat plate upside down over the pan. Re-insert the tortilla in the pan with a little more oil (cooked side up).

4. Cook for about 5 minutes over low heat, or until it sets. Remove from the heat and set aside for 5 minutes before turning out onto a board to serve warm or cold. Cut the wedges in half.

Nutrition Fact: Calories Per Serving 498: Total Fat 28.5g: Cholesterol 0mg: Sodium 602mg: Total Carbohydrate 78.1g: Dietary Fiber 26.1g: Sugars 20.8g: Protein 21.8g

52. CHICKEN MISO SOUP

Preparation Time: 10 minutes
Cooking Time: 15 Minute
Total Time: 25 Minutes

INGREDIENTS
- 2 x 15g Japanese miso paste sachets (we used Clearspring)
- 1 chicken breast, skinned and sliced
- 1 clove garlic, crushed
- ½ tsp grated ginger
- 8 shiitake mushrooms, sliced
- Dash of soy sauce
- ¼ Savoy cabbage, finely shredded

DIRECTION
1. In a saucepan, pour 600ml (1 pint) boiling water and whisk in the miso paste.

2. Simmer for 10 minutes with the rest of the ingredients, except the cabbage.

3. Add the cabbage and cook for 3 minutes before serving.

Nutrition Fact: Calories Per Serving 498: Total Fat 28.5g: Cholesterol 0mg: Sodium 602mg: Total Carbohydrate 78.1g: Dietary Fiber 26.1g: Sugars 20.8g: Protein 21.8g

53. TARKA DHAL

Preparation Time: 10 minutes
Cooking Time: 1 Hours
Total Time: 1Hours, 10 Minutes

INGREDIENTS

- For The Dhal:
- 250g rinsed chana dhal (yellow dried split peas).
- 2 garlic cloves, crushed
- 1 tbsp ginger (freshly grated)
- 1 tsp turmeric powder
- a couple of bay leaves
- Sodium chloride.

For Tarka's sake:

- 2 tbsp. ghee (clarified butter) or vegetable oil
- 12 tsp cumin seeds
- 1 peeled and sliced onion
- 1 garlic clove, crushed
- a pinch of red pepper flakes

DIRECTION

1. 1 litre water, chana dhal, garlic, ginger, turmeric, and bay leaves, brought to a boil. Return the mixture to a boil, skimming off any scum that has risen to the surface. Cover the pan with a lid and cook, stirring occasionally, for 45-60 minutes, or until the mixture thickens.

2. In a pan, heat the oil or ghee, then add the cumin seeds and cook for a few seconds. Toss in the onion, garlic, and chilli. Cook for 10-15 minutes over medium heat, or until the onion has softened. Turn off the heat in the pan.

3. Remove the pan lid if the dhal mixture is still runny, and increase the heat to reduce the liquid, stirring constantly.

4. Season with salt once the dhal has softened and is almost smooth. Serve with a spoonful of tarka on top, reheated if necessary. Stir the tarka into the dhal and freeze it for up to a month. Before reheating, defrost.

Nutrition Fact: Calories Per Serving 498: Total Fat 28.5g: Cholesterol 0mg: Sodium 602mg: Total Carbohydrate 78.1g: Dietary Fiber 26.1g: Sugars 20.8g: Protein 21.8g

54. MIXED BEAN SALAD WITH MUSTARD DRESSING

Preparation Time: 25 minutes
Cooking Time: 5 Minute
Total Time: 30 Minutes

INGREDIENTS

- 90g (3oz) trimmed and halved green beans
- 1 peeled and chopped red onion
- 2 celery sticks, chopped

- 410g rinsed and drained cannellini beans
- Borlotti beans, rinsed and drained, 410g
- 6 halved cherry tomatoes

To Prepare the Dressing
- 2 tbsp mustard (whole grain)
- 1 tbsp honey that is runny
- 1 lemon, finely grated zest and juice
- 4 tbsp extra virgin olive oil
- Black pepper, salt, and freshly ground black pepper

DIRECTION
1. 2 tbsp water + 2 tbsp green beans in a heatproof bowl Microwave on high for 2 minutes after covering with cling film and piercing. Place in a large mixing bowl after rinsing in cold water.
2. Add the chopped red onion to the bowl after rinsing it in a sieve to remove the strong flavor.
3. Toss in the celery, canned beans, and tomatoes gently.
4. To make the dressing, combine all of the ingredients in a mixing bowl. Combine the oil, mustard, honey, and lemon zest and juice in a small jar. Season with salt and pepper, then shake to combine. Drizzle the dressing over the salad and toss gently to combine.

Nutrition Fact: Calories Per Serving 498: Total Fat 28.5g: Cholesterol 0mg: Sodium 602mg: Total Carbohydrate 78.1g: Dietary Fiber 26.1g: Sugars 20.8g: Protein 21.8g

55. PRAWN SALAD WITH PICKLED CUCUMBER

Preparation Time: 25 minutes
Cooking Time: 5 Minute
Total Time: 30 Minutes

INGREDIENTS
- 1 cucumber
- 2 tsp sea salt
- 4 handfuls of baby spinach leaves
- 3 tsp sesame oil
- 280g pack raw tiger prawns
- For The Dressing:
- 1 clove garlic, peeled and finely chopped
- ½ small red chilli or ½-1 large red chilli, deseeded and finely diced
- 1 tsp brown sugar
- ½ tsp sesame oil

- 1 tbs fish sauce
- 4 tbs lime juice (juice from 2 limes)
- 1 tbs freshly chopped mint leaves
- 2 tbs freshly chopped coriander leaves, plus extra for garnish

DIRECTION

1. Cut the cucumber into fine slices on the diagonal after peeling it.
2. Mix all of the ingredients in a large mixing bowl. Under cold running water, quickly rinse the cucumber and pat dry with a clean tea towel.
3. Toss the cucumber into the dressing and gently fold it in. Season with salt and pepper as needed. Place spinach leaves in four bowls and top with pickled cucumber.
4. 1 tsp sesame oil, 1 tsp sesame oil, and the prawns in a hot pan; cook for a few minutes until pink and tinged with brown. Spoon on top of the salad, along with any leftover dressing and the remaining oil. Serve immediately after garnishing with coriander.

Nutrition Fact: Calories Per Serving 498: Total Fat 28.5g: Cholesterol 0mg: Sodium 602mg: Total Carbohydrate 78.1g: Dietary Fiber 26.1g: Sugars 20.8g: Protein 21.8g

56. MASALA OMELETTE

Preparation Time: 10 minutes
Cooking Time: 10 Minute
Total Time: 20 Minutes

INGREDIENTS

- 2 whole eggs plus 2 egg whites
- 5 halved cherry tomatoes
- spinach, a handful
- 12 red chilies, small
- 12 tsp garam masala
- 12 tsp turmeric
- 12 tsp cumin
- 1 tablespoon extra virgin olive oil
- 1 sliced onion
- 2 chopped spring onions
- 12 bunch chopped coriander

DIRECTION

1. Add salt and pepper to the eggs. Stir in the tomatoes, spinach, and spices until everything is well combined.
2. In a frying skillet, heat the oil and fry the onion and spring onion until softened. Let flow the egg mixture into a skillet and swirl it around with a spatula to ensure that the

eggs cook evenly, then set aside until almost set. Fold in half so that the outside is firm and the middle is soft.

3. To serve, garnish with fresh coriander and a pinch of extra chilli.

Nutrition Fact: Calories Per Serving 498: Total Fat 28.5g: Cholesterol 0mg: Sodium 602mg: Total Carbohydrate 78.1g: Dietary Fiber 26.1g: Sugars 20.8g: Protein 21.8g

57. SPANISH-STYLE PRAWNS

Preparation Time: 10 minutes
Cooking Time: 25 Minute
Total Time: 35 Minutes

INGREDIENTS
- 1 tablespoon extra virgin olive oil
- 1 or 2 garlic cloves, peeled and finely sliced
- 1 fennel bulb, thinly sliced
- a handful of parsley sprigs with flat leaves
- 500g vine-ripened cherry tomatoes
- 5 tbsp sherry de manzanilla
- 1 tbsp tomato paste (sun-dried).
- 10-15 large raw prawns, peeled but not deveined.
- Season with salt and freshly ground black pepper.
- Bread is ready to be served.

DIRECTION
1. In a large, shallow pan, heat the oil. Fry for 12-15 minutes, until the garlic, fennel, and parsley stalks are tender. Combine the cherry tomatoes, sherry, and tomato paste in a mixing bowl. Reduce to a low heat and continue to cook for 25 minutes, or until the sauce has thickened.
2. Cook for 2 minutes after pushing the prawns into the sauce. Cook for another 1-2 minutes, or until they're pink all over. For serving, season with salt and pepper and garnish with parsley leaves. Serve with bread chunks.

Nutrition Fact: Calories Per Serving 498: Total Fat 28.5g: Cholesterol 0mg: Sodium 602mg: Total Carbohydrate 78.1g: Dietary Fiber 26.1g: Sugars 20.8g: Protein 21.8g

58. CRUSHED POTATO SALAD

Preparation Time: 10 minutes
Cooking Time: 15 Minutes
Total Time: 25 Minutes

INGREDIENTS

- 500 grams of new potatoes
- 1 small diced red onion
- 2 tablespoons capers, diced if large
- 4-6 small sliced gherkins
- 2-3 tbsp mint, freshly chopped
- 4 tablespoons mayonnaise
- Garnish with mint sprigs.

DRESSING INGREDIENTS:

1. 1 tsp powdered vegetable stock
2. 1 tsp mustard (Dijon).
3. 2 tbsp balsamic vinegar
4. 4 tablespoons olive oil
5. Season with salt and pepper.

DIRECTION

1. Bring to boil a pot with the potatoes in it. Cook for 12-15 minutes, or until the potatoes are just tender.
2. In the meantime, combine the vegetable stock powder, 100ml boiling water, mustard, vinegar, oil, salt, and pepper in a mixing bowl.
3. Drain the potatoes, lightly crush them, then combine with the dressing and set aside to cool.
4. After the onion, capers, gherkins, mint, and mayonnaise have cooled, stir in the onion, capers, gherkins, mint, and mayonnaise.

Nutrition Fact: Calories Per Serving 498: Total Fat 28.5g: Cholesterol 0mg: Sodium 602mg: Total Carbohydrate 78.1g: Dietary Fiber 26.1g: Sugars 20.8g: Protein 21.8g

59. SWEET POTATO PASTA

Preparation Time: 10 minutes
Cooking Time: 15 Minutes
Total Time: 25 Minutes

INGREDIENTS

- 300g peeled and cut into small cubes sweet potato
- Pasta shapes weighing 300g
- 100g peas, frozen
- 2 tbsp milk, semi-skimmed

- 150g natural low-fat yoghurt
- 40 g fat-free Finely grated Parmesan or mature cheese
- black pepper, ground

DIRECTION

1. Cook the sweet potato chunks for 12-15 minutes, or until tender, in a saucepan of simmering water. Drain thoroughly.
2. Cook the pasta shapes in a large saucepan for 6-8 minutes, or until tender, according to package directions. Return to the saucepan after draining well.
3. Toss the pasta with the sweet potato chunks and frozen peas. Heat the milk and yogurt for 1-2 minutes on low heat. Serve with a sprinkling of cheese and freshly ground black pepper.

Nutrition Fact: Calories Per Serving 498: Total Fat 28.5g: Cholesterol 0mg: Sodium 602mg: Total Carbohydrate 78.1g: Dietary Fiber 26.1g: Sugars 20.8g: Protein 21.8g

60. CHINESE VEGETABLE CHOW MEIN

Preparation Time: 15 minutes
Cooking Time: 20 Hours
Total Time: 35 Minutes

INGREDIENTS

- 2 tbsp vegetable or groundnut oil
- 125g sliced oyster mushrooms in a packet
- 1 deseeded and sliced red pepper
- 125g tenderstem broccoli, cut into pieces from a packet
- 1 carrot, peeled and sliced
- 1 tablespoon soy sauce
- 1 tbsp vinegar (rice)
- 1 to 2 tablespoons oyster sauce
- 300g medium egg noodles, ready to eat
- 1 lime (for serving)

DIRECTION

1. Heat the oil in large frying pan. After adding the vegetables, cook for another 2-3 minutes. In a bowl, mix the soy sauce, vinegar, and oyster sauce. Then heat the noodles until they are hot.
2. Serve immediately, garnished with a squeeze of lime.

Nutrition Fact: Calories Per Serving 498: Total Fat 28.5g: Cholesterol 0mg:

Sodium 602mg: Total Carbohydrate
78.1g: Dietary Fiber 26.1g: Sugars
20.8g: Protein 21.8g

DINNER

1. CAULIFLOWER AND RIBEYE STEAK FAJITAS

Preparation Time: 20 minutes
Cooking Time: 30minutes
Total Time: 50 Minutes

INGREDIENTS:
- 6 ounce ribeye steak
- 1/2 medium head of cauliflower
- 1/4 cup avocado oil
- 1 tablespoon apple cider vinegar
- 1 tsp of sea salt
- 1 medium zucchini
- 1 tablespoon chopped cilantro

DIRECTIONS:
1. Preheat the oven to 375 degrees
2. Cut the cauliflower and courgettes
3. Add oil, avocado, apple cider vinegar and salt.
4. Season the steak with salt
5. Cook the steak for 3-4 minutes in a skillet over medium heat.
6. Remove the steak from the heat and cover it with foil. Let it rest for 5 minutes.
7. Cilantro, chopped, should be added to the remaining oil mixture.
8. Serve atop the roasted vegetables, sliced against the grain. Drizzle the olive oil mixture over the whole dish.

Nutrition Fact: Calories Per Serving 498: Total Fat 28.5g: Cholesterol 0mg: Sodium 602mg: Total Carbohydrate 78.1g: Dietary Fiber 26.1g: Sugars 20.8g: Protein 21.8g

2. NO-BEAN KETO CHILI

Preparation Time: 30 minutes
Cooking Time: 1 Hour
Total Time: 1Hour, 30 Minutes

INGREDIENTS:
- 1 pound grass-fed ground beef or lamb
- 4 cloves garlic, minced
- 1 onion finely diced, or 2 shallots finely sliced
- 1 cup chicken or beef broth
- 1 zucchini, finely diced
- 2 Tbsp. tomato paste
- 1-2 tsp. chili powder
- 1/2-1 tsp. cayenne pepper
- 1 tsp. cumin

- 1 tsp. salt
- 1/2 tsp. black pepper
- 1-2 Tbsp. Bulletproof Collagelatin
- 2 Tbsp. Bulletproof Grass-Fed Ghee
- 1 tsp. fresh herbs for garnish (we used chives)
- 1/2 tsp. chili flakes
- 1 generous scoop of quality coconut yogurt
- Optional: 1/2 bell pepper, finely diced
- Optional: 1 jalapeño, sliced

DIRECTIONS:

1. Preheat the frying pan to medium-high heat. 1 tablespoon ghee, onion or shallots, and garlic, fried until golden brown
2. 1 tbsp. ghee, ground beef (or lamb), bell peppers, and jalapeo (if using), sauté until meat is browned.
3. Season with spices, salt, pepper, tomato paste, and broth. Stir all together and cook for 30 minutes to an hour. Add 1-2 tablespoons Bulletproof Collagelatin to speed up the thickening process.
4. If required, season chili with more chili powder or cayenne pepper.
5. Serve in a bowl of chives and chili flakes on top. Enjoy with a dollop of coconut yogurt on top!

Nutrition Fact: Calories Per Serving 498: Total Fat 28.5g: Cholesterol 0mg: Sodium 602mg: Total Carbohydrate 78.1g: Dietary Fiber 26.1g: Sugars 20.8g: Protein 21.8g

3. KETO FISH CAKES WITH AVOCADO LEMON DIPPING SAUCE

Preparation Time: 5minutes
Cooking Time: 15minutes
Total Time: 20 Minutes

INGREDIENTS:

- 1 pound raw white boneless fish (preferably local and wild caught)
- 1/4 cup cilantro (leaves and stems)
- Pinch of salt
- Pinch of chili flakes
- 1-2 garlic cloves (optional)
- 1-2 tablespoons coconut oil or grass-fed ghee for frying
- Neutral oil for greasing your hands, such as avocado oil

DIPPING SAUCE INGREDIENTS:

- 2 ripe avocados
- 1 lemon, juiced
- Pinch of salt
- 2 tablespoons water

DIRECTIONS:

1. Combine the fish, vegetables, garlic (if using), flour, chili, and fish in a food processor. Blitz until it is evenly mixed.
2. Add coconut oil or ghee to a big frying pan over medium-high heat and swirl to coat.
3. Roll the fish mixture into 6 patties with oiled paws.
4. Place the cakes in the hot frying pan.
5. While the fish cakes are frying, combine all dipping sauce ingredients in a small food processor or blender (starting with the lemon juice) and blitz until smooth and fluffy. If needed, add more lemon juice or salt to the mixture.
6. When the fish cakes are finished, steam them up and serve with a dipping sauce.

Nutrition Fact: Calories Per Serving 498: Total Fat 28.5g: Cholesterol 0mg: Sodium 602mg: Total Carbohydrate 78.1g: Dietary Fiber 26.1g: Sugars 20.8g: Protein 21.8g

4. ZOODLES WITH KETO ALFREDO SAUCE

Preparation Time: 10 minutes
Cooking Time: 10minutes
Total Time: 20 Minutes

INGREDIENTS:

- 1 cup soaked, raw, unsalted cashews (reflected in nutrition) or 1.5 cups cooked cauliflower, to remain keto-friendly
- 1/2 cup homemade chicken bone broth
- 3 Tbsp. Bulletproof Grass-Fed Ghee or butter + extra for frying
- 2 Tbsp. Bulletproof Unflavored Collagen Powder
- 3/4 tsp. mustard powder
- 3/4 tsp. garlic powder
- 1/4-1/2 tsp. onion powder
- Salt, to taste
- 2 brown onions, diced
- 4-5 rashers of chemical-free bacon, diced

- 2 garlic cloves, crushed
- Enough zoodles for two people (2 medium-sized zucchini squashes per person)

DIRECTIONS:

1. In a mixer, mix soaked (and strained) cashews or cooked cauliflower, bone broth, ghee (or butter), collagen powder, garlic, onion, and mustard powder. Blitz until smooth. It's about the taste. Then season with salt to taste.
2. In ghee, fry onions until golden brown. Add the bacon to the frying pan and cook until it begins to crisp up. Stir in the garlic, which has been crushed. Remove from heat until all ingredients are golden brown and bacon is crispy.
3. In a medium saucepan, steam zoodles until they are cooked to your taste.
4. Meanwhile, warm the alfredo sauce in another small saucepan over medium heat.
5. Start plating until everything is packed. Divide the cooked zoodles into two bowls. Serve with fried bacon and onions on top of the sauce. If required, top with fresh herbs and a pinch of salt and pepper.
6. Serve right away and enjoy!

Nutrition Fact: Calories Per Serving 498: Total Fat 28.5g: Cholesterol 0mg: Sodium 602mg: Total Carbohydrate 78.1g: Dietary Fiber 26.1g: Sugars 20.8g: Protein 21.8g

5. EASY PALEO BAKED MEATBALLS

Preparation Time: 5 minutes
Cooking Time: 25minutes
Total Time: 30 Minutes

INGREDIENTS:

- 1 1/4 pounds pastured ground beef
- 2 tablespoons Grass-Fed Ghee
- 1 tablespoon apple cider vinegar
- 1/2 tsp pepper
- 1 tsp salt
- 1/2 medium yellow onion, minced
- 2 garlic cloves, minced
- 1/4 cup fresh rosemary, roughly chopped

- Optional: One tsp crushed red pepper flakes

DIRECTIONS:

1. Preheat the oven to 350 degrees Fahrenheit.
2. Place all the meatball ingredients in a bowl.
3. Blend it together with your hands.
4. Roll the mixture into small balls on a baking tray lined with parchment paper, using just over a tablespoon of mixture per meatball.
5. Bake for 15 minutes.
6. Enable to cool before serving, then store in an airtight jar in the fridge or freezer.

Nutrition Fact: Calories Per Serving 498: Total Fat 28.5g: Cholesterol 0mg: Sodium 602mg: Total Carbohydrate 78.1g: Dietary Fiber 26.1g: Sugars 20.8g: Protein 21.8g

6. TURMERIC PULLED PORK CURRY AND CILANTRO CAULIFLOWER RICE

Preparation Time: 10 minutes
Cooking Time: 30minutes
Total Time: 40 Minutes

INGREDIENTS:

Curry
- 2 pounds pork shoulder roast
- 2 tablespoons avocado oil
- 1 can organic full-fat coconut milk
- 2 tsps of curry powder
- 5 minced garlic cloves
- 1 tsp turmeric
- 1 tablespoon of red curry paste
- 1/2 tablespoon of ginger powder
- 1/2 tablespoon of smoked paprika
- 15 dashes of fish sauce
- 2 tsps sea salt
- 2 sliced bell peppers
- 2 cups of cubed butternut squash

Rice
- 3 cups cauliflower, chopped
- 1 tablespoon avocado oil
- 1 tablespoon cumin
- 1/2 tsp salt
- 1/2 cup fresh cilantro
- 1/2 lime, juiced

Sauce
- 1 avocado
- 1/2 can coconut milk
- 1/2 tsp of paprika
- 1/2 tsp of cayenne
- 1/2 tsp of sea salt

DIRECTIONS:

Curry
1. Cook each side of the strak for 3 minutes.
2. In an instant pot, combine 1 tablespoon avocado oil and the

minced garlic; cook until the garlic is translucent, then turn off the burner.

3. Cook for 60 minutes on high pressure on the manual setting with coconut milk, turmeric, curry paste, ginger powder, paprika, fish sauce, cinnamon, and browned pork bits.

4. Allow 15 minutes for the pot to naturally release the steam, after which you can manually release the pressure.

5. Add the peppers and squash, set the timer for 10 minutes on manual, and then manually release the pressure.

Rice

1. Over medium heat, add 1 tablespoon avocado oil to the plate.

2. Cook for 3-5 minutes, or until mildly crispy, with the cauliflower rice, cumin, and salt in the pan.

3. Toss the rice in a cup with the minced cilantro and a squeeze of lime on top.

4. ketchup

5. Blend the avocado, coconut milk, paprika, cayenne, and salt in a high-powered blender until creamy.

Nutrition Fact: Calories Per Serving 498: Total Fat 28.5g: Cholesterol 0mg: Sodium 602mg: Total Carbohydrate 78.1g: Dietary Fiber 26.1g: Sugars 20.8g: Protein 21.8g

7. SLOW COOKER MEXICAN SHREDDED BEEF

Preparation Time: 20 minutes
Cooking Time: 30minutes
Total Time: 50 Minutes

INGREDIENTS:

- 3 1/2 pounds pastured beef short ribs or beef shank
- 2 tsps turmeric powder
- 1 tsp sea salt
- 2 tsps ground cumin and 1/2 tsp pepper
- 2 tsps coriander powder
- half a cup of water
- 1 cup coarsely chopped cilantro stems
- Alternate: 4 crushed garlic cloves, 1 tsp chipotle powder, 2 tsps paprika

DIRECTIONS:

1. Combine the dry ingredients in a shallow cup.

2. In a slow cooker, place the short ribs and gently coat each slice in the spice mixture.
3. Garnish the ribs with cilantro stems and optional garlic. Carefully pour in the water, not rinsing the spices off the beef.
4. Cook for 6-7 hours on medium, or before it falls apart. Check the meat after 6 hours and cook it until it is tender.
5. Drain cooking liquid into a small saucepan and reduce over medium heat for 10-15 minutes if necessary.
6. Pull the meat out with two forks and shred the beef.
7. Serve with Bulletproof guacamole, tacos made with silverbeet leaves, roasted pumpkin, cucumbers, green beans, and new cilantro.

Nutrition Fact: Calories Per Serving 498: Total Fat 28.5g: Cholesterol 0mg: Sodium 602mg: Total Carbohydrate 78.1g: Dietary Fiber 26.1g: Sugars 20.8g: Protein 21.8g

8. SLOW COOKER POT ROAST

Preparation Time: 30 minutes
Cooking Time: 8 Hours
Total Time: 8 Hours, 30 Minutes

INGREDIENTS:
- 1 pound grass-fed sirloin or skirt steak
- 2 tbsp sea salt 1 tbsp ground turmeric
- 1 tsp. dried oregano
- 2 tbsp. Brain Octane Oil (or MCT oil)
- 3 tbsp unsalted grass-fed butter
- 1 1/2 tbsp apple cider vinegar

DIRECTIONS:
1. Sprinkle the salt, turmeric, and oregano over the beef.
2. Pour the Brain Octane Oil over the aged steak in the slow cooker.
3. Cook on low for 6 to 8 hours, or until the meat is shreddable, after adding the butter.
4. When the meat is finished, shred it with a fork and toss it with the vinegar.

9. KALE QUINOA SALAD

Preparation Time: 10 minutes
Cooking Time: 35minutes, 59 seconds
Total Time: 45 Minutes

INGREDIENTS

- 1 1/2 cups water
- 1/2 cup tomato juice
- 1 cup quinoa rinsed
- 1 piece small onion chopped
- 1 tbsp olive oil
- 1 clove garlic minced
- 1/2 tsp crushed red pepper flakes
- 6 cups fresh kale coarsely chopped
- 1/4 cup pine nuts or sunflower kernels
- 1/4 cup raisins or dried cranberries
- 1 tbsp balsamic vinegar
- 1 tsp lemon juice
- 1 tsp grated lemon zest
- 1/4 tsp salt
- 1/8 tsp pepper

DIRECTIONS

1. Add the water and tomato juice to a pan.
2. Lower the heat and add the quinoa.
3. Cover and cook for about 20 minutes. Remove the quinoa from the heat with a fork.
4. Fry the onion in a pan with a little extra virgin olive oil. Add garlic and chilli.
5. Combine the pine nuts and raisins in a bowl. Cook for another 3 minutes.
6. Cook for another 3 minutes after adding the vinegar, lemon juice, zest, salt and pepper.
7. Leave to cool before serving.

Nutrition Fact: Calories Per Serving 498: Total Fat 28.5g: Cholesterol 0mg: Sodium 602mg: Total Carbohydrate 78.1g: Dietary Fiber 26.1g: Sugars 20.8g: Protein 21.8g

10. BEEF STIR FRY RECIPE

Preparation Time: 5 minutes
Cooking Time: 15minutes
Total Time: 25 Minutes

INGREDIENTS:

- 1 tbsp olive oil
- 250 g beef sirloin, cut into strips
- 5 button mushrooms, sliced
- 1 cm fresh ginger, grated
- ½ tsp chinese five spice
- 1 garlic clove, peeled and crushed
- 200 g broccoli, cut into small florets
- 1 red pepper (capsicum), chopped

- 1 bunch pakchoi, chopped
- 1 ½ tbsp tamari sauce
- sea salt
- black pepper

DIRECTIONS:

1. In a big wok, heat half a tablespoon of olive oil over medium heat for around 2 minutes. Brown the beef in the wok, then cut it and set it aside.
2. Cook for about 4 minutes in the remaining olive oil with the mushrooms, ginger, five spice, and garlic.
3. Cook for an extra 5 minutes after adding the broccoli, capsicum, and pakchoi.
4. Return the beef strips to the pan, stir in the soy sauce, and cook for another 2 minutes, or until heated through.
5. Divide the stir-fry in half and store in an airtight tub in the refrigerator.
6. Place the remaining stir-fry half in a serving dish, season with salt and pepper, and serve.

Nutrition Fact: Calories Per Serving 498: Total Fat 28.5g: Cholesterol 0mg: Sodium 602mg: Total Carbohydrate 78.1g: Dietary Fiber 26.1g: Sugars 20.8g: Protein 21.8g

11. CAJUN RED BEANS AND RICE (VEGETARIAN)

Preparation Time: 4 minutes
Cooking Time: 5minutes, 59 seconds
Total Time: 10 Minutes

Ingredients:

- Three tbsp olive oil
- 1 big chopped onion
- 1/2 cup diced green bell pepper 3 minced garlic cloves
- 1/2 tsp salt 1 celery stalk, including green leaves
- 1 tablespoon cumin
- 1 tsp chili powder
- 1/2 tsp fresh thyme
- 2 cans (15 oz.) Dark red kidney beans, rinsed and drained
- 20 1/2 cup cooked rice

DIRECTION

Garnish with fresh parsley

1. In a pan, heat the olive oil. Over medium heat, cook the onions,

garlic, bell pepper, and celery in the oil until the onions are translucent (roughly 7 minutes). Combine the flour, cumin, chili powder, and thyme in a mixing bowl. To mix, stir all together.

2. Mix in the beans thoroughly. Cook until the beans are hot. To avoid sticking, make sure to stir regularly.

3. Add the rice and stir well to combine all of the ingredients. Until eating, heat the rice for about 5 minutes to get it up to temperature. Garnish with parsley sprigs and serve.

Nutrition Fact: Calories Per Serving 498: Total Fat 28.5g: Cholesterol 0mg: Sodium 602mg: Total Carbohydrate 78.1g: Dietary Fiber 26.1g: Sugars 20.8g: Protein 21.8g

12. ULTRA-SATISFYING CHICKEN NOODLE SOUP

Preparation Time: 4 minutes
Cooking Time: 5minutes, 59 seconds
Total Time: 10 Minutes

Instead of cooking a whole chicken, boneless, skinless chicken thighs are used in this faster variation of homemade chicken noodle soup. The soup is still delicious, filling, and traditional. This chicken soup from scratch can be made on a weeknight thanks to the drastically shortened cook time. We suggest using chicken thighs for this recipe because of their flavor and soft texture when baked, but chicken breasts will also fit.

Makes 6 servings

INGRIDEINTS

- 2 tbsp. butter, fat from chicken, or olive oil
- 1 big chopped onion
- 2 big carrots, diced
- 2 celery stalks, chopped (optional)
- a heaping tablespoon of minced garlic (4 cloves)
- two bay leaves
- 3 sprigs new thyme (optional) a half tsp dried thyme
- 1 pound chicken breasts, skinless and boneless (4 or 5 thighs)
- 8 cups low sodium chicken stock or broth (or homemade stock)
- 5 oz. egg noodles (or pasta of choice)
- Season with salt and pepper to taste.
- 1/4 cup finely chopped new parsley
- As required, add more water or stock.

DIRECTIONS

1. In a big pot or Dutch oven, melt the butter over medium heat. Combine the onions, carrots, and celery in a large mixing bowl. Cook, stirring occasionally, until the vegetables soften, around 5 to 6 minutes.

2. Combine the garlic, bay leaves, and thyme in a mixing bowl. Cook for 1 minute while swirling the garlic around the grill.

3. Add the chicken stock and reduce to a low heat. Season the broth with salt and pepper after tasting it. You can need to add 1 or more tsps of salt depending on the stock used.

4. Submerge the chicken thighs in the soup until they are fully covered by the broth. Return the soup to a low boil, then cover the pot partially with a lid and cook, stirring occasionally, until the chicken thighs are cooked through.

5. If the broth seems to be running low at this period, add a splash of stock or a splash of water. Reduce the heat to a low setting.

6. Place the fried chicken on a serving tray. Cook, stirring sometimes, until the noodles are tender, 6 to 10 minutes depending on the form of noodles used.

7. When the noodles are cooking, shred or dice the chicken into strips or cubes. Return the chicken to the pot, then season with salt and pepper to taste. As required, season with more salt and pepper. Serve with a garnish of parsley.

8. NOTE Noodle Soup: The noodles soak up the soup broth as it lies. Add a splash of excess chicken stock or water if you don't have any for reheating.

9. Chicken Noodle Soup Doesn't Freeze Well: The noodles don't freeze well. Remove the part of the soup you want to ice before adding the noodles if you want to freeze it. The soup, chicken, and vegetables can all be frozen. When you're about to reheat the soup, add the dry noodles and cook until they're cooked.

10. Seasoning the Broth: If you think the soup is lacking in zing, season it with a pinch of salt. A squeeze of fresh lemon juice, a dab of fish sauce (we sometimes use this trick for store-bought stocks and broths), or Worcestershire sauce may also be used to add flavor.

13. WALDORF SALAD

Preparation Time: 15 minutes
Cooking Time: 15minutes
Total Time: 25 Minutes

INGREDIENTS

- 6 tablespoons mayonnaise (or plain yogurt)
- 1 tablespoon lemon juice
- A half tsp of salt
- 1 tsp freshly ground black pepper
- 2 cored and diced sweet apples
- 1 cup sliced red seedless grapes (or 1/4 cup raisins)
- 1 cup thinly sliced celery
- 1 cup walnuts, diced and finely toasted
- The lettuce

DIRECTIONS

1. Whisk together the mayonnaise (or yogurt), lemon juice, salt, and pepper in a medium mixing cup. Combine the apple, celery, grapes, and walnuts in a mixing bowl. On a bed of new lettuce, serve.

Nutrition Fact: Calories Per Serving 498: Total Fat 28.5g: Cholesterol 0mg: Sodium 602mg: Total Carbohydrate 78.1g: Dietary Fiber 26.1g: Sugars 20.8g: Protein 21.8g

14. MEDITERRANEAN ROAST VEGETABLES

Preparation Time: 5 minutes
Cooking Time: 15minutes
Total Time: 25 Minutes

INGREDIENTS

- 1 zucchini
- 3 peppers
- 10 cherry tomatoes
- 2 small red onions
- 2 tbsp olive oil
- ½ tsp parsley
- 1 tsp basil
- ½ tsp garlic powder
- ½ tsp salt
- ½ tsp dried oregano

DIRECTIONS

2. Preheat the oven to 425 degrees Fahrenheit / 220 degrees Celsius / 210 degrees Celsius fan oven.

3. Both of the vegetables should be diced and chopped into similar-sized chunks. Combine them with the other ingredients in a mixing cup.

4. Stir before the oil and spices are evenly distributed in the vegetables. Bake for 10-15 minutes, or until all the vegetables have softened and cooked through, on a baking dish.

5. For the best outcomes, serve the vegetables when they are still soft.

NOTES

1. Make use of your favorite vegetables! This recipe can be used to roast almost every kind of vegetable. If you're going to use potatoes or other root vegetables, parboil them first so they take longer to cook though.

2. Your vegetables can take slightly longer or shorter to roast than the estimated time due to the fact that different ovens cook at different temperatures. Have your eyes out for them!

3. Leftover roasted vegetables can be held in an airtight jar for up to 4 days in the refrigerator. You should serve them cold in a salad or reheat them for a few minutes in the oven to use as a side dish in potential meals.

Nutrition Fact: Calories Per Serving 498: Total Fat 28.5g: Cholesterol 0mg: Sodium 602mg: Total Carbohydrate 78.1g: Dietary Fiber 26.1g: Sugars 20.8g: Protein 21.8g

15. HONEY MUSTARD CHICKEN SALAD

Preparation Time: 4 minutes
Cooking Time: 5minutes, 59 seconds
Total Time: 10 Minutes

INGREDIENTS

- ⅓ cup honey (115 g)
- ¼ cup dijon mustard (65 g)
- 2 tablespoons olive oil
- 2 cloves garlic, minced
- 2 tsps salt
- 1 tsp pepper
- 4 boneless, skinless chicken thighs
- ¼ cup bacon (60 g), chopped
- 4 cups romaine lettuce (300 g), chopped

- 1 cup cherry tomatoes (200 g), halved
- ¼ red onion, sliced
- 1 avocado, pitted and sliced

DIRECTION

- Combine the sugar, mustard, oil, garlic, salt, and pepper in a shallow bowl or liquid measurement cup.
- Place the chicken thighs in a dish and pour half of the marinade over them, reserving the other half for another day.
- Turn the chicken thighs over and coat them fully in the marinade.
- Refrigerate the dish for 30 minutes to an hour after covering it with plastic wrap.
- Place the chicken thighs in a big skillet and heat over medium heat.
- Cook for 5 minutes on either side or until the chicken is thoroughly cooked.
- Remove the chicken from the pan and set it aside.
- Return the pan to the heat after wiping it clean.
- Heat the sliced bacon in the pan for about ten minutes, or until crispy.
- To drain the bacon, place it on a paper towel-lined tray.

- Stir in three tablespoons of water to the marinade that has been set aside.
- Chicken can be sliced into strips.
- Drizzle the leftover honey mustard dressing over the romaine, cherry tomatoes, red onion, avocado, fried bacon, and chicken in a cup.

Nutrition Fact: Calories Per Serving 498: Total Fat 28.5g: Cholesterol 0mg: Sodium 602mg: Total Carbohydrate 78.1g: Dietary Fiber 26.1g: Sugars 20.8g: Protein 21.8g

16. BAKED COD WITH BROCCOLI AND TOMATOES

Preparation Time: 15 minutes
Cooking Time: 15 minutes
Total Time: 30 Minutes

INGREDIENTS

- 6 (6-oz) cod fillets
- ¼ cup olive oil, divided
- 2 tsp Italian seasoning
- 1 pint grape tomatoes, halved
- 1 (12-oz) pkg broccoli florets
- 1 Tbsp minced garlic

- 2 tsp lemon zest
- 3 Tbsp lemon juice
- 3 Tbsp chopped fresh basil
- 1 Tbsp honey

DIRECTIONS

1. Preheat the oven to 425 degrees Fahrenheit. Place the fish on a wide baking sheet with a rim. Drizzle 1 tbsp oil over the top and season with Italian seasoning. Season with salt and pepper to taste.
2. In a big mixing bowl, combine tomatoes, broccoli, 3 tablespoons oil, and garlic; season lightly with salt and pepper. Surround the fish with the tomato mixture.
3. Bake for 12 to 18 minutes, or until the fish flakes easily with a fork and the broccoli is soft. In the meantime, whisk together the lemon zest, lemon juice, basil, and honey; drizzle over the fish and vegetables.

Nutrition Fact: Calories Per Serving 498**:** Total Fat 28.5g**:** Cholesterol 0mg**:** Sodium 602mg**:** Total Carbohydrate 78.1g**:** Dietary Fiber 26.1g**:** Sugars 20.8g**:** Protein 21.8g

17. AVOCADO AND PRAWN SALAD RECIPE

Preparation Time: 10 minutes
Cooking Time: 10minutes
Total Time: 20 Minutes
Avocado and prawns are combined in this super salad, which is served with a tarragon dressing and lemon crumbs.
Serves 6

INGREDIENTS

- 3 tbsp extra virgin olive oil
- 50g fresh breadcrumbs
- 1 lemon, zested and juiced
- ½ tsp Dijon mustard
- ¼ bunch tarragon, leaves roughly chopped
- 1 x 80g bag watercress or lamb's lettuce
- 3 spring onions, thinly sliced, to serve
- 2 x avocados, peeled and sliced
- 18 fresh or frozen, cooked tiger or jumbo king prawns (defrosted if frozen)

DIRECTIONS

1. In a frying pan, heat 1 tablespoon olive oil, then add the breadcrumbs and roast, stirring constantly, until golden brown. Season with salt and pepper, then whisk in the lemon zest.
2. Create the dressing in a separate bowl by combining the mustard, 2 tsp lemon juice, remaining olive oil, tarragon, and some seasoning.

3. Arrange the salad leaves, spring onions, and avocado slices on a serving platter or divide between dishes. Place the prawns on top and toss with a little of the seasoning. Drizzle the remaining dressing over the salad and top with lemon crumbs.

Nutrition Fact: Calories Per Serving 498: Total Fat 28.5g: Cholesterol 0mg: Sodium 602mg: Total Carbohydrate 78.1g: Dietary Fiber 26.1g: Sugars 20.8g: Protein 21.8g

18. SMOKED SALMON & RYVITA

Preparation Time: 5 minutes
Cooking Time: 5minutes
Total Time: 10 Minutes
Number of Servings: 1

INGREDIENTS
Serves 1

- 2 tbsp. Philadelphia Greek Style Cream Cheese
- 2 slices Smoked Salmon
- Black pepper
- ½ Lemon, juiced
- 2 Original Rye Crispbread

DIRECTIONS
1. Spread Philadelphia Greek Style on the rye crispbread.
2. Arrange the smoked salmon on top.

3. Finish with a splash of lemon juice and freshly cracked black pepper to taste.

Nutrition Fact: Calories Per Serving 498: Total Fat 28.5g: Cholesterol 0mg: Sodium 602mg: Total Carbohydrate 78.1g: Dietary Fiber 26.1g: Sugars 20.8g: Protein 21.8g

19. SPINACH TOMATO OMELETTE RECIPE

Preparation Time: 5 minutes
Cooking Time: 10 minutes
Total Time: 20 Minutes

INGREDIENTS

- 2 servings
- 2 tomato
- 1 tsp vegetable oil
- 3 tablespoon shredded cheese cubes
- Salt as required
- 1 cup spinach
- 1 onion
- 4 egg
- Powdered black pepper as required

DIRECTION

1. To make this nutritious breakfast, start by slicing the onion and roughly chopping it into small pieces. Also, wash and chop the tomatoes and spinach leaves. Set aside the cut vegetables.

2. Now, boil some oil in a pan over a medium flame. In the same grill, add the sliced onions and tomatoes and cook for 1-2 minutes.

3. In the same pan, add the sliced spinach leaves and cook until they begin to wilt. Remove the pan from the heat and pass the sauteed vegetables to a mixing bowl.

4. Split the eggs in a separate dish. Beat the eggs, then add them to the bowl with the sauteed vegetables and stir well. It's worth noting that you can add some water if necessary.

5. After that, heat a nonstick skillet or tawa over medium heat. Grease the pan with some grease, then add the egg mixture on top and stir it around a little.

6. Allow the omelette to cook before it begins to set. Season with salt and black pepper and sprinkle some cheese on top of the egg mixture. Finally, after setting the flame to low, flip the omelette and let the other side cook.

7. Cover the pan and continue to cook the omelette until the eggs are fully set. Serve shortly after transferring the spinach tomato omelette to a pan.

Nutrition Fact: Calories Per Serving 498: Total Fat 28.5g: Cholesterol 0mg: Sodium 602mg: Total Carbohydrate 78.1g: Dietary Fiber 26.1g: Sugars 20.8g: Protein 21.8g

20. GREEK SALAD

Preparation Time: 15 minutes
Cooking Time: 15minutes
Total Time: 30 Minutes

Serves 4

INGREDIENTS

- 1 tablespoon extra-virgin olive oil
- Three tbsp of red wine vinegar
- 1 minced garlic clove
- 1 tsp dry oregano, with more for sprinkling
- 1 tablespoon dijon mustard

- A quarter tsp of sea salt
- Black pepper, freshly roasted
- To make the salad.
- One english cucumber, cut lengthwise, seeded, and 14-inch thickly sliced
- One orange bell pepper, cut into 1-inch cubes
- 2 cups cherry tomatoes, halved
- Five oz. Feta cheese, cubed into 12 inch cubes
- 1/3 cup red onion, thinly sliced
- A third of a cup pitted kalamata olives
- A third of a cup new mint leaves

DIRECTIONS

1. To make the dressing, combine all ingredients in a mixing bowl. Whisk together the olive oil, vinegar, garlic, oregano, mustard, salt, and a few grinds of pepper in a shallow cup.
2. Arrange the cucumber, green pepper, cherry tomatoes, feta cheese, red onions, and olives on a big platter. Drizzle the dressing over the salad and toss gently. Add a few generous pinches of oregano and the mint leaves to finish. Season with salt and pepper to taste, then serve.

Nutrition Fact: Calories Per Serving 498: Total Fat 28.5g: Cholesterol 0mg: Sodium 602mg: Total Carbohydrate 78.1g: Dietary Fiber 26.1g: Sugars 20.8g: Protein 21.8g

21. BLACK OLIVE AND TUNA SALAD

Preparation Time: 5 minutes
Cooking Time: 5minutes
Total Time: 10 Minutes

INGREDIENTS

- 2 (5 to 6 oz.) Cans white tuna in water
- 1/4 cup chopped ripe pitted or greek kalamata pitted olives
- 2 tablespoons olive oil
- 1 tablespoon balsamic vinegar
- 1 tablespoon fresh lemon juice
- 1/4 red onion, chopped
- 1 tsp capers (optional)
- Sea salt and freshly ground black pepper to taste

DIRECTIONS

1. Cut open the tuna cans with a can opener, but keep the lids on. Holding the cans over a sink or a tub, press the tuna fish lid onto the tuna and tip the container to

remove all of the oil. Remove the lids from the tuna fish and place it in a big mixing bowl.

2. Toss the tuna fish with the olives, oil, balsamic vinegar, lemon juice, red onion, capers (if using), salt, and a few cracks of fresh black pepper.

3. Toss all together with a fork, breaking up any big bits of tuna as you go. Taste and adjust the amount of all of the ingredients to your liking.

4. Serve right away or keep refrigerated for up to 3 days in an airtight container.

Nutrition Fact: Calories Per Serving 498: Total Fat 28.5g: Cholesterol 0mg: Sodium 602mg: Total Carbohydrate 78.1g: Dietary Fiber 26.1g: Sugars 20.8g: Protein 21.8g

22. HOISIN CHICKEN STIR-FRY

Preparation Time: 10 minutes
Cooking Time: 15minutes
Total Time: 25 Minutes

INGREDIENTS

- 3 Tbs. vegetable or peanut oil
- 1 medium onion, cut in half and sliced
- 1 red bell pepper, cored, seeded, and thinly sliced
- 1 lb. boneless, skinless chicken breasts, cut into 3/4-inch chunks
- Salt and freshly ground black pepper
- 6 oz. snow peas, trimmed
- Crushed red chile flakes
- 1 to 2 tsp. minced fresh ginger (optional)
- 1/3 cup hoisin sauce
- 2 Tbs. water
- 1/3 cup dry-roasted peanuts or cashews

DIRECTION

1. In a big skillet, heat 2 tablespoons of oil over medium-high heat. Cook for 2 or 3 minutes after adding the onion. Cook, stirring occasionally, until the bell pepper and onion are browned around the edges, around 4 to 6 minutes. Take the vegetables out of the skillet and set them aside. In the same skillet, pour the remaining 1 tablespoon of oil. Season the chicken with salt and pepper, then add it to the oil and roast, stirring constantly, for 2 to 3 minutes, or until both sides are golden brown. Add the snow peas and red chile flakes and mix well. For using, add the ginger. Reduce the heat to low and add the hoisin sauce and water, stirring

constantly. To wilt the snow peas and finish cooking the chicken (don't overcook it), simmer for 1 minute. a pinch of salt

Nutrition Fact: Calories Per Serving 498: Total Fat 28.5g: Cholesterol 0mg: Sodium 602mg: Total Carbohydrate 78.1g: Dietary Fiber 26.1g: Sugars 20.8g: Protein 21.8g

23. CAPRESE SALAD

Preparation Time: 10 minutes
Cooking Time: 15minutes
Total Time: 25 Minutes
Serves 4 to 6

INGREDIENTS

- 3 to 4 medium heirloom tomatoes, sliced
- 1 (8-ounce) ball fresh mozzarella, sliced
- Fresh basil leaves
- Extra-virgin olive oil, for drizzling
- Flaky sea salt and freshly ground black pepper
- Optional additions/variations:
- Drizzle of balsamic vinegar or reduced balsamic
- Dollops of pesto
- Sliced peaches
- Mint leaves
- Avocado slices
- Strawberries

DIRECTIONS

2. Arrange the tomatoes, mozzarella, and basil leaves on a platter. Drizzle with olive oil and sprinkle with sea salt and freshly ground black pepper.
3. If desired, add ingredients from the variations list.

24. CHICKEN CAESAR SALAD

Preparation Time: **10** minutes
Cooking Time: 15 minutes, 59 seconds
Total Time: 25 Minutes

INGREDIENTS

- 1 ciabatta loaf, medium (or 4 thick slices crusty white bread)
- 3 tablespoons olive oil
- 2 chicken breasts, skinless and boneless
- 1 big cos or romaine lettuce, divided leaves
- To make the dressing

- 1 clove garlic
- 2 tins anchovies medium block parmesan or Grano Padano cheese for grating and shaving (you won't need any of it)
- 5 tablespoons mayonnaise
- 1 tablespoon of sparkling wine vinegar

DIRECTIONS

1. Preheat the oven to 200°C/fan 180°C/gas mark 6 6. 1 medium ciabatta, torn into big, ragged croutons, or sliced with a bread knife if you choose. 2 tablespoons olive oil, spread out on a big baking sheet or tray.

2. If desired, rub the oil onto the bread and season with a pinch of salt (sea salt crystals are best for this). Bake for 8-10 minutes, rotating the croutons a few times to ensure even browning.

3. 1 tbsp olive oil, 2 skinless, boneless chicken breasts, season Heat pan for 1 minute over medium heat, or until hot but not smoking. Place the chicken on the pan and cook for 4 minutes (it can sizzle if it's hot enough).

4. Cook for another 4 minutes after turning the bird. Poke the thickest section with the tip of a sharp knife to see if it's cooked; there should be no pink and the juices should run free.

5. Peel the skin off 1 garlic clove with the flat of a knife. Using a garlic crusher, smash the garlic cloves. With a spear, mash 2 anchovies against the side of a shallow tub.

6. Combine a pinch of parmesan cheese, ginger, anchovies, 5 tablespoons mayonnaise, and 1 tablespoon white wine vinegar in a mixing bowl. Season with salt and pepper to taste. It should be the consistency of yogurt; if it isn't, thin it with a few tsps of water.

7. Using a peeler, shave the cheese. 1 big cos or romaine lettuce, torn into large sections, placed in a large mixing bowl. Cut the chicken into bite-size strips and sprinkle half of the croutons over the leaves.

8. Toss in the most of the dressing through your thumbs. Drizzle the leftover sauce over the remainder of the chicken and croutons. Serve immediately with a sprinkling of parmesan cheese on top.

Nutrition Fact: Calories Per Serving 498: Total Fat 28.5g: Cholesterol 0mg: Sodium 602mg: Total Carbohydrate 78.1g: Dietary Fiber 26.1g: Sugars 20.8g: Protein 21.8g

25. GRILLED BBQ TOFU VEGETABLE KEBABS

Preparation Time: 25 minutes
Cooking Time: 20minutes
Total Time: 45 Minutes

INGREDIENTS
For the Tofu:
- 14 oz (395g) Firm Tofu I like Wildwood
- 1/2 C (105g) Smoky Bourbon BBQ Sauce
- For the Vegetables:
- 1 Pint (435g) Cherry Tomatoes
- 8oz (250g) Zucchini about one large
- 6oz (170g) Crimini Mushrooms
- 1/2 (155g) Red Bell Pepper large
- 1/2 (155g) Green Bell Pepper large
- 1/2 (175g) Purple Onion large
- 2 Tbs Olive Oil
- 1/2 tsp Fine Sea Salt
- Fresh Ground Pepper

DIRECTIONS
1. To make way for flavor, we need to press the water out of the tofu, which we can do ahead of time if needed. Using a tea towel to press the tofu by placing it under and on top of it. Arrange it on a tray. To press the water out, place something heavy on top, such as a cutting board, another tray, or an empty wine box. We don't want it to be too hard or the tofu will be squashed. Move the tea towel to a dryer part of the towel a few times to allow it to retain more water. Press for 20-30 minutes, or up to an hour if time allows.

2. Preheat the oven to 425 degrees Fahrenheit (218C). Silpat or parchment paper can be used to line a sheet pan. Cut the tofu into 32 bits of 1/2" (1.27cm) cubes. Arrange the tofu in a single layer on the sheet plate. Preheat oven to 200°F and bake for 20-22 minutes. Tofu should be golden in color but also fuzzy.

3. Pour the BBQ sauce over the warm tofu in a medium mixing cup, then give it a good swirl. Allow for at least 30 minutes, but up to eight hours, of marinating time. Remove from the equation.

4. Soak the bamboo skewers in water as you cook the vegetables. Place the vegetables in a big mixing bowl, cut into bite-size bits. Season the vegetables with salt and

pepper after drizzling the olive oil over them. Toss the vegetables together in a large mixing bowl.

5. Preheat the grill to 400-450 degrees Fahrenheit (204-232C). Using the remaining BBQ sauce, skewer the vegetables and tofu. Place the kebabs on the grill and cook for around 15-20 minutes overall, slathering with more BBQ sauce and turning every four to five minutes to ensure that the vegetables and tofu are evenly cooked on all sides (15 = more tender crisp / 20 = softer, throughly cooked). Charring is a positive thing!

6. Serve immediately after they've been removed from the barbecue. They have a tendency to cool off fast. If necessary, keep the kebabs warm on the grill for a few minutes after they've been thoroughly cooked, but with the grill switched off.

7. Keep leftovers in a sealed fridge in the refrigerator for up to three days. This recipe is successful.

Nutrition Fact: Calories: 69kcal | Carbohydrates: 7g | Protein: 3g | Fat: 3g | Saturated Fat: 1g | Sodium: 182mg | Potassium: 202mg | Fiber: 1g | Sugar: 5g | Vitamin A: 345IU | Vitamin C: 18.5mg | Calcium: 45mg | Iron: 0.7mg

26. TOFU & VEGETABLE SKEWERS

Preparation Time: 10 minutes
Cooking Time: 20minutes
Total Time: 30 Minutes

INGREDIENTS

- For 4 skewers
- ½ cup water (120 ml)
- ¼ cup maple syrup (55 g)
- 3 tablespoons soy sauce
- 2 tablespoons bbq sauce
- 1 tablespoon oil
- 1 tablespoon garlic powder
- 1 tablespoon sriracha
- 1 tsp black pepper
- 15 oz firm tofu (425 g), or extra firm tofu
- Pepper
- Onion
- Zucchini

DIRECTION

1. To avoid fire, soak wooden skewers in a shallow dish of water.

2. Place the tofu on a plate lined with paper towels. Add another paper towel and a tray on top. 3 minutes in the microwave

3. Tofu can be cut into 9-12 cubes and put aside.

4. Stir together the water, maple syrup, soy sauce, barbecue sauce, oil, garlic powder, Sriracha, and pepper.

5. Refrigerate the tofu for at least 1 hour after placing it in the marinade.

6. Let the tofu out of the marinade. Cook for about 10 minutes over low heat, before the marinade decreases and thickens.

7. Assemble the skewers, mixing tofu and vegetables.

8. Cook each skewer for 3-4 minutes on each side in a hot pan or grill.

Nutrition Fact: Calories Per Serving 498: Total Fat 28.5g: Cholesterol 0mg: Sodium 602mg: Total Carbohydrate 78.1g: Dietary Fiber 26.1g: Sugars 20.8g: Protein 21.8g

27. BEANS AND CHEESE ON TOAST

Preparation Time: 5 minutes
Cooking Time: 15minutes
Total Time: 20 Minutes

INGREDIENTS

- 4 slices Co-op farmhouse loaf
- 1 x 420g Co-op baked beans
- 60g Co-op mature Cheddar cheese, grated

DIRECTIONS

1. Heat the beans according to the package directions.

2. Serve with lots of grated cheese on top of hot buttered toast.

3. Until eating, make sure your meal is thoroughly cooked and piping hot.

Nutrition Fact: Calories Per Serving 498: Total Fat 28.5g: Cholesterol 0mg: Sodium 602mg: Total Carbohydrate 78.1g: Dietary Fiber 26.1g: Sugars 20.8g: Protein 21.8g

28. CHICKEN MEATBALLS AND GREEN BEANS IN TOMATO BROTH

Preparation Time: 4 minutes
Cooking Time: 5minutes, 59 seconds
Total Time: 10 Minutes

Ingredients
MEATBALLS

- 1 pound ground chicken (dark meat preferred)
- 4 finely chopped scallions
- A single big egg
- 2 tbsp miso (red or white)

- 1 tsp kosher salt
- Black pepper, freshly roasted

BROTH AND ASSEMBLY
- 3 tbsp olive oil (extra-virgin)
- 2 thinly sliced shallots or 1 small onion
- 4 finely sliced garlic cloves
- 1 tbsp. Tomato paste, double-concentrated
- 1 pound of cherry tomatoes
- 2 tbsp miso (red or white)
- 12 oz. Cut green beans or other pole beans, cut into 2–3" lengths
- Kosher salt is kosher salt.
- Basil leaves torn (for serving; optional)

Direction

MEATBALLS
1. In a medium mixing dish, combine the chicken, scallions, egg, miso, salt, and few grinds of pepper. Mix vigorously with a fork until thoroughly mixed (it may appear moist at first, but persevere) and mildly sticky; set aside.

BROTH AND ASSEMBLY
1. In a big saucepan, heat the oil over medium heat. Cook, stirring often, until shallots are softened, around 5 minutes. Cook, stirring occasionally, until garlic is softened and just starting to turn golden around the edges, around 3 minutes. Cook, stirring constantly, until the tomato paste has darkened slightly in color and is starting to sizzle in the fat, around 2 minutes. 4 cups sugar, cherry tomatoes, and miso Bring to a boil, stirring constantly and mashing miso against pot's side to melt, and cook, stirring regularly, until most of the tomatoes have burst open, around 5 minutes (it's fine to support them along with a spoon).
2. Cook for 6–8 minutes, or until green beans are tender. Drop gumball-size balls of reserved meat mixture into simmering broth with two spoons. Cook, stirring regularly, until all of the meatballs have been added and are cooked through, about 5 minutes. Season with salt and pepper.
3. Fill bowls halfway with meatballs, onions, and broth, and finish with basil if desired.

29. ALMOND LENTIL STEW

Preparation Time: 20 minutes
Cooking Time: 30minutes
Total Time: 50 Minutes

INGREDIENTS

- 2 tbsp olive oil, plus extra for frying the almonds
- 1 carrot, chopped
- 1 stalk celery, chopped
- 1 onion, chopped
- 1 turnip, chopped
- 2 garlic cloves, chopped
- 150g/5½oz baby button mushrooms, halved
- 250g/9oz green lentils
- litres/2 pints vegetable stock
- 1 bay leaf
- 1 sprig rosemary
- 4 sprigs thyme
- handful almonds
- 1 tbsp ground cinnamon
- 10 cherry tomatoes, quartered

DIRECTIONS

2. In a large pan, heat the olive oil and fry the carrot, celery, onion, and turnip until softened, about 5 minutes.

3. Combine the garlic and mushrooms in a mixing bowl. Cook for an additional five minutes.
4. In the same skillet, add the lentils. Pour in the stock and season with the herbs. Bring to a boil, then reduce to a low heat and continue to cook for 45 minutes.
5. In a separate pan, fry the almonds in a splash of olive oil with the cinnamon for two minutes just before the stew finishes frying.
6. Heat the cherry tomatoes in the pan.
7. Toss the lentil stew with the almonds and tomatoes before serving.

Nutrition Fact: Calories 351 kcal, 20g protein, 37g carbohydrate (of which 7.5g sugars), 14g fat (of which 1.5g saturates), 11.5g fibre and 1.9g salt per portion.

30. COURGETTE AND MINT FRITTATA

Preparation Time: 25 minutes
Cooking Time: 35minute
Total Time: 1Hour

INGREDIENTS

- 4 tsp olive oil
- 1 red onion, thinly sliced
- 375g/13oz courgettes, diced
- 6 free-range eggs
- 2 tbsp chopped mint
- Salt and freshly ground black pepper

DIRECTIONS

1. In a big nonstick frying pan with a flameproof handle, heat the oil. Fry the onion and courgettes for 5 minutes over low heat, or until finely browned and fried.
2. Preheat the grill to medium-high heat.
3. Combine the eggs, 2 tsps of water, and the minced mint in a mixing bowl. Salt and freshly ground black pepper to taste.
4. Fill the frying pan with the egg mixture. Cook for 4-5 minutes, or until the frittata is almost set and the underside is golden brown, without stirring.
5. Place the pan under a hot grill for 3-4 minutes, or until the top is golden and the frittata is fully cooked.
6. Serve wedges cut into wedges.

Nutrition Fact: Calories 256 kcal, 13g protein, 3.5g carbohydrate (of which 3g sugars), 21.4g fat (of which 4.3g saturates), 1.6g fibre and 0.3g salt per portion.

31. SPRING VEGETABLE SALAD

Preparation Time: 30minutes
Cooking Time: 10minutes
Total Time: 40 Minutes

INGREDIENTS

- 200g/7oz fresh or frozen peas
- 200g/7oz asparagus, trimmed
- 200g/7oz sugar-snap peas
- 2 courgettes, cut into long, thin ribbons
- 1 fennel bulb, thinly sliced
- For the dressing
- 1 lemon, grated rind and juice
- 1 tsp Dijon mustard
- 1 tsp clear honey
- 1 tbsp chopped flat leaf parsley
- 2 tbsp olive oil
- For the garlic bread
- 4 ciabatta rolls, halved
- 1 garlic clove, left whole

DIRECTIONS

1. A big pot of salted water should be brought to a boil. Simmer for 3 minutes with the tomatoes, asparagus, and sugar snap peas in the pan. Drain and then rinse under cool running water to refresh.
2. Mix the vegetables, courgette ribbons, and fennel together in a big mixing dish.
3. In a separate dish, combine the lemon rind and juice, mustard, butter, parsley, and half of the oil for the sauce. In a large mixing bowl, toss the vegetables with the dressing.
4. Preheat the grill to medium-high heat.
5. To make the garlic bread, rub the cut sides of the rolls with the garlic clove, then drizzle with the remaining oil and toast on both sides on a baking sheet under the grill.
6. Place the salad on four plates and top with the chicken..

Nutrition Fact: Calories 296 kcal, 13.2g protein, 38.9g carbohydrate (of which 7.2g sugars), 9.2g fat (of which 1.5g saturates), 8.4g fibre and 0.9g salt per portion.

32. LENTIL STEW WITH SWEET ONIONS

Preparation Time: 20 minutes

Cooking Time: 40minutes
Total Time: 1Hour

INGREDIENTS
- A good handful, chopped unsmoked bacon or pancetta
- 4 medium sized onions
- 3 small carrots
- ½ tsp mild paprika
- ½ tsp ground cinnamon
- ½ nutmeg, for grating
- 300g/10oz puy lentils
- 500ml/1pint stock
- A handful parsley
- Knob of butter
- 100g/4oz crème fraîche

DIRECTIONS
1. Allow the fat to slowly ooze out of the bacon or pancetta in a deep pan over a moderate fire. Two of the onions should be roughly chopped and added to the pan. Apply the carrots to the pan after cutting them into pieces. Cover and set aside for a few minutes to steam. Add the paprika, cinnamon, and 12 nutmeg gratings. Cover and set aside the lentils, stock, and 500ml

water for 30 minutes, or until the lentils have softened.

2. As that is heating, dice the remaining two onions and cook them slowly in butter in a separate pan until golden brown. Finish with a nutmeg grate.

3. A pinch of sliced parsley is the last addition to the lentils. Serve with a dollop of crème fraiche and a heaping helping of caramelized onions.

Nutrition Fact: Calories 471 kcal, 25g protein, 51g carbohydrate (of which 13.5g sugars), 19g fat (of which 10.5g saturates), 14g fibre and 1.5g salt per portion.

33. EDAMAME FALAFEL

Preparation Time: 30 minutes
Cooking Time: 45 minutes
Total Time: 1 Hour, 5 Minutes

INGREDIENTS
For the falafels
- 500g/1lb 2oz frozen soya beans, defrosted
- 1 small red onion, finely chopped
- 2 garlic cloves, crushed
- ½ small bunch coriander, leaves and stalks finely chopped
- 1-2 tsp ras-el-hanout, to taste
- 1 free-range egg, beaten
- 2 tbsp toasted sesame seeds
- 2 tbsp dry breadcrumbs
- Sea salt and freshly ground black pepper.
- Olive oil cooking spray
- For the vegetables
- 1 red pepper, seeds removed, quartered
- 1 yellow pepper, seeds removed, quartered
- 2 courgettes, cut into long batons
- 1 aubergine, halved lengthways then sliced into half moons
- 1 tsp sweet smoked paprika
- 1-2 tsp sherry vinegar, to taste
- ½ small bunch coriander, torn
- For the dip
- ⅓ cucumber, roughly peeled, seeds removed, finely chopped
- 1 small garlic clove, crushed
- 100g/3½oz fat-free greek yoghurt
- 1 lemon, juice of ½, remainder cut into wedges for serving
- Small handful mint, leaves shredded

DIRECTIONS
1. Preheat the oven to 200 degrees Celsius/400 degrees Fahrenheit/Gas 6. To extract as

much extra moisture as possible, pat the soy beans dry with kitchen paper. Blend the beans into a gritty paste in a food processor. Combine the remaining falafel ingredients (except the olive oil) in a mixing bowl and season to taste.

2. Place the mixture on a baking tray and roll it into golf ball-sized pieces. Bake for 15-20 minutes, or until golden brown, after spraying with a little oil.

3. Place the tomatoes on a baking tray with the vegetables. Spray the smoked paprika with a little olive oil and layer it on top. Season with salt and pepper and bake for 20 minutes alongside the falafel in a preheated oven.

4. In the meantime, prepare the dip. Season to taste with salt and pepper after combining the cucumber, garlic, yoghurt, lemon, and mint.

5. Pick the falafel from the oven when the vegetables are tender and the falafel is golden brown and crisp on the bottom. Drizzle sherry vinegar over the roasted vegetables and toss in the coriander. Serve with a side of yoghurt dip and a wedge of lemon.

Nutrition Fact: Calories 363 kcal, 25.5g protein, 30g carbohydrate (of which 10g sugars), 15.5g fat (of which 1.5g saturates), 11g fibre and 0.3g salt per portion.

34. LEMON AND POMEGRANATE COUSCOUS

Preparation Time: 20 minutes
Cooking Time: 30minutes
Total Time: 50 Minutes

INGREDIENTS
- 1 large or 2 small pomegranates
- 200g/7oz couscous
- 250ml/9fl oz pints boiling chicken stock or water
- sea salt and freshly ground black pepper
- 2 lemons, juice only
- 6 tbsp olive oil
- 4 tbsp chopped, fresh mint or coriander

DIRECTIONS
1. Break the white membrane around the seeds by cutting the pomegranates in half and scooping out the seeds with a tsp.

2. In a dish, position the couscous. Pour the couscous with the boiling stock or water, then add the olive oil and lemon juice. Season with freshly ground black pepper and sea salt.

3. Cover the couscous closely with clingfilm and set aside for 5-10 minutes, or until the liquid has been absorbed. Remove the clingfilm and use a fork to fluff the kernels. Allow for full cooling of the couscous.

4. Toss the couscous with the chopped herbs and pomegranate seeds. To taste, add more olive oil, salt, pepper, and spices.

Nutrition Fact: Calories 300 kcal, 5g protein, 31g carbohydrate (of which 6g sugars), 17g fat (of which 2.5g saturates), 2.3g fibre and 0.5g salt per portion.

35. SEA BREAM WITH A COURGETTE SALAD WITH FRESH MINT AND ROCKET

Preparation Time: 25 minutes
Cooking Time: 55minutes
Total Time: 1 Hour, 20 Minutes

INGREDIENTS
For the sea bream
- 4 x 200g/7oz sea bream fillets
- 1 lemon, juice only
- Six tbsp extra virgin olive oil
- 2 garlic cloves, finely chopped
- 1 tbsp capers
- 4 anchovies
- 200ml/7floz white wine
- 300g/10½oz cherry tomatoes, halved, deseeded
- salt and freshly ground black pepper
- 150g/5oz black olives, pitted
- 1 handful parsley, finely chopped
- 1 pinch oregano
- For the courgette salad
- 125ml/4fl oz extra virgin olive oil
- 4 tbsp balsamic vinegar
- 1 garlic clove, finely chopped
- handful fresh mint, finely chopped
- 4 small courgettes
- 2-3 handfuls of rocket leaves

DIRECTIONS
1. Place the bream fillets in a cup, squeeze over the lemon juice, and set aside for 30 minutes to marinate.

2. Preheat the oven to 200 degrees Celsius/400 degrees Fahrenheit/Gas 6. In a large frying pan, heat the olive oil, then add the garlic, capers, and anchovy fillets and cook for five minutes over medium heat, until the anchovies have dissolved.

3. Simmer before half of the wine has evaporated, then add the tomatoes, squashing them gently.
4. Cook for five minutes after seasoning with salt and freshly ground black pepper, then add the olives and cook for another ten minutes.
5. Season the fish with salt and freshly ground black pepper in an ovenproof bowl. Cover with foil and add the parsley, the remaining white wine, the sauce, a drizzle of olive oil, and the oregano. Preheat the oven to 350°F and bake for 20 minutes, removing the foil halfway through.
6. Prepare the salad in the meantime. In a small cup, whisk together the olive oil, vinegar, garlic, and mint. Set aside.
7. Trim the courgettes' ends and slice them lengthwise into wafer-thin strips using a potato peeler or mandolin.
8. Mix in the courgette slices with the dressing and set aside for at least 10 minutes to marinate.
9. Serve the rocket and courgettes together on serving dishes. Allow one minute for the fish to rest before serving it with the salad.

Nutrition Fact: Calories 551 kcal, 39g protein, 11g carbohydrate (of which 8g sugars), 36g fat (of which 4.5g saturates), 2.6g fibre and 1.7g salt per portion.

36. PIEDMONTESE ROAST PEPPERS

Preparation Time: 30 minutes
Cooking Time: 40minutes
Total Time: 1 Hour

INGREDIENTS
- 8-12 ripe plum tomatoes
- 4 red peppers, stalks left on (for decoration), cut lengthways in half, seeds removed
- 4 garlic cloves, sliced
- 5-6 tbsp extra virgin olive oil
- salt and freshly ground black pepper
- 8 large canned anchovies, cut in half lengthways
- small handful fresh basil

DIRECTIONS
1. Preheat the oven to 190 degrees Celsius/375 degrees Fahrenheit/Gas 5.

2. Pour boiling water over the plum tomatoes, wait 10 seconds, then carefully remove them from the water and place them in a bowl of cold water to cool down. Remove the skins from the tomatoes.

3. Cut-side up, place the halved peppers cut-side up in an ovenproof dish (preferably one that will be nice to show later).

4. Place the garlic inside the peppers, followed by the tomatoes, gently pressing them into the room. Sprinkle with a tablespoon of salt and freshly ground black pepper. Place in the oven after sprinkling the olive oil on top. Bake for 45 minutes to an hour, turning the heat down if the peppers are scorching too much.

5. Pull the peppers from the oven until they have softened and partially fallen. Crisscross each pepper half with an anchovy, baste with the oily juices, and set aside to cool.

6. Serve with basil leaves on top.

Nutrition Fact: Calories 231 kcal, 6.2g protein, 16g carbohydrate (of which 15g sugars), 16g fat (of which 2.5g saturates), 6g fibre and 1g salt per

37. HEALTHY CHICKEN PASTA

Preparation Time: 30 minutes

Cooking Time: 30 minutes
Total Time: 1 Hour

INGREDIENTS

- 1–2 chicken breasts, boneless, skin removed
- 1 tbsp olive oil, plus extra for rubbing
- 2 garlic cloves, finely chopped
- Pinch chilli flakes
- 1 tbsp tomato purée
- 300g/10½oz tomato passata
- sea salt and freshly ground black pepper
- 200g/7oz whole wheat penne pasta
- 200g/7oz broccoli, sliced into bite-sized chunks
- 125g/4½oz baby spinach, washed (optional)
- ½ bunch basil, leaves picked (optional)
- 1–2 tbsp finely grated Parmesan (optional)

DIRECTIONS

1. Slice the breast about in half horizontally, stopping just short of cutting open on the other side. Keep the edge intact and open up the breast as though it were a

novel. This would mean that the meat is uniformly thick, allowing for easy and even cooking.

2. Over medium–low heat, heat a big saucepan. In the same cup, add the olive oil. Cook for 2 minutes after adding the garlic and chilli flakes, then stir in the tomato purée and cook for another 2 minutes. Add the passata to the plate, season with pepper, whisk well to combine, and reduce to a low heat. Allow to cook as you finish the rest of the meal gently.

3. Bring a big pot of salted water to a boil, then add the pasta and cook according to the directions on the package. 3 minutes before the end of the cooking time, add the broccoli. Drain the water completely.

4. Meanwhile, preheat a griddle pan over high heat until it begins to smoke. Griddle the chicken for 3–5 minutes on each side after rubbing it with a little oil and seasoning it with a pinch of salt and pepper. Allow for 5 minutes of resting time before slicing into bite-sized bits.

5. Toss the cooked pasta and broccoli with the tomato sauce in a pan (if the sauce has thickened too much while simmering then add a little hot water from the pasta). Stir well to combine, then add the chicken, spinach, and basil leaves (if using). Enable the spinach and basil to wilt after seasoning with plenty of black pepper. Serve with a sprinkling of Parmesan cheese, if desired.

38. MA'S MACADAMIA SALAD

Preparation Time: 25 minutes
Cooking Time: 40minutes
Total Time: 1Hour, 5 Minutes

INGREDIENTS

- 2 red onions, halved, cut into wedges
- 2 red peppers, seeded, cut into chunks
- 1-2 tbsp extra virgin olive oil
- 120g/4½oz macadamia nuts
- ½ cucumber, peeled
- 3 spring onions, finely chopped
- 2 shallots, finely chopped
- 2 chicory heads, hearts removed, coarsely chopped
- ½ fennel bulb, chopped
- 1 tart green apple (such as braeburn or granny smith) peeled, chopped
- 3 baby gem lettuces, chopped
- Sea salt and freshly ground black pepper
- For the french dressing
- 3 shallots, very finely sliced

- 1 tsp wholegrain mustard
- 1 tbsp brown sugar
- 2 tbsp white wine vinegar
- Large pinch maldon sea salt
- Freshly ground black pepper
- 75ml/3fl oz extra virgin olive oil

DIRECTIONS

1. Preheat the oven to 200 degrees Celsius/400 degrees Fahrenheit/Gas 6.
2. Roast the onion and red pepper in the oven for 30 minutes after tossing them in the olive oil.
3. In the same oven, toast the macadamia nuts in a small roasting pan for 5-7 minutes, or until they have turned a lovely caramel color. Remove the macadamia nuts from the oven and coarsely cut them before setting them aside to cool while the onion and pepper finish frying.
4. Cut the cucumber lengthwise into quarters. Slice each length down the middle, removing the seeds (which are watery and would make your salad wishy-washy). Remove the remaining flesh and chop it.
5. In a glass jar with a screw-top lid, combine all of the dressing ingredients except the olive oil for the French dressing. Shake vigorously to melt the sugar, then set aside for ten minutes (this takes

the onion punch out of the shallot and softens its flavour). Shake in the oil some more.
6. To eat, toss all of the salad ingredients in a bowl with the French dressing, seasoning with salt and freshly ground black pepper.

Nutrition Fact: Calories 321 kcal, 4g protein, 16g carbohydrate (of which 14g sugars), 27g fat (of which 4g saturates), 5g fibre and 0.3g salt per

39. QUINOA SALAD WITH MINT AND MANGO

Preparation Time: 20 minutes
Cooking Time: 30minutes
Total Time: 50 Minutes

INGREDIENTS

- 110g/4oz quinoa, cooked according to packet Directions
- 1 tbsp chopped fresh mint
- 4 spring onions, including the green parts, chopped

- 2 tbsp chopped fresh coriander
- 1 mango, peeled, finely chopped
- 2 tbsp olive oil
- ½ lemon, juice only

DIRECTIONS
1. In a mixing cup, combine all of the ingredients and stir well.
2. Serve with surplus meats, such as grilled halloumi, chicken, or fish.

Nutrition Fact: Calories 340 kcal, 9g protein, 45g carbohydrate (of which 18g sugars), 14g fat (of which 2g saturates), 4g fibre and 0.1g salt per portion.

40. CHICKEN WITH RED KIDNEY BEANS

Preparation Time: 15 minutes
Cooking Time: 35minutes
Total Time: 10 Minutes

INGREDIENTS
- Low-calorie cooking spray
- 1 onion, roughly chopped
- 1 red pepper, cored, deseeded and roughly chopped
- 1 garlic clove, halved
- 250g/9oz boneless, skinless chicken thighs, cut into 3cm/1¼in chunks
- 2 tsp mild chilli powder
- 200g/7oz easy-cook long-grain rice
- 400g can red kidney beans, rinsed and drained
- 400g can cherry tomatoes, in natural juice
- 200ml/7fl oz chicken stock
- Salt and freshly ground black pepper
- To garnish
- Fresh coriander leaves, roughly chopped
- Lime wedges

DIRECTIONS
1. Spray a large frying pan with a flameproof handle with oil and heat over medium heat. Combine the onion, red pepper, garlic, and chicken in a large mixing bowl. Cook for 3 minutes and constantly stirring.
2. Preheat the grill to medium-high heat.
3. In a large skillet, combine the chilli powder, flour, beans, tomatoes, and stock. Season with salt and freshly ground black pepper to taste. Bring to a boil, then reduce to low heat and continue to cook for 15 minutes.

4. Heat the pan under the grill until golden brown.
5. Serve with lime wedges, divided among four plates and garnished with coriander.

Nutrition Fact: Calories 386 kcal, 23.3g protein, 59.1g carbohydrate (of which 8.7g sugars), 5.2g fat (of which 1.1g saturates), 7.8g fibre and 1.2g salt per portion.

41. TAMARIND AND LEMONGRASS BEEF

Preparation Time: 20 minutes
Cooking Time: 30minutes
Total Time: 50 Minutes

INGREDIENTS
- 1 tbsp oil
- 500g/1lb 2oz lean beef, cut into strips
- Two lemongrass stalks, chopped
- Six shallots, chopped
- Two green chillies, chopped
- 3 tbsp tamarind paste
- 2 tbsp lime juice
- 2 tsp Thai fish sauce
- 2 tsp brown sugar
- 200g/7oz shredded green papaya

DIRECTIONS
1. In a wok or frying pan, heat the oil, throw in the meat, and cook for 2-3 minutes over high heat.
2. Stir-fry for 5 minutes, or until the meat is well browned, with lemongrass, shallots, and chillies.
3. Stir-fry for 4 minutes with the tamarind paste, lime juice, fish sauce, sugar, and papaya.
4. Serve by dividing the mixture into four bowls.

Nutrition Fact: Calories 232 kcal, 30g protein, 13.4g carbohydrate (of which 10.8g sugars), 6.3g fat (of which 1.7g saturates), 1.7g fibre and 0.8g salt per portion.

42. MEDITERRANEAN-STYLE LAMB CHOP TRAYBAKE

Preparation Time: 20 minutes
Cooking Time: 30minutes
Total Time: 50 Minutes

INGREDIENTS

- 2 tbsp chopped fresh mint
- 1 tsp finely chopped fresh rosemary
- Three garlic cloves
- 2 tbsp olive oil
- Four lean lamb chops or cutlets
- One aubergine, sliced
- Four courgettes, sliced
- Two red peppers, cut into large chunks
- Two yellow peppers, cut into large chunks
- 85g/3oz feta cheese, crumbled
- 250g/9oz cherry tomatoes
- To serve
- Mixed leaf salad

DIRECTIONS

1. Preheat the oven to 180 degrees Celsius/355 degrees Fahrenheit/Gas 4.
2. Combine the mint, rosemary, and garlic in a pestle and mortar or food processor, and apply one tablespoon of olive oil. Using your hands, smear the herb mixture all over the lamb chops.
3. On a baking dish, arrange the aubergine, courgette, and peppers. Drizzle the remaining olive oil over the lamb chops and serve. Place in the oven for 20-25 minutes to roast.
4. Remove the chops from the oven and cover with feta cheese, then apply the cherry tomatoes to the plate. Return to the oven for another 10 minutes, or before the cheese begins to brown and the lamb chops are completely cooked.
5. Serve the chops with grilled vegetables and a salad with mixed greens.

Nutrition Fact: Calories 200 kcal, 9g protein, 15g carbohydrate (of which 14g sugars), 11.5g fat (of which 4g saturates), 7g fibre and 0.8g salt per portion.

43. SUNSHINE MUFFINS

Preparation Time: 30 minutes
Cooking Time: 30minutes
Total Time: 1 Hour

INGREDIENTS

- One free-range egg
- 125ml/4fl oz natural yoghurt
- 2 tbsp vegetable oil
- 150g/5oz plain wholemeal flour

- 2 tbsp porridge oats
- 1 tbsp dark soft brown sugar
- 1½ tsp mixed spice
- 2 tsp baking powder
- 200g/7oz mango, chopped into small pieces
- 2 tbsp pumpkin seeds

DIRECTIONS

1. Preheat the oven to 220 degrees Celsius (425 degrees Fahrenheit)/Gas 7. Using paper muffin boxes, line six holes in a muffin tray.
2. In a jug, whisk together the egg, yoghurt, and vegetable oil.
3. In a mixing dish, combine the rice, peas, sugar, mixed spice, and baking powder. Mix both the mango and the egg mixture until it is well mixed.
4. Sprinkle the pumpkin seeds over the top of the mixture in the muffin tins, gently pressing them in.
5. Bake for 20-25 minutes, or until golden brown and raised, and a cake tester inserted in the centre comes out clean.

44. BLACKENED SALMON WITH SALSA

Preparation Time: 25 Minutes
Cooking Time: 30 minutes

Total Time: 55 Minutes

INGREDIENTS

- 3 tbsp Cajun seasoning
- 1 tsp dried oregano
- Four salmon fillets, about 75g/3oz each
- Sunflower oil, to brush
- Lime wedges, to garnish
- For the salsa
- 400g tin black-eyed beans, rinsed and drained
- 2 tbsp olive oil
- One avocado, peeled, stoned and chopped
- Two plum tomatoes, finely chopped
- One yellow pepper, deseeded and finely chopped
- 2 tbsp lime juice
- Salt and freshly ground black pepper

DIRECTIONS

1. In a small dish, combine the Cajun seasoning and oregano.

2. Brush all sides of the salmon with a little oil and then spray with the seasoning mixture, making sure it is fully coated. Remove from the equation.
3. Meanwhile, make the salsa by combining all of the ingredients in a mixing cup. Season with salt and pepper to taste then set aside.
4. Dry fry the salmon for 4 minutes on either side in a frying pan over medium heat.
5. Serve the salmon with the salsa spooned over it, garnished with lime wedges.

Nutrition Fact: Calories 362 kcal, 21.6g protein, 18.3g carbohydrate (of which 6.8g sugars), 22.6g fat (of which 4.1g saturates), 9.9g fibre and 2.7g salt per portion.

45. TOASTED CRUMPETS AND WARM SPICED BERRIES WITH YOGHURT AND HONEY

Preparation Time: 30 minutes
Cooking Time: 10minutes
Total Time: 40 Minutes

Serves 2

INGREDIENTS

- Four crumpets
- 100g/3½oz fat-free Greek yoghurt
- 150g/5½oz ripe strawberries, hulled and sliced
- 50g/2oz raspberries
- 50g/2oz blueberries
- Two big pinches ground mixed spice
- 2 tsp runny honey for drizzling

DIRECTIONS
1. Toast the crumpets until finely browned in a toaster or under the grill.
2. In a mixing cup, whisk the yoghurt until it is shiny.
3. Place all of the fruit in a nonstick frying pan over medium-high heat. Cook for a minute, flipping sometimes until the fruit is softened but still holds its form. This will pull out the flavour without having to add any more sugar.
4. On two plates, divide the sweet, toasted crumpets. Enable some of the fruit to fall onto the plates while you spoon it over the end. Drizzle a little honey over the yoghurt and serve.

Nutrition Fact: Calories Per Serving 498: Total Fat 28.5g: Cholesterol 0mg: Sodium 602mg: Total Carbohydrate

78.1g: Dietary Fiber 26.1g: Sugars 20.8g: Protein 21.8g

46. SALMON AND BULGUR WHEAT PILAF

Preparation Time: 20 minutes
Cooking Time: 30minutes
Total Time: 50 Minutes

Serves 4

INGREDIENTS

- 475g/1lb 1oz salmon, boned and skinned
- 250g/8oz bulgur wheat
- 85g/3oz frozen peas
- 200g/7oz runner beans, chopped
- 2 tbsp chopped chives
- 2 tbsp chopped flat-leaf parsley
- salt and freshly ground black pepper
- To serve
- Two lemons halved
- 4 tbsp low-fat yoghurt

DIRECTIONS

1. Preheat the oven to 180 degrees Celsius/160 degrees Celsius fan/Gas 4.
2. Cook for 15 minutes, or until the salmon is cooked through, wrapped in foil.
3. Meanwhile, in a medium-sized lidded jar, put the bulgur wheat. 1cm/12in above the bulgur wheat, pour the boiling broth. Cover and cook for 12-15 minutes over medium heat or until the bulgur wheat is soft and has absorbed the liquid.
4. Cook the peas and beans until they're cooked to your taste in a pot of boiling water, then rinse.
5. Flake the salmon and toss it with the peas and beans in the bulgur wheat. Combine the chives and parsley in a bowl. Salt and freshly ground black pepper to taste.
6. Serve with milk and lemon halves.

Nutrition Fact: Calories 461 kcal, 32g protein, 49g carbohydrate (of which 1.7g sugars), 14.6g fat (of which 2.4g saturates), 2.5g fibre and 0.1g salt per portion.

47. TURKEY SAUSAGE WITH PEPPER AND ONIONS

Preparation Time: 10 minutes
Cooking Time: 15minutes

Total Time: 25 Minutes

INGREDIENTS

- 1 pound turkey rope sausage cut into thick half-moons
- 1/2 tablespoon olive oil
- 1 cup green pepper sliced
- 1 cup yellow pepper sliced
- 1 cup red onion sliced

Directions

1. Combine all of the ingredients in a big skillet over medium-high heat. Cook, often stirring until the peppers and onions soften slightly.
2. Serve with quinoa or brown rice as a side dish. Have fun!

Nutrition Fact: Serving: 0.75cup | Calories: 363kcal | Carbohydrates: 6g | Protein: 18g | Fat: 30g | Saturated Fat: 9g | Cholesterol: 79mg | Sodium: 841mg | Fiber: 1g | Sugar: 3g | SmartPoints (Freestyle): 12

48. CHICKEN NOODLE MISO SOUP

Preparation Time: 15 minutes
Cooking Time: 25minutes
Total Time: 40 Minutes

INGREDIENTS

- Low-calorie cooking spray
- 5cm/2in piece fresh root ginger, chopped
- Three garlic cloves, crushed
- Pinch of crushed chillies
- 3 tbsp miso paste
- 2 tbsp lime juice
- 200g/7oz fine egg noodles
- Two chicken breasts, 125g/4½oz each, thinly sliced
- 125g/4½oz shiitake mushrooms, sliced
- 70g/2½oz baby sweetcorn, chopped
- 200g/7oz sugar-snap peas, halved
- 85g/3oz watercress, tough stems removed
- Soy sauce, to serve

DIRECTIONS

1. Heat a big saucepan over medium heat, sprayed with oil. Stir in the ginger, garlic, and chillies for 1 minute.
2. Bring 1.7 litres (3 pints) of boiling water to a simmer. Cook for 1 minute after adding the miso paste, lime juice, and noodles. Set back, protected.

3. Stir-fry the chicken, mushrooms, and sweetcorn for 2-3 minutes in a big wok or frying pan sprayed with oil. Cook for 2 minutes, or until the chicken is cooked through, before adding the peas.

4. Pour the soup into four bowls and top with the vegetables and chicken. to the top with watercress and serve with soy sauce on the side.

Nutrition Fact: 331 kcal, 26g protein, 42g carbohydrate (of which 3.3g sugars), 6.7g fat (of which 1.5g saturates), 4g fibre and 1.4g salt per portion

49. POTATO DROP SCONES WITH GRILLED BACON AND TOMATO

Preparation Time: 15 minutes
Cooking Time: 20minutes
Total Time: 25 Minutes

INGREDIENTS

- 550g/1lb2oz large potatoes, cut into small chunks
- Eight rashers of bacon, visible fat removed
- Four tomatoes, halved
- 1½ tsps baking powder
- Two medium free-range eggs
- 5 tbsp milk
- vegetable oil, for frying
- salt and freshly ground black pepper

DIRECTIONS

1. Bring a large pot of salted water to a boil, then add the potatoes and roast for 15 minutes, or until tender. Drain well, then return to the saucepan and mash to a smooth consistency. Allow cooling slowly before serving.

2. Preheat the grill to medium-high heat in the meantime. Cook the bacon rashers for 5-6 minutes, or until mildly crispy, on a foil-lined grill tray. Grill the tomatoes until they are tender, seasoning them with salt and freshly ground black pepper. Keep yourself wet.

3. In a mixing bowl, combine the mashed potatoes, baking powder, eggs, and milk: salt and freshly ground black pepper to taste. Continue to beat until all of the ingredients are equally mixed.

4. In a heavy-bottomed frying pan, heat a little oil. Drop heaping dessertspoons of the mixture into the pan, spaced slightly apart, and

cook for 3-4 minutes, stirring once, until golden brown.

5. Hold warm on a serving plate as you finish frying the rest of the potato mixture.

6. Divide the scones among four plates and top with two rashers and two tomato halves on each.

50. SLOW COOKER HEARTY VEGETABLE AND BEAN SOUP

Preparation Time: 5minutes
Cooking Time: 1 hour
Total Time: 1hour, 5 minutes

INGREDIENTS

- One sweet onion diced
- Two garlic cloves minced
- One sweet potato medium, peeled and cut into 1-inch cubes (white or red potato optional)
- Two carrots peeled and sliced into 1-inch pieces
- Two celery stalks diced
- 1 cup whole kernel corn optional
- kosher or sea salt to taste
- 1/2 tsp black pepper
- 1/8 tsp allspice
- One tsp paprika
- One bay leaf
- Half tsp crushed red pepper flakes
- 2 cups green beans frozen or fresh
- 4 cups vegetable broth low sodium (chicken broth can be substituted)
- 1/4 cup parsley freshly chopped
- 14 1/2 ounce diced tomatoes can
- 31-ounce cannellini beans cans - drained (navy, black, or pinto can be substituted)

DIRECTIONS

1. In a slow cooker, mix all of the above ingredients, whisk to combine, cover, and cook on low for 8-10 hours, or until carrots are tender.

2. Observations

3. Simply add 1 pound chicken fillets (cut into 1 inch cubes) to the slow cooker with the other ingredients to make this a meat dish.

4. Tip: If you want a thicker broth, cut 1/2 cup of the soup (liquid and veggies) at the end of the cooking period and mix with 1-2 tablespoons flour or corn starch, puree, and return to the slow cooker. To mash the ingredients, including the flour or cornstarch, use a fork. Allowing the hot mixture to spin out is dangerous. Cook for another 15 minutes or before the soup thickens.

Nutrition Fact: Serving: 1.5cups | Calories: 183kcal | Carbohydrates: 17g | Protein: 6g | Fat: 4g | Saturated Fat: 1g | Cholesterol: 47mg | Sodium: 253mg | Fiber: 4g | Sugar: 5g | SmartPoints (Freestyle): 6

51. SLOW COOKER CREAM OF CHICKEN AND RICE SOUP

Preparation Time: 10 minutes
Cooking Time: 8 hours, 10 minutes
Total Time: 8 hours, 20 Minutes

We love how rich and flavorful this nutritious soup is, adding warmth to your day without wreaking havoc on your waistline.

INGREDIENTS

- 1/2 cup long-grain brown rice this is not the quick type of rice
- Three carrots peeled and sliced
- One potato large, cut into 1-inch cubes
- One stalk celery diced
- One yellow onion or sweet onion, diced
- Two garlic cloves minced
- 1/2 tsp black pepper
- 1/4 tsp crushed red pepper flakes
- 1/2 tsp kosher or sea salt more or less to taste
- Two fresh sprigs of thyme stem removed
- 1 pound boneless and skinless chicken breast about two breast filets, cut into 1 inch pieces
- 4 cups chicken broth recommend bone broth
- 1 cup milk I used 1%, skim is not recommended for this recipe
- One tablespoon cornstarch

DIRECTIONS

1. Stir together all of the ingredients in the slow cooker, except the milk and cornstarch. Cook for 6 to 8 hours on medium, or until chicken is fried and carrots and rice are tender.
2. Add the milk just before turning off the slow cooker and mix to blend—Cook for about 10 minutes more.
3. If you like a smoother broth, combine the milk and one tablespoon cornstarch in a mixing bowl. Toss in the milk mixture and whisk well. Cook, covered, for another 10 minutes or until the soup has thickened.
4. Notes Saute diced onion in 1 tablespoon olive oil until soft,

about 5 minutes. Put all in the slow cooker.

Nutrition Fact: Serving: 1cup | Calories: 180kcal | Carbohydrates: 13g | Protein: 17g | Fat: 5g | Saturated Fat: 2g | Cholesterol: 45mg | Sodium: 339mg | Fiber: 2g | Sugar: 1g | SmartPoints (Freestyle): 4

52. SLOW COOKER VEGETABLE OMELETTE

Preparation Time: 15 minutes
Cooking Time: 2 hours, 15minutes
Total Time: 2Hours, 30 Minutes

INGREDIENTS
- Eight eggs
- 1/2 cup parmesan cheese grated
- 1/2 tsp salt
- 1/4 tsp pepper
- One tablespoon extra virgin olive oil
- One onion medium, coarsely chopped
- 1/2 cup carrots peeled and diced
- 1/4 cup string beans end discarded and coarsely chopped
- 1/2 cup potatoes peeled and diced
- 1/2 cup zucchini diced
- 1/4 cup red bell peppers diced

DIRECTIONS
1. Whisk together the eggs, Parmesan cheese, salt, and pepper in a medium mixing dish.
2. In a saucepan of extra virgin olive oil over medium heat, sauté the onions for 2 minutes before adding the rest of the vegetables. Cook for 10 minutes, or until the vegetables are almost tender.
3. Place the vegetables in the slow cooker and pour the egg mixture over them, making sure they are fully coated.
4. Set the timer for 2 hours on big.

Nutrition Fact: Serving: 0.167omelette | Calories: 168kcal | Carbohydrates: 8g | Protein: 11g | Fat: 10g | Saturated Fat: 4g | Cholesterol: 224mg | Sodium: 421mg | Potassium: 273mg | Fiber: 1g | Sugar: 2g | Vitamin A: 2411IU | Vitamin C: 16mg | Calcium: 143mg | Iron: 1mg | SmartPoints (Freestyle): 5

53. MUSHROOM STEW

Preparation Time: 10 minutes
Cooking Time: 15minutes
Total Time: 25 Minutes

Servings: 4

This mushroom stew is a filling, family-friendly, one-pot meal that takes less than 30 minutes to prepare. It goes well with spaghetti, quinoa, corn, or mashed potatoes and can be eaten all year.

INGREDIENTS

- One tablespoon any vegetable oil
- One onion diced
- Two carrots diced
- Two garlic cloves minced
- One tablespoon all-purpose flour or corn starch if gluten-free
- Three tomatoes diced
- 1 pound (450 grams) mushrooms sliced
- 1 ½ cups (350 ml) vegetable stock
- One tablespoon soy sauce reduced-sodium (or tamari if gluten-free)
- One tsp oregano dried
- One tablespoon parsley fresh, to garnish

DIRECTIONS

1. In a medium saucepan, heat the oil.
2. Cook, often stirring, until the onion is smooth and translucent.
3. Cook for a few minutes after adding the carrots.
4. Cook for a minute or until the garlic is fragrant and golden in colour.
5. Mix in the flour thoroughly (or corn starch if gluten-free).
6. Then, cover with vegetable stock and add the tomatoes and sliced mushrooms.
7. Soy sauce can be added (or tamari if gluten-free).
8. Cook, covered, for 5 minutes or until the carrots are softened, adding oregano or any other herbs if desired.
9. Change the seasonings to your liking after tasting the stew.
10. Garnish with new parsley and serve immediately.

Nutrition Fact: Calories Per Serving 498: Total Fat 28.5g: Cholesterol 0mg: Sodium 602mg: Total Carbohydrate 78.1g: Dietary Fiber 26.1g: Sugars 20.8g: Protein 21.8g

54. KETO SHRIMP COCONUT CURRY

Preparation Time: 5 minutes
Cooking Time: 20minutes
Total Time: 25 Minutes

This keto shrimp coconut curry recipe will astound you with how tasty and easy it is to prepare. This curry recipe, made with a delectable ethnic blend of spices, explodes with flavours that will make your taste buds squeal with delight!

INGREDIENTS

- 1 lb shrimp
- 1 tbsp coconut oil
- 1 cup coconut milk
- ½ tsp ginger
- 1 tsp curry powder
- ½ onion
- One clove garlic
- ½ tsp cinnamon powder
- ¼ tsp ground cumin
- ½ tsp cayenne pepper
- 1 tsp black pepper
- ½ tsp salt
- Parsley Or Cilantro To Garnish

DIRECTIONS

1. Place aside the shrimp that have been marinated in salt, black pepper, and cayenne pepper.
2. For 2-3 minutes, fry onions, garlic, and ginger in coconut oil.
3. Add the coconut milk, cumin, curry, and cinnamon, and bring to a boil for around 5 minutes.
4. Combine the shrimp and the marinade in a mixing bowl.
5. Allow cooking until the shrimp is cooked (approximately 10 mins).
6. If the sauce becomes too thick and the shrimp aren't cooked, add about a quarter cup of water.
7. Taste for salt and season with more if necessary.
8. Serve over cauliflower rice garnished with parsley or cilantro.

Notes

1. There are 4 servings in this dish, each with two net carbs.
2. If the shrimp aren't done yet, and the sauce is being too thick, add around a quarter cup of water. Add a small amount at a time.
3. If the curry becomes too watery, thicken it by mixing one tablespoon arrowroot powder with two tablespoons water and pouring it into the curry. Allow for 2-3 minutes of cooking time.

Nutrition Fact: Calories: 138kcal | Carbohydrates: 3g | Protein: 23g | Fat: 3g

| Sodium: 168mg | Potassium: 210mg | Fiber: 1g | Sugar: 1g | Vitamin A: 3IU | Calcium: 3mg | Iron: 1mg

55. WARM CHICKEN SALAD OVER ARUGULA WITH CREAMY DILL DRESSING

Preparation Time: 10 minutes
Cooking Time: 15minutes
Total Time: 25 Minutes

INGREDIENTS

- One tablespoon olive oil
- 8 to 12 ounces boneless and skinless chicken breasts cut into 1-inch cubes
- 1 cup asparagus fresh, cut into 1-inch pieces
- 1/2 cup grape tomatoes cut in half
- 1/4 tsp kosher salt
- 1/4 tsp ground black pepper
- 1/2 cup Greek yoghurt
- One tsp dry dill
- Two tablespoons lemon juice
- One tablespoon red wine vinegar
- One tablespoon Dijon mustard
- One tablespoon whole-grain mustard
- 4 cups baby arugula

DIRECTIONS

1. Heat the olive oil in a big skillet over medium-high heat. When the pan is heated, add the chicken and cook for 5 minutes, or until the chicken is almost done. Combine the asparagus and tomatoes in a large mixing bowl. Increase the fire too strong and season with salt and pepper. Cook for another 5 minutes, or until the chicken is cooked through and the tomatoes have blistered.
2. Combine the cream, dill, lemon juice, vinegar, and all mustards in a mixing bowl. Set aside after thoroughly mixing.
3. Arugula can be divided into serving cups. Toss about three tablespoons of the yoghurt dressing into the warm chicken and toss well to coat the chicken. Pour the dressing over the arugula. If needed, drizzle with more dressing.

Nutrition Fact: Calories: 167kcal | Carbohydrates: 5g | Protein: 20g | Fat: 8g | Saturated Fat: 2g | Cholesterol: 57mg | Sodium: 254mg | Fiber: 1g | Sugar: 3g | SmartPoints (Freestyle): 4

56. CREAMY SKINNY COLESLAW RECIPE

Preparation Time: 10 minutes
Cooking Time: 15 minutes
Total Time: 25 Minutes

INGREDIENTS

- 2/3 cup plain nonfat Greek yoghurt
- Two tablespoons apple cider vinegar
- half tbsp lemon juice, preferably new
- Two tablespoons granulated sugar
- 1/4 tsp celery seed
- to taste, kosher salt and black pepper (I like mine peppery).
- Shredded coleslaw blend, 10 oz.
- 1/3 cup finely diced red onion or shallots
- Two tbsp sliced green onions

DIRECTIONS

1. Combine Greek yoghurt, vinegar, lemon juice, sugar, celery seed, salt, and pepper in a big mixing cup. In a mixing bowl, whisk together all of the ingredients before a dressing emerges.
2. Combine the coleslaw blend, red onion, and green onions in a mixing bowl. Toss to blend, making sure to coat all of the coleslaw.
3. Until serving, cover and chill for at least 1 hour—season with salt and pepper to taste.

Nutrition Fact: Calories Per Serving 498: Total Fat 28.5g: Cholesterol 0mg: Sodium 602mg: Total Carbohydrate 78.1g: Dietary Fiber 26.1g: Sugars 20.8g: Protein 21.8g

57. FRENCH ONION TART

Preparation Time: 20 minutes
Cooking Time: 1 Hour
Total Time: 1Hour. 20 Minutes

INGREDIENTS

- 4-5 Onion medium
- 1 Shortcrust OR puff pastry sheet *See Notes
- 1 Tablespoon Butter to saute onion
- For the savory cusard filling:
- 2 Egg
- 1 cup Liquid Cream
- 1 Tablespoon Thyme dried
- ½ Tsp Salt
- ¼ Tsp Black Pepper

DIRECTIONS

1. Onion, peeled and sliced Set aside for now.
2. To make the savory custard filling, combine all of the ingredients in a mixing bowl. In a mixing cup, whisk together the egg, liquid cream, thyme, cinnamon, and black pepper until smooth. Set aside for now.
3. Place the rolled out pastry dough in a tart pan and trim the excess pastry dough around the edges. To make little holes in the pastry, poke it with a fork. This prevents the pastry from deforming when baking blind.
4. Preheat the oven to 400 degrees Fahrenheit/ 200 degrees Celsius.
5. Hold beans or pie weights on a cut out circular baking sheet that fits into the tart frame. Bake the crust alone (blind baking) at 400 degrees Fahrenheit/ 200 degrees Celsius for 15 minutes. *If you want to miss this stage, see the notes.
6. Melt the butter in a skillet and soften the onions. This could take up to 10-15 minutes (time added to total cooking time in recipe)
7. Cooked onions should be uniformly distributed across the tart crust. Over the onions, pour the savory custard mixture.
8. Preheat oven to 400-430 degrees Fahrenheit/ 200-220 degrees Fahrenheit and bake tart for 30 minutes.

Observations
1. Use 1 rolled out shortcrust pastry (traditional version), puff pastry (for a flakier version), or filo pastry (for a lighter version).
2. If you're in a hurry or want to save time and money, you should miss the blind baking of your pastry crust. Add 15 minutes to the baking time for the filled tart. In that case, the total time for the tart would be 45 minutes (15 minutes for the crust + 30 minutes for the filling). However, bear in mind that baking the crust blind has its benefits. The pastry will be more evenly baked and will not distort.
3. Preheat your oven to the appropriate temperature for baking. Ovens aren't always created equal. Start with a higher heat setting and change as required.

Nutrition Fact: Calories Per Serving 498: Total Fat 28.5g: Cholesterol 0mg: Sodium 602mg: Total Carbohydrate 78.1g: Dietary Fiber 26.1g: Sugars 20.8g: Protein 21.8g

58. CRUNCHY ROASTED CHICKPEAS

Preparation Time: 10 minutes

Cooking Time: 40minutes
Total Time: 50 Minutes

INGREDIENTS

- 1 15 oz can chickpeas
- ½ tsp ground cumin
- ½ tsp smoked paprika
- ½ tsp garlic powder
- ¼ tsp onion powder
- ¼ tsp ground corriander
- ½ tsp sea salt
- ¼ tsp freshly ground black pepper
- ½ to 1 TBS olive oil

DIRECTIONS

1. Preheat the oven to 400 degrees Fahrenheit.
2. Using non-stick oil, lightly coat a baking dish. Remove from the equation.
3. Rinse and rinse the chickpeas thoroughly.
4. Combine cumin, paprika, garlic powder, sea salt, onion powder, and pepper in a shallow cup. Remove from the equation.
5. Bake dried chickpeas for 15 minutes on a lined baking sheet in a preheated oven (do not add any other ingredients yet)!
6. Remove the chickpeas from the oven and drizzle 12 tablespoons olive oil over them, swirling to cover evenly. If possible, drizzle in a little more olive oil until all of the chickpeas are finely covered.
7. Stir the spices into the chickpeas until they are finely cooked.
8. Bake for another 10 minutes at 400 degrees, then stir.
9. Return the stirred chickpeas to the oven for a final 5-10 minutes of baking, or until optimal crispiness is reached (a total of 35-40 minutes of baking).
10. Switch off the oven and open the door slightly. Allow chickpeas to cool fully in the oven for optimum crispiness.

Nutrition Fact: Calories Per Serving 498: Total Fat 28.5g: Cholesterol 0mg: Sodium 602mg: Total Carbohydrate 78.1g: Dietary Fiber 26.1g: Sugars 20.8g: Protein 21.8g

59. KETO SWEET CHILLI PORK LETTUCE WRAPS

Preparation Time: 7 minutes
Cooking Time: 8minutes
Total Time: 15 Minutes
INGREDIENTS

- 9 oz lean pork, minced
- 3 garlic cloves, peeled, chopped
- 1 red chilli, deseeded, chopped
- 1 tbsp soy sauce
- 4 baby gem lettuces
- Low Carb sweet chilli sauce
- Lemon Juice

- 1 tbsp sunflower oil
- 5 spring onions, finely chopped
- 8 fresh mint leaves
- Parsley

DIRECTIONS

1. Heat the sunflower oil and add the pork mince. Cook for 2-3 minutes after breaking it off.
2. Cook for another minute or two after adding the garlic and chili.
3. Fry until the meat is almost finished, then add the soy sauce.
4. Finally, finely cut fresh mint leaves and toss them in with the bacon. Half of the spring onions and half of the parsley can be used in the same way. Add a squeeze of lemon juice to finish.
5. 2 minutes in the oven
6. Place equivalent quantities of pork on each lettuce leaf and top with a drizzle of sweet chili sauce. Garnish with the remaining spring onion, mint, and parsley if desired.

Nutrition Fact: Amount Per Serving: Calories: 192Total Fat: 13gSaturated Fat: 3.8gTrans Fat: 0gUnsaturated Fat: 8.5gCholesterol: 44mgSodium: 276mgCarbohydrates: 4.2gNet Carbohydrates: 3.1gFiber: 1.1gSugar: 1.7gProtein: 13g

60. BAKED PESTO TOFU

Preparation Time: 10 minutes
Cooking Time: 15minutes,
Total Time: 25 Minutes

INGREDIENTS

- 1 pound super firm tofu drained and cut into 1/2-inch cubes
- 1 tablespoon olive oil
- 1/4 tsp garlic powder
- 1/8 tsp ground black pepper
- 1/8 tsp sea salt
- 3 tablespoons vegan basil pesto

DIRECTIONS

1. Preheat the oven to 350 degrees Fahrenheit.
2. Toss cubed tofu into a medium mixing cup.
3. Toss in the olive oil to coat.
4. Garlic powder, ground black pepper, and sea salt are all good additions. Toss once more to spread seasonings equally.
5. Arrange tofu in an even layer on a parchment-lined baking dish. Keep the mixing bowl out of the way; you'll need it again.
6. Bake for 40 minutes in a preheated oven, gently stirring halfway through.
7. Remove the baked tofu from the oven and put it in a mixing bowl.
8. Toss in the pesto and toss gently to cover.

9. Hot, room temperature, or chilled is fine.

Nutrition Fact: Calories: 138kcal | Carbohydrates: 3g | Protein: 9g | Fat: 10g | Saturated Fat: 2g | Cholesterol: 1mg | Sodium: 249mg | Potassium: 175mg | Fiber: 1g | Sugar: 1g | Vitamin A: 227IU | Calcium: 53mg | Iron: 1mg

SNACKS

1. CHILLI BEEF AVOCADO BURGER

Preparation Time: 15 minutes
Cooking Time: 15minutes
Total Time: 30 Minutes
Makes: 2 burgers

This is maybe our favourite! This dish can also be made without the bun if you're worried about maintaining intermittent fasting or on a ketogenic diet; you don't have to give up one for the other. Here's an example of how you can get the health benefits of both diets in one dish!

INGREDIENTS:

- 400 grams lean beef mince
- 2 red chilies
- Burger bun (optional)
- Sea salt
- Black pepper
- One ripe medium avocado
- Two sundried tomatoes
- Juice of 1 lemon

DIRECTION

1. In a large mixing bowl, combine the beef with half of the chopped chilies, season with salt and pepper, and divide into four balls. Set aside after flattening each into a thin patty.
2. Round the avocados in half, scoop out the flesh, and mash with a fork in a dish.
3. Combine the mashed avocados with leftover chili, sundried tomatoes, and lemon juice.
4. Place a tablespoon of the avocado mixture in the middle of each of the patties, then cover with the remaining patties. To keep the avocado in the center of the sandwich, press down the ends.
5. Cook the burgers for 5 minutes on either side until cooked through in a griddle pan over high heat. In a large mixing bowl, combine the beef with half of the chopped chillies, season with salt and pepper, and divide into four balls. Set aside after flattening each into a thin patty.
6. Round the avocados in half, scoop out the flesh, and mash with a fork in a dish.

222

7. Combine the mashed avocados with leftover chilli, sundried tomatoes, and lemon juice.

8. Place a tablespoon of the avocado mixture in the middle of each of the patties, then cover with the remaining patties. To keep the avocado in the centre of the sandwich, press down the ends.

9. Cook the burgers for 5 minutes on either side until cooked through in a griddle pan over high heat.

10. If you're using buns, just sandwich the cooked avocado patties between two buns (you can use only one if you want to reduce the number of calories). Try using a full-grain bun to keep you feeling fuller for longer.

Nutrition Fact: 74 calories; protein 1g; carbohydrates 12.6g; fat 2.6g; sodium 62.1mg. Full Nutrition

2. CHEWY CINNAMON ROLLS (VEGETARIAN)

Preparation Time: 45 minutes
Dough to Rise: 1 Hour 45minutes
Cooking time: 20 minutes
Total Time: 2 Hours, 50 Minutes
Makes: 24 rolls

The smell of cinnamon and freshly baked bread to get the day started. These chewy cinnamon rolls are as soft, chewy, and sweet as their name suggests.

INGREDIENTS:
Rolls:
- 1 cup whole-wheat flour
- 3 cups all-purpose flour
- ¼ ounce active dry yeast
- 1 cup plain soymilk or milk
- ¾ cup of sugar
- ¼ cup of vegetable oil
- One tsp salt
- Four egg whites
- ¼ cup trans-fat-free margarine
- Two tsps cinnamon

Glaze:
- 1 cup powdered sugar
- ½ tsp pure vanilla extract
- Two tablespoons soymilk or milk

DIRECTION
1. In a big mixing bowl, combine the whole wheat flour, 1 cup all-

223

purpose flour, and the yeast. Remove from the equation.

2. In a saucepan, combine the soymilk, 14 cup sugar, oil, and salt and cook on low until wet. Add to the flour and yeast mixture after stirring to combine. In a separate bowl, whisk together the egg whites.

3. For around 4 minutes, beat on high speed, pausing briefly to scratch down the sides.

4. To make a hard dough, stir in the majority of the remaining all-purpose flour.

5. Place the dough on a floured surface after removing it from the mixing tub. Knead for about 10 minutes, adding more flour by the tablespoon as required to keep the dough from sticking.

6. Place the dough in an oiled bowl and turn it to coat the top of the dough bowl with oil. Cover with a towel and set aside to climb until it has doubled in size (roughly an hour).

7. Punch down the risen dough and cut it in half. Every piece of dough should be rolled into a 14-inch-thick rectangle.

8. Brush the margarine onto the dough rectangle after it has melted. Combine the cinnamon and the remaining 12 cup sugar in a small cup, and spread the mixture uniformly over all dough rectangles.

9. Starting at the widest ends, roll up the rectangles. Using your thumbs, pinch the ends shut and drive the seams into the dough.

10. Break the rolls into 1-inch slices and put them cut side down in two oiled baking dishes or nonstick 9-inch round pans. Cover each dish with a towel or waxed paper and let the rolls rise until doubled in size in a warm position (roughly 45 minutes). Preheat oven to 375 degrees Fahrenheit.

11. Preheat oven to 350°F and bake for 20 minutes.

12. Prepare the glaze by combining confectioner's sugar, vanilla, and 1 tablespoon soymilk while the rolls are baking. Apply more soymilk in 1 tsp intervals until the glaze is dense but pourable. Drizzle the glaze over the warm rolls and serve immediately.

Nutrition Fact: 74 calories; protein 1g; carbohydrates 12.6g; fat 2.6g; sodium 62.1mg. Full Nutrition

3. MINI AUBERGINE PIZZAS

Preparation Time: 5 minutes
Cooking Time: 15minutes
Total Time: 20 Minutes

Serves 4

INGREDIENTS

- 1 aubergine or eggplant
- 1/2 tbsp olive oil
- 1/2 cup tomato sauce or pizza sauce
- 1/2 cup fresh spinach
- 1 cup grated cheddar cheese
- 6–7 cherry tomatoes

DIRECTIONS

1. Preheat the oven to 180 degrees Celsius (250 degrees Fahrenheit). Using parchment paper, line a baking tray.
2. Cut the aubergine into half-inch to 3/4-inch thick circular strips. Brush the slices with olive oil and place them on the baking tray. Preheat the oven to 350°F and bake for 10 minutes.
3. Switch the aubergine slices to a grill pan and top with tomato sauce, spinach, cheese, and tomatoes after they've finished cooking.
4. Grill the pan for 3 or 4 minutes, or until the cheese has melted.
5. Serve directly with a sprig of fresh basil on top (optional).

Nutrition Fact: Calories Per Serving 568: Total Fat 28.5g: Cholesterol 0mg: Sodium 602mg: Total Carbohydrate 78.1g: Dietary Fiber 26.1g: Sugars 20.8g: Protein 21.8g

4. OMELET MUFFINS

Preparation Time: 10 minutes
Cooking Time: 15minutes
Total Time: 25 Minutes

INGREDIENTS

- 8 large eggs
- 1/2 cup milk I use skim or low fat, but whole milk also works
- 1 cup shredded cheddar cheese
- 1 cup bell peppers diced (I used a mix of red, orange and green)
- 1/2 cup baby spinach roughly chopped
- 1/4 tsp salt
- 2 scallions thinly sliced

DIRECTIONS

1. Preheat the oven to 350 degrees Fahrenheit. Coat the inside of a nonstick muffin pan with cooking spray.
2. Combine the eggs and milk in a medium mixing cup. Whisk until

the consistency is consistent. In a large mixing bowl, combine the cheese, bell peppers, spinach, salt, scallions, and any other omelet ingredients you're using.

3. Fill muffin tins nearly all the way to the bottom with batter. You should be able to make 12 muffins with the batter.

4. Bake for 20-25 minutes, or until the eggs are completely cooked. The muffins will bubble up at first, but will settle down when they cool.

5. To extract the muffins from the tray, loosen the edges with a small spatula. Eat when it's still warm. Keep those muffins that haven't been consumed in the fridge or freezer.

NOTES

1. Grease a nonstick muffin pan before pouring the batter in. Since the egg muffins adhere to the pan, using a nonstick muffin pan and lightly greasing it would make it easier to remove the muffins.

2. Both of the omelet's ingredients can be cut into very small sections. Bell peppers, for example, can be cut into 1/2-inch squares. They will be able to cook more easily as a result of this.

3. While I did not use beef in this recipe, you might use ham or bacon instead. If you're using beef, make sure it's already baked until you put it in the muffin batter.

4. Estimated nutritional value based on skim milk.

Nutrition Fact: serving: 1muffin, calories: 93kcal, carbohydrates: 1g, protein: 7g, fat: 6g, saturated fat: 3g, cholesterol: 134mg, sodium: 160mg, potassium: 109mg, sugar: 1g, vitamin a: 820iu, vitamin c: 16.6mg, calcium: 103mg, iron: 0.8mg, net carbs: 1g

5. APPLE AND RAISIN MUFFINS

Preparation Time: 20 minutes
Cooking Time: 30minutes
Total Time: 50 Minutes

INGREDIENTS

- 3 tbsp runny honey
- 2 medium Braeburn apples, peeled and diced
- 1 tsp Chinese five-spice powder
- 1 tsp ground mixed spice

- 2 large free-range eggs, beaten
- 3 tbsp toasted sesame oil
- 200ml/7fl oz semi-skimmed milk
- 2 small bananas, mashed
- 300g/10½oz self-raising flour
- 2–3 tsp granulated sweetener
- 1 tsp bicarbonate of soda
- 40g/1½oz raisins
- 1 tbsp rolled oats
- 1 tbsp light brown sugar

DIRECTIONS

1. Preheat the oven to 200 degrees Celsius/180 degrees Celsius fan/gas 6 and line a 12-hole muffin tray with big muffin cases.
2. Heat the honey in a small nonstick saucepan over medium heat for 2–3 minutes, or before it turns a rich golden-brown color and only starts to smoke.
3. Cook for 3–4 minutes, or until slightly softened, after adding the apples and spices. Remove the pan from the heat and allow to cool.
4. In a mixing cup, whisk together the eggs, sesame oil, and milk. Add the mashed bananas to the mix.
5. Combine the flour, sweetener, bicarbonate of soda, and raisins in a big mixing cup. In the middle, make a well and pour in the egg mixture. In a large mixing bowl, combine the apples and any

remaining liquid from the tub. Fill muffin tins halfway with the batter.
6. Combine the oats and sugar in a small bowl and spread on top of each muffin.
7. Preheat oven to 350°F and bake for 20 minutes, or when a skewer inserted in the center comes out clean. Cool on a wire rack and serve hot, or store in an airtight jar for up to 3 days and reheat in a 200C/180C Fan/Gas 6 oven for 5 minutes.

Nutrition Fact: Calories 190 kcal, 5g protein, 33g carbohydrates (of which 13g sugars), 5g fat (of which 1g saturates), 1.5g fibre and 0.5g salt.

6. NO-BAKE RAWIES

Preparation Time: 4 minutes
Cooking Time: 5 minutes, 59 seconds
Total Time: 10 Minutes

INGREDIENTS
- 400g pitted Medjool dates
- 85g (1 cup) desiccated coconut
- 35g (1/3) cup cocoa

- 90g (2/3 cup) dry roasted almonds, plus 30, extra, to decorate
- 1 tsp ground cinnamon
- 2 tsps vanilla extract

DIRECTIONS

1. In a food processor, add all ingredients until well mixed. Make balls out of level tablespoonfuls of the mixture. Flatten each one slightly and place a roasted almond in the middle. Refrigerate for up to 2 weeks in an airtight jar.

Nutrition Fact: Calories Per Serving 498: Total Fat 28.5g: Cholesterol 0mg: Sodium 602mg: Total Carbohydrate 78.1g: Dietary Fiber 26.1g: Sugars 20.8g: Protein 21.8g

7. PUMPKIN AND SPINACH QUICHES

Preparation Time: 15minutes
Cooking Time: 25minutes, 59 seconds
Total Time: 40 Minutes

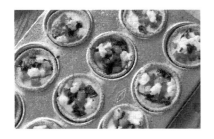

INGREDIENTS

- 2 tsp olive oil
- 1/2 small brown onion, finely chopped
- 300g butternut pumpkin, peeled, diced
- 50g baby spinach
- 24 slices wholemeal bread, crusts removed
- Olive oil spray
- 3 eggs
- 1/4 cup reduced-fat milk
- 50g reduced-fat fresh ricotta, crumbled

DIRECTIONS

2. Preheat the oven to 200 degrees Celsius/180 degrees Celsius fan-forced.

3. In a big frying pan, heat the oil over medium-high heat. Toss in the onion. Cook for 3 minutes, stirring sometimes, or until softened. Toss in a pumpkin. Cook for 5 minutes, or until the pumpkin is soft. Toss in the spinach. Cook for 5 minutes, or until the spinach has wilted. Remove the pan from the sun. Allow 10 minutes for cooling.

4. Place 1 slice of bread on a flat surface in the meantime. Flatten the bread mildly with a rolling pin. Cut 1 round from bread with a 7.5cm round cutter. In two 12-hole, 1 1/2 tablespoon-capacity

round-based patty pans, press round into 1 hole. Rep with the rest of the bread. Using a light spray of oil, lightly coat the bread. Bake for 5–6 minutes, or until golden brown. Remove the dish from the oven.

5. In a jug, whisk together the eggs and milk. Salt and pepper to taste. Evenly divide the spinach mixture between the bread cups. Ricotta cheese should be sprinkled on top. Pour the egg mixture over it. Preheat oven to 350°F and bake for 12 to 15 minutes, or until golden and set. Serve the food.

Nutrition Fact: Calories Per Serving 498: Total Fat 28.5g: Cholesterol 0mg: Sodium 602mg: Total Carbohydrate 78.1g: Dietary Fiber 26.1g: Sugars 20.8g: Protein 21.8g

8. DATE HEDGEHOGS

Preparation Time: 10minutes
Cooking Time: 25minutes,
Total Time: 35 Minutes

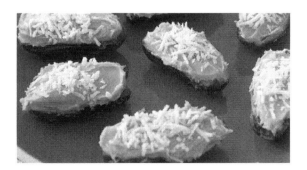

INGREDIENTS
- 4 fresh dates
- 1 tablespoon peanut butter
- 1 tablespoon shredded coconut

DIRECTIONS
1. Cut dates in half lengthwise with a thin, sharp knife. Remove the stones with your fingertips. Get rid of the bricks. Fill each date half with peanut butter. On a big pan, spread the coconut out. Coat 1 date half in the almond, peanut butter side down. Place on a serving platter. Rep with the rest of the date halves and coconut. Serve the food.

Nutrition Fact: Calories Per Serving 498: Total Fat 28.5g: Cholesterol 0mg: Sodium 602mg: Total Carbohydrate 78.1g: Dietary Fiber 26.1g: Sugars 20.8g: Protein 21.8g

9. MINI CHOC-LIME CUPCAKES

Preparation Time: 20 minutes
Cooking Time: 30minutes,
Total Time: 50 Minutes

INGREDIENTS
- 40g dark chocolate (70% cocoa), chopped
- 2 tablespoons coconut oil
- 80ml (1/3 cup) maple syrup

- 270ml can Ayam Premium Coconut Milk
- 2 limes, rind finely grated, juiced
- 30g (1/4 cup) almond meal
- 2 tablespoons raw cacao powder
- 1 tablespoon coconut flour
- 1 tablespoon buckwheat flour
- 1 1/4 tsps baking powder
- 2 eggs, separated
- 1 tablespoon coconut sugar
- 1 tablespoon boiling water
- 2 tsps powdered gelatine
- Finely grated lime rind, extra, to serve

DIRECTIONS

1. Preheat the oven to 180 degrees Celsius/160 degrees Celsius fan pushed. Paper cases should be lined in a 24-hole, 1 tbs capacity mini muffin tub. In a shallow saucepan over low heat, combine the chocolate, coconut oil, 1/4 cup maple syrup, 1 1/2 tablespoons coconut milk, and the juice and rind of 1 lime. Cook, stirring constantly, for 3 minutes, or until smooth and melted. Place in a bowl and set aside for 5 minutes to cool.

2. In a large mixing bowl, combine the almond meal, cacao powder, coconut flour, buckwheat flour, baking powder, and egg yolks. In a clean cup, beat egg white and coconut sugar with electric beaters until soft peaks form. Part of the egg white mixture should be folded into the chocolate mixture. Combine the remaining egg white mixture with the remaining egg white mixture until just mixed. Distribute among the prepared pans. Preheat the oven to 350°F and bake for 12-14 minutes, or when a skewer inserted in the middle comes out clean. Allow 5 minutes for cooling in the pan. Allow to cool full on a wire rack.

3. In a large mixing bowl, combine the almond meal, cacao powder, coconut flour, buckwheat flour, baking powder, and egg yolks. In a clean cup, beat egg white and coconut sugar with electric beaters until soft peaks form. Part of the egg white mixture should be folded into the chocolate mixture. Combine the remaining egg white mixture with the remaining egg white mixture until just mixed. Distribute among the prepared pans. Preheat the oven to 350°F and bake for 12-14 minutes, or when a skewer inserted in the middle comes out clean. Allow 5 minutes for cooling in the pan. Allow to cool full on a wire rack.

Nutrition Fact: Calories Per Serving 498: Total Fat 28.5g: Cholesterol 0mg: Sodium 602mg: Total Carbohydrate 78.1g: Dietary Fiber 26.1g: Sugars 20.8g: Protein 21.8g

10. NO-COOK HALVA TRUFFLES

Preparation Time: 5minutes
Cooking Time: 15minutes,
Total Time: 20 Minutes

INGREDIENTS

- 2/3 cup sultanas
- 1/2 cup almond meal
- 1/4 cup Nestle Baking Cocoa, plus 2 tbsp extra (optional)
- 1/4 cup tahini
- 1 tbsp black chia seeds
- 2 tbsp desiccated coconut or shredded coconut (optional)
- 2 tbsp sesame seeds, toasted (optional)

DIRECTIONS

1. In a food processor, pulse the sultanas until finely chopped. Combine the almond meal, cocoa powder, tahini, and chia seeds in a food processor and process until smooth. Make 2-tsp balls out of the mixture.
2. Layer coconut, sesame seeds, and extra cocoa powder on three different plates to decorate the truffles. Every truffle should be rolled in coconut, sesame seeds, or cocoa powder.

Nutrition Fact: Calories Per Serving 498: Total Fat 28.5g: Cholesterol 0mg: Sodium 602mg: Total Carbohydrate 78.1g: Dietary Fiber 26.1g: Sugars 20.8g: Protein 21.8g

11. FRUIT LEATHER

Preparation Time: 20 minutes
Cooking Time: 5 Hours
Total Time: 5hrs 20 Minutes

INGREDIENTS

- 1 cup sugar
- 4 cups apple, peeled, cored, and chopped
- 4 cups pears, peeled, cored, and chopped
- ¼ cup lemon juice

DIRECTIONS

1. Preheat the oven to 150 degrees Fahrenheit (60 degrees Celsius) (65 degrees C). Plastic wrap or

parchment paper should be used to cover a baking sheet.

2. Blend the sugar, lemon juice, apple, and pear together in a blender container. Puree until smooth with a lid on. On the prepared pan, spread evenly. Preheat the oven to 400°F and place the pan on the top rack.

3. Preheat the oven to 350°F and bake for 5 to 6 hours, with the door slightly ajar. When the surface of the fruit is no longer tacky and can be ripped like leather, it is dry. Wrap the plastic wrap around the roll and place it in an airtight jar.

Nutrition Fact: Calories Per Serving 498: Total Fat 28.5g: Cholesterol 0mg: Sodium 602mg: Total Carbohydrate 78.1g: Dietary Fiber 26.1g: Sugars 20.8g: Protein 21.8g

12. TOMATO-CHEDDAR CHEESE TOAST

Preparation Time: 5 minutes
Cooking Time: 5minutes,
Total Time: 10 Minutes

INGREDIENTS
- 1 whole-wheat baguette, sliced diagonally (1/4 inch thick).
- 2 small tomato slices
- ½ tablespoons (1/2 ounce) shredded Cheddar cheese
- A pinch of black pepper, cracked

DIRECTIONS
1. Bread should be toasted. Add tomato, cheese, and pepper to taste. If desired, melt the cheese in a toaster oven (or broil).

Nutrition Fact: Calories Per Serving 498: Total Fat 28.5g: Cholesterol 0mg: Sodium 602mg: Total Carbohydrate 78.1g: Dietary Fiber 26.1g: Sugars 20.8g: Protein 21.8g

13. VEGAN CHOCOLATE-DIPPED FROZEN BANANA BITES

Preparation Time: 30 minutes
Cooking Time: 2hrs 30minutes,
Total Time: 2hrs 30 Minutes

INGREDIENTS
- Thress large bananas
- ¾ cup vegan chocolate chips
- ¼ cup natural peanut butter (chunky or smooth)

DIRECTIONS

1. Each peeled banana should be cut in half lengthwise. Spread peanut butter on both halves. Make banana "sandwiches" by sandwiching the banana halves together. Each banana "sandwich" should yield 8 rounds. Freeze the banana bites for at least 2 hours or overnight on a parchment paper or wax paper-lined baking sheet or tray.
2. Microwave chocolate chips in a microwave-safe bowl for 15 seconds at a time on High until melted (1 to 1 1/2 minutes total). Half of each frozen banana bite should be dipped in chocolate. Allow to cool until the chocolate has hardened. Return to the freezer if not serving right away.

Nutrition Fact: Calories Per Serving 340**:** Total Fat 28.5g**:** Cholesterol 0mg**:** Sodium 602mg**:** Total Carbohydrate 78.1g**:** Dietary Fiber 26.1g**:** Sugars 20.8g**:** Protein 21.8g

14. HEALTHIER BRAN MUFFINS

Preparation Time: 15 minutes
Cooking Time: 20 minutes,
Total Time: 35 Minutes

INGREDIENTS

- ½ tsp salt
- 2 tablespoons brown sugar, packed
- a quarter cup of all-purpose flour
- 1 tablespoon powdered baking soda
- 1 ½ cup bran cereal (whole)
- 1 ½ cup soy milk with vanilla flavor
- 1 tablespoon extra virgin olive oil
- 2 beaten egg whites

DIRECTIONS

1. Preheat the oven to 400 degrees Fahrenheit (200 degrees C).
2. In a large mixing bowl, sift together the salt, sugar, flour, and baking powder. Combine the bran cereal and soy milk in a separate bowl; set aside for 5 minutes before whisking in the olive oil and egg whites. Combine the dry and wet ingredients in a mixing bowl. Fill muffin cups halfway with batter.
3. Bake for 20 minutes in a preheated oven until lightly browned.

Nutrition Fact: Calories Per Serving 498: Total Fat 28.5g: Cholesterol 0mg: Sodium 602mg: Total Carbohydrate 78.1g: Dietary Fiber 26.1g: Sugars 20.8g: Protein 21.8g

15. GRILLED PINEAPPLE SLICES

Preparation Time: 10 minutes
Cooking Time: 12minutes,
Total Time: 22 Minutes

INGREDIENTS

- ¼ cup canned coconut milk
- One fresh pineapple - peeled, cored and cut into rings
- ½ cup cinnamon sugar

DIRECTIONS

1. Preheat the grill to medium. Lightly oil the grill grate once it's hot.
2. Separate the coconut milk from the cinnamon sugar in two dishes. Slices of pineapple are dipped in coconut milk and then dusted with cinnamon sugar.
3. Cook for 6 minutes on each side on the grill. Transfer to plates to serve.

Nutrition Fact: Calories Per Serving 498: Total Fat 28.5g: Cholesterol 0mg:

Sodium 602mg: Total Carbohydrate 78.1g: Dietary Fiber 26.1g: Sugars 20.8g: Protein 21.8g

16. WWII OATMEAL MOLASSES COOKIES

Preparation Time: 20 minutes
Cooking Time: 10 minutes,
Total Time: 30 Minutes

INGREDIENTS

- 2 cups flour (all-purpose)
- 2 cups of oats
- 1 tsp bicarbonate of soda
- 1 tsp powdered baking soda
- 1 tsp kosher salt
- 1 pound of sugar
- ¾ cup shortening
- 2 eggs, beaten
- 5 tablespoons molasses (light)
- 2 tsp vanilla bean extract
- ½ cup chopped walnuts (Optional)
- ½ cup raisins (Optional)

DIRECTIONS

1. Preheat the oven to 350 degrees Fahrenheit (175 degrees C).
2. Combine the flour, oatmeal, baking soda, baking powder, and salt in a large mixing bowl.
3. In a separate large mixing bowl, cream together the sugar and shortening until smooth and creamy; stir in the beaten eggs, molasses, and vanilla extract. Mix in the dry ingredients gradually. Combine walnuts and raisins in a mixing bowl. Drop by tspfuls onto baking sheets that haven't been greased. Bake for 10–12 minutes, or until golden brown. Allow 5 minutes for cookies to cool on the baking sheet before transferring to a wire rack to cool completely.

Nutrition Fact: Calories Per Serving 498: Total Fat 28.5g: Cholesterol 0mg: Sodium 602mg: Total Carbohydrate 78.1g: Dietary Fiber 26.1g: Sugars 20.8g: Protein 21.8g

17. DONUT MUFFINS

Preparation Time: 15 minutes
Cooking Time: 15minutes,
Total Time: 30 Minutes

INGREDIENTS
- 1 cup all-purpose flour
- ¼ cup margarine, melted
- ½ cup white sugar
- One tsp ground cinnamon
- ½ cup white sugar
- ¼ cup margarine, melted
- ¾ tsp ground nutmeg
- ½ cup milk
- One tsp baking powder

DIRECTIONS
1. Preheat the oven to 375 degrees Fahrenheit (190 degrees C). Grease 24 mini-muffin cups with cooking spray.
2. In a large mixing bowl, combine 1/2 cup sugar, 1/4 cup margarine, and nutmeg. In a separate bowl, whisk together the milk, baking powder, and flour until thoroughly combined. Half-fill the mini muffin cups that have been prepared.
3. 15 to 20 minutes in a preheated oven until the tops are lightly golden.
4. Place 1/4 cup melted margarine in a bowl while the muffins are baking. Combine 1/2 cup sugar and the cinnamon in a separate bowl. Remove the muffins from their cups and roll them in the sugar-cinnamon mixture after dipping them in the melted

margarine. Allow to cool before serving.

Nutrition Fact: Calories Per Serving 498: Total Fat 28.5g: Cholesterol 0mg: Sodium 602mg: Total Carbohydrate 78.1g: Dietary Fiber 26.1g: Sugars 20.8g: Protein 21.8g

18. SRIRACHA-BUFFALO CAULIFLOWER BITES

Preparation Time: 10 minutes
Cooking Time: 20 minutes,
Total Time: 30 Minutes

INGREDIENTS
- 2 tablespoons hot sauce, such as Frank's RedHot
- 1-2 tablespoons Sriracha
- 1 tablespoon butter, melted
- 1 tablespoon lemon juice
- 1/2-inch cauliflower florets One 8 cups
- 2 tablespoons extra-virgin olive oil
- ¼ tsp kosher salt

DIRECTIONS
1. Preheat the oven to 450 degrees Fahrenheit. Using cooking spray, coat a large rimmed baking sheet.
2. In a large mixing bowl, combine the cauliflower, oil, and salt. Reserve the bowl and spread the mixture on the prepared baking sheet. Roast the cauliflower for 15 minutes, or until it begins to soften and brown on the bottom.
3. Meanwhile, in a large mixing bowl, combine the hot sauce, Sriracha to taste, butter, and lemon juice. Toss in the roasted cauliflower to coat. Return the cauliflower to the baking sheet and roast for another 5 minutes, or until hot.

Nutrition Fact: Calories Per Serving 327: Total Fat 28.5g: Cholesterol 80mg: Sodium 602mg: Total Carbohydrate 90.1g: Dietary Fiber 26.1g: Sugars 20.8g: Protein 21.8g

19. PROSCIUTTO E MELONE (ITALIAN HAM AND MELON)

Preparation Time: 10 minutes
Cooking Time: 10 minutes
INGREDIENTS
- 1 cantaloupe - seeded and cut into 8 wedges
- 8 thin slices prosciutto

DIRECTIONS

1. Remove the flesh from the cantaloupe rind; wrap a slice of ham around each piece of cantaloupe. Allow to cool before serving.

Nutrition Fact: Calories Per Serving 476: Total Fat 58.5g: Cholesterol 0mg: Sodium 602mg: Total Carbohydrate 78.1g: Dietary Fiber 26.1g: Sugars 20.8g: Protein 21.8g

20. GARLIC PITA BREAD BITES

Preparation Time: 15 minutes
Cooking Time: 10 minutes,
Total Time: 25 Minutes

INGREDIENTS

- 1 (10 ounce) package pita bread, cut in half
- 3 tablespoons unsalted butter
- 1 tsp garlic, crushed
- 1 tsp Italian-style seasoning, dried
- 2 tblsp. Parmesan cheese, grated

DIRECTIONS

1. Preheat the oven to 350 degrees Fahrenheit (175 degrees C).
2. Pita bread halves should be opened and roughly cut into 2 inch pieces. Place on a medium baking sheet to cool.

3. Melt butter in a small saucepan over medium heat, then add garlic and dried Italian seasoning. Over the pita bread pieces, pour the mixture.
4. Adjust the amount of Parmesan cheese on the bread as desired. Bake for 10 minutes, or until lightly browned in a preheated oven.

Nutrition Fact: Calories Per Serving 762: Total Fat 38.5g: Cholesterol 0mg: Sodium 602mg: Total Carbohydrate 78.1g: Dietary Fiber 26.1g: Sugars 20.8g: Protein 76.8g

21. QUICK BAKED ZUCCHINI CHIPS

Preparation Time: 5 minutes
Cooking Time: 10 minutes

INGREDIENTS

- ½ cup seasoned dry bread crumbs
- ⅛ tsp ground black pepper
- 2 medium zucchini, cut into 1/4-inch slices
- Two tablespoons grated Parmesan cheese
- Two egg whites

DIRECTIONS

1. Preheat oven to 475 degrees Fahrenheit (245 degrees C).

237

2. Combine the bread crumbs, pepper, and Parmesan cheese in a small mixing bowl. In a separate bowl, separate the egg whites. After dipping zucchini slices in egg whites, coat them in the breadcrumb mixture. Place on a baking sheet that has been greased.

3. In a preheated oven, bake for 5 minutes, then flip and bake for another 5 to 10 minutes, until browned and crispy.

Nutrition Fact: Calories Per Serving 129**:** Total Fat 67.5g**:** Cholesterol 0mg**:** Sodium 602mg**:** Total Carbohydrate 78.1g**:** Dietary Fiber 26.1g**:** Sugars 20.8g**:** Protein 21.8g

22. TOFU HIYAYAKKO

Preparation Time: 10 minutes
Cooking Time: 10 minutes,
Total Time: 20 Minutes

INGREDIENTS

- One tablespoon soy sauce
- One tsp white sugar
- One pinch bonito shavings (dry fish flakes)
- One pinch toasted sesame seeds
- ½ tsp dashi granules
- ½ tsp water
- ¼ (12 ounce) package silken tofu
- 1 ½ tsps grated fresh ginger root
- ¼ tsp thinly sliced green onion

DIRECTIONS

1. In a small bowl, whisk together the soy sauce, sugar, dashi granules, and water until the sugar dissolves. Top the tofu with ginger, green onion, and bonito shavings on a small plate. Drizzle the soy sauce over the top and top with sesame seeds.

Nutrition Fact: Calories Per Serving 498**:** Total Fat 28.5g**:** Cholesterol 0mg**:** Sodium 602mg**:** Total Carbohydrate 78.1g**:** Dietary Fiber 26.1g**:** Sugars 20.8g**:** Protein 21.8g

23. SALMON DEVILED EGGS WITH HOMEMADE MAYONNAISE

Preparation Time: 20 minutes
Cooking Time: 20 minutes,
Total Time: 40 Minutes

INGREDIENTS

Homemade Mayonnaise:

- Two tablespoons red wine vinegar, or to taste
- Twelve eggs
- One shallot, minced
- 1 (6 ounce) can salmon, drained and flaked
- One pinch salt and pepper to taste
- Two egg yolks, room temperature
- 1 clove garlic, pressed
- ½ cup vegetable oil
- One pinch salt and pepper to taste

DIRECTIONS

1. In a medium mixing bowl, beat the egg yolks with an electric mixer or a hand blender to make the mayonnaise. Slowly drizzle in the oil, a tablespoon at a time, while constantly mixing. Continue to add oil until it reaches a consistency similar to regular mayonnaise. Garlic cloves should be pierced and stirred around in the mixture until they release their juice. Season with salt and pepper after removing the garlic cloves. 1 tsp at a time, add the red wine vinegar. Slowly drizzle in the mayonnaise to thin it out.

2. In a large pot, cover the eggs with enough water to cover them. Bring to a boil, then reduce to a low heat for 10 minutes. Remove the pan from the heat, drain, and set aside to cool. Remove the shells from the eggs and cut them in half lengthwise. Remove the yolks from the egg and place them in a medium mixing bowl. On a serving plate, arrange the egg whites.

3. Add the shallot, salmon, 1/2 cup mayonnaise, salt, and pepper to the yolks. Mix until everything is well combined. If the mixture appears to be dry, add more mayonnaise. Fill the egg white halves with the mixture and chill or serve.

Nutrition Fact: Calories Per Serving 546: Total Fat 55g: Cholesterol 0mg: Sodium 602mg: Total Carbohydrate 78.1g: Dietary Fiber 26.1g: Sugars 20.8g: Protein 70.8g

24. CARROT AND TUNA BITES

Preparation Time: 10 minutes
Cooking Time: 15minutes,
Total Time: 25 Minutes

INGREDIENTS

- Three green onions, chopped
- One tablespoon mayonnaise
- One large carrot, sliced diagonally into 1/4-inch-thick slices
- One (5 ounce) can tuna packed in water, drained

DIRECTIONS

1. Place carrot slices on a plate or serving tray. Combine the tuna, green onions, and mayonnaise in a small bowl. Spoon some onto each carrot slice and serve right away.

Nutrition Fact: Calories Per Serving 250: Total Fat 73g: Cholesterol 0mg: Sodium 602mg: Total Carbohydrate 78.1g: Dietary Fiber 26.1g: Sugars 20.8g: Protein 21.8g

25. LADYBUGS ON A LOG

Preparation Time: 10 minutes
Cooking Time: 10 minutes,
Total Time: 20 Minutes

INGREDIENTS

- ¼ cup dried cranberries
- Six stalks celery, cut into 3-inch pieces
- ½ cup raspberry flavored cream cheese

DIRECTIONS

1. Top each celery stick with 3 or 4 dried cranberries and raspberry-flavored cream cheese.

Nutrition Fact: Calories Per Serving 674: Total Fat 45.5g: Cholesterol 0mg: Sodium 602mg: Total Carbohydrate 78.1g: Dietary Fiber 26.1g: Sugars 20.8g: Protein 29.8g

26. DIRTY DIAPERS

Preparation Time: 20 minutes
Cooking Time: 20 minutes,
Total Time: 45 Minutes

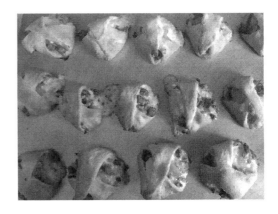

INGREDIENTS

- One pound ground beef
- One small onion, finely chopped

- One (10 ounce) can refrigerated crescent roll dough
- Eight slices Cheddar cheese
- Thirty Two slices dill pickle

DIRECTIONS

1. Preheat the oven to 350°F (180°C) (175 degrees C).
2. In a skillet over medium-high heat, brown the ground beef. Cook, stirring constantly to prevent crumbling, until the meat is no longer pink. Cook and stir the onion in the skillet until it is tender. Grease should be removed.
3. On a clean surface, unroll the crescent roll dough. Cut each triangle in half diagonally to make two smaller triangles after separating the triangles. Stack the cheese slices and cut into four triangles diagonally. Place one cheese triangle on each dough triangle. Place about a tablespoon of ground beef on top of the cheese, followed by a slice of pickle. Place the dough on a baking sheet and fold the points towards the center like a diaper.
4. In a preheated oven, bake for 10 to 15 minutes, or until golden brown.

Nutrition Fact: Calories Per Serving 238: Total Fat 56.5g: Cholesterol 0mg: Sodium 602mg: Total Carbohydrate 78.1g: Dietary Fiber 26.1g: Sugars 20.8g: Protein 21.8g

27. MEXICAN JICAMA SNACK

Preparation Time: 10 minutes
Cooking Time: 10minutes,
Total Time: 20 Minutes

INGREDIENT

- One large jicama
- Two lime, juiced
- One tablespoon crushed red pepper, or to taste

DIRECTIONS

1. Jicama should be peeled and cut into french fry-sized sticks. Toss in a medium bowl with the lime juice and cayenne pepper to coat. As a finger food, serve.

Nutrition Fact: Calories Per Serving 498: Total Fat 28.5g: Cholesterol 0mg: Sodium 602mg: Total Carbohydrate 78.1g: Dietary Fiber 26.1g: Sugars 20.8g: Protein 21.8g

28. FRIED FARFALLE CHIPS

Preparation Time: 15 minutes
Cooking Time: 15minutes,
Total Time: 30 Minutes

At parties, these crispy and unusual snacks are a big hit. They're a nice change of pace from chips and pretzels. When making this recipe, use bow ties or your favorite pasta shapes.

INGREDIENTS

- One tsp chili powder
- One tsp garlic powder
- One tsp dry mustard
- Two cups bow tie pasta
- Four tablespoons vegetable oil
- Two tablespoons grated Parmesan cheese

DIRECTION

1. A large pot of lightly salted water should be brought to a boil. Cook for 8 to 10 minutes, or until pasta is al dente; drain and rinse under cold water. Water should be drained completely from the pasta.
2. Heat oil to 375 degrees F (190 degrees C) in a large skillet and fry about 1 cup of pasta at a time until golden. Using paper towels, absorb any excess liquid.
3. Combine the Parmesan, chili powder, garlic powder, and dry mustard in a large mixing bowl. Toss with the pasta that has been drained. Serve the food.

Nutrition Fact: Calories Per Serving 537: Total Fat 67.5g: Cholesterol 0mg: Sodium 602mg: Total Carbohydrate 78.1g: Dietary Fiber 26.1g: Sugars 20.8g: Protein 37.8g

29. GRANDMA OLGA'S KOLACKY

Preparation Time: 45 minutes
Cooking Time: 20minutes,
Total Time: 1 Hour, 5 Minutes

INGREDIENTS

- One tsp white sugar
- ¼ cup warm water (100 degrees)
- Four egg yolks
- 1 cup sour cream
- Three (10 ounce) jars apricot or other fruit filling (such as Baker® Fine Dessert Filling)
- ½ cup confectioners' sugar, for dusting
- Two (.25 ounce) packages active dry yeast
- Four cups sifted all-purpose flour
- 1 cup margarine, softened

DIRECTIONS

1. Add the sugar in warm water in a mixing bowl, then stir in the yeast. Allow for 3 minutes for the yeast to form a creamy layer. Take bowl, mix together the flour and margarine until smooth, then add the egg yolks one at a time. Stir in the yeast mixture until completely combined, then add the sour cream to make a soft but not sticky dough.
2. Preheat the oven to 375 degrees.
3. . Refrigerate the remaining dough pieces. Cut the square into 12 smaller squares, each about 2 inches on a side, using a pastry cutter or pizza roller. 2 tsps fruit filling in the center of each square. To partially enclose the filling, pinch the corners together. Place the filled kolacky on the baking sheets that have been prepared.
4. Bake the cookies to 375 degrees until golden brown. Confectioners' sugar should be sprinkled over the kolacky.

Nutrition Fact: 85calories; protein 40g; carbohydrates 35.6g; fat 78.6g; sodium 62.1mg. Full Nutrition

30. GUILT-FREE SNACK MIX

Preparation Time: 10 minutes
Cooking Time: 10 minutes,

Total Time: 20 Minutes

Here's a quick and easy party or trail mix that's free of chocolate and salty snacks! It's delicious to eat under any circumstances.

INGREDIENTS
- Four cups crispy corn cereal squares
- One cup dried mixed fruit, chopped
- ¼ cup yogurt covered raisins
- ⅓ cup chopped mixed nuts
- Sixty Six cup of banana chips

DIRECTIONS
1. Combine crispy corn cereal squares, dried fruit mix, yogurt-covered raisins, mixed nuts, and banana chips in a medium mixing bowl. Store in airtight, sealed containers.

Nutrition Fact: 74 calories; protein 1g; carbohydrates 12.6g; fat 2.6g; sodium 62.1mg. Full Nutrition

Do Not Go Yet; One Last Thing To Do

If you enjoyed this book or found it useful, I'd be very grateful if you'd post a short review on Amazon. Your support does make a difference, and I read all the reviews personally so I can get your feedback and make this book even better.

Thanks for your help and support!

Made in the USA
Las Vegas, NV
07 October 2021